REASON
and
HUMAN ETHICS

Alan E. Johnson

Philosophia Publications
Pittsburgh, Pennsylvania

Copyright © 2022 by Alan E. Johnson
All rights reserved. Published 2022

For permissions or other information,
contact Alan E. Johnson at
https://alanjohnson.academia.edu/contact.

Print ISBN: 978-0-9701055-5-4
Digital ISBN: 978-0-9701055-6-1
Library of Congress Control Number: 2022911684

Cover images

Portrait of Confucius made during the
Yuan dynasty (1279-1368) (public domain).

Roman sculpture of Socrates after a Greek original (Creative Commons Attribution 2.5 Generic license; no changes were made to the image).

Published by

Philosophia Publications
301 South Hills Village Drive
Suite LL200-112
Pittsburgh, Pennsylvania 15241
USA
http://www.PhilosophiaPublications.com

To Char and Robin

Zilu asked how to serve the spirits and gods. Confucius said, "You are not yet able to serve men, how could you serve the spirits?"

Zilu said, "May I ask you about death?" Confucius said, "You do not yet know life, how could you know death?"

—*Analects of Confucius*[1]

But numbers and motions, and the beginning and end of all things, were the subjects of the ancient philosophy down to Socrates, who was a pupil of Archelaus, who had been the disciple of Anaxagoras. These made diligent inquiry into the magnitude of the stars, their distances, courses, and all that relates to the heavens. But Socrates was the first who brought down philosophy from the heavens, placed it in cities, introduced it into families, and obliged it to examine into life and morals, and good and evil.

—Cicero[2]

Contents

Preface vi
Chapter 1. What is the Basis of Human Ethics? 1
Chapter 2. Human Reason 31
Chapter 3. Individual Ethics 63
Chapter 4. Social Ethics 88
Chapter 5. Citizen and Media Ethics 115
Chapter 6. Political Ethics 132
Epilogue 159
Appendix. Conflicts among the Claims to Revelation 161
Notes 183
Selected Bibliography 224
Index 243
About the Author 250

PREFACE

This work, like all my books, is written for advanced general readers as well as scholars. I avoid academic jargon to the extent possible and define any needed technical terms in plain language.

This book argues that a secular, biological, teleological basis of human ethics exists and that reasoning and critical thinking about both ends and means are essential to human ethics. It examines how these principles apply in the contexts of individual ethics, social ethics, citizen ethics, media ethics, and political ethics.

Chapter 1 ("What Is the Basis of Human Ethics?") discusses the various theories of the basis of ethics over the millennia. It concludes with my position that ethics is properly founded on a secular, biological, teleological understanding of human nature. This chapter is directed especially to those with a scholarly interest in this question. Others may wish to skim through or skip over it. Some may find it of interest after they have read the remainder of the book.

Chapter 2 ("Human Reason") is, in a way, the core of this book. All the subsequent chapters refer, explicitly or implicitly, back to it. The chapter begins with a discussion of how reason relates to secular teleology. I argue that reason is, contrary to much of modern philosophy and science, properly directed to human ends as well as means. I explain the differences between abstract and practical reasoning and between formal and informal logic. Unlike mathematics and physics, ethics involves practical reasoning and informal, nonsymbolic logic. The chapter concludes with an extended discussion of common fallacies and the importance of critical thinking.

Chapter 3 ("Individual Ethics") addresses the appropriate ethical orientation toward ourselves as individuals. It explains why we should want to be rational, how human reason is related to cerebral maturation, the life of reason, and general departures from a rational life. It concludes with a discussion of the ethical mean of Confucius and Aristotle and how that mean properly applies to such moral virtues as courage and moderation.

Chapter 4 ("Social Ethics") considers how individuals should think and act regarding other human and nonhuman beings. This chapter discusses when we should or should not *express* ethical judgments about others, the merits and limitations of the Golden Rule, prejudice and discrimination, veracity, friendship, romantic relationships, family, work, business ethics, environmental ethics, the ethical treatment of nonhuman animals, and issues regarding force and fraud.

Chapter 5 ("Citizen and Media Ethics") discusses, among other things, the long-forgotten concept of public virtue, the ethical imperative of reason in public discourse and conduct, ideologies of the far Right and far Left, and media ethics.

Chapter 6 ("Political Ethics") is about the ethics of political leadership. The first major section is on authoritarian, tyrannical, and totalitarian political leaders, with a discussion of Plato's account of oligarchical and tyrannical rulers in his *Republic* and *Seventh Letter* and the examples of Joseph Stalin, Adolph Hitler, and Vladimir Putin. The second section addresses irrational democratic-republican political leadership, with examples being the self-acknowledged "gut instinct" leadership styles of U.S. presidents George W. Bush and Donald J. Trump and the latter's advanced flirtation with authoritarian ideology and practice. The concluding section is about rational democratic-republican political leadership: what it would be and a possible example in President John F. Kennedy's leadership during the 1962 Cuban Missile Crisis.

An epilogue sums it all up, and the appendix discusses the theological and violent conflicts among the claims to revelation.

Reason and Human Ethics is the second book of my planned three-volume philosophical trilogy on free will, ethics, and political philosophy. The first in this series, *Free Will and Human Life*, was published in 2021. The third, titled *Reason and Human Government*, will be completed and published sometime within the next few years.

The present work has been many decades in the making. It replaces my 2000 book, *First Philosophy and Human Ethics: A Rational Inquiry*, which is no longer in print. More than twenty years later, I no longer agree with some of the statements I made in the earlier book. The valuable portions of that book have been incorporated, directly or indirectly, into the present work, and I accordingly request that the 2000 book be totally disregarded.

Preface

When I discuss or cite other writers in the present book, my agreement or disagreement with them should not be construed to extend to issues other than those being immediately addressed. It is not unusual for me to agree with other thinkers on some matters and disagree with them on others.

I thank my wife, Mimi Lindauer, for reviewing and commenting on drafts of this book and for our numerous substantive discussions regarding ethical and political questions over the years. Among other things, she has called my attention to the scholarly literature on evolutionary biology; her information (including her own online essay on the subject) is discussed and cited in the section on evolutionary biology in Chapter 1. Additionally, she is more knowledgeable than I about environmental and nonhuman animal ethics, and she wrote most of the section on those issues in Chapter 4.

I also express appreciation to my sisters, Char and Robin, to whom I have dedicated this book, for reading and commenting on draft chapters of it and for our discussions of ethical and political matters over the decades.

I am, of course, solely responsible for the final product, and the views expressed herein should not be attributed to anyone else, except as noted above regarding my wife's direct contribution to a section of Chapter 4.

When I discuss a particular work in the present book, I sometimes put cited page numbers of that writing in textual parentheses instead of in endnotes. In all such cases, these citations refer to the book or paper last mentioned in the text.

Preface

Citations to Plato are to the traditional Stephanus numbers. Citations to Aristotle are to the standard Bekker pagination, with the conventional book and chapter numbers prefixed to the Bekker notation. The indicated line numbers of the Bekker edition are approximate.

The page numbers of the print edition of this book are inserted in italicized braces (*{}*) at the appropriate locations of the ebook edition. The page numbers identified in the index of the ebook refer to these italicized page numbers, and that index is accordingly identical to the index in the printed book.

This book sometimes uses the terms "democratic republic" or "democratic-republican" to denote what is often alternatively called "constitutional democracy." Unlike the direct democracies of ancient Greece, modern democracies have constitutional limitations on majority rule, including representation, bills of rights, separations of powers, and checks and balances. Accordingly, they can appropriately be called democratic republics. When capitalized, the term "Democratic-Republican" refers to the Jeffersonian political party founded in the 1790s.

I will post errata and supplemental comments, if any, at https://chicago.academia.edu/AlanJohnson/Books,-Book-Excerpts,-and-Errata-Supp-Comments.

The images on the cover of this book are of Confucius and Socrates. The portrait of Confucius (ca. 551–ca. 479 BCE) was created during the Yuan dynasty (1297–1368 CE). The Roman sculpture of Socrates (ca. 470–399 BCE) is based on a Greek original of about 350 BCE, often attributed to Lysippos. I selected these cover

Preface

images when thinking about which philosophers are closest to my own ideas about ethics. These are the two I selected, though there are others whom I have favorably quoted or cited in the text and endnotes of this work.

Alan E. Johnson
June 21, 2022

Chapter 1

What Is the Basis of Human Ethics?

> Zilu, I am going to teach you what knowledge is. To take what you know for what you know, and what you do not know for what you do not know, that is knowledge indeed.
> —Confucius[1]

> What I don't know, I don't think I know.
> —Socrates[2]

The first question in a philosophical examination of ethics is whether it has any basis. This chapter explores and evaluates different theories of the foundation of ethics: relativism, classical reason, religion, emotion/sentiment, Kant's categorical imperative, utilitarianism, virtue ethics, evolutionary biology, and a secular teleological understanding of human nature.

Ethical Relativism

Ethical relativism is "the assertion that all ends are relative to the chooser and hence equal . . . ."[3] Under the positivist interpretation of ethical relativism, "Reason can tell us which means are conducive to which ends; it cannot tell us which attainable ends are to be preferred to other attainable ends."[4]

Individual Ethical Relativism

The Greek sophist Protagoras (ca. 490–ca. 420 BCE) famously wrote in his lost book *Truth* that a human being is the measure of all things. Plato quoted the opening of this work as follows: "A human being is the measure of all things, of the things which are, that they are, and of the things which are not, that they are not."[5] We do not know how Protagoras elaborated on this sentence, and it is not entirely clear what he meant by it. Nevertheless, his pronouncement is often considered the earliest-known statement of relativism, including individual ethical relativism.[6]

During the twentieth century, a form of the doctrine of individual relativism emerged under the rubric of "emotivism," which has been defined as "the doctrine that all evaluative judgments and more specifically all moral judgments are *nothing but* expressions of preference, expressions of attitude or feeling, insofar as they are moral or evaluative in character."[7] The argument that scientific facts can be known whereas ethical views are mere subjective preferences is the basis of the fact-value dichotomy posited by Max Weber and others.[8] The present book will later elaborate and critically assess this academically popular doctrine.

Cultural Relativism; Historicism

Cultural relativism has been defined as "[t]he view that what is true, rational, justified, good, etc. varies with and is dependent on cultural frameworks of different societies or historic periods."[9] The notion that ethical relativism applies to different historical periods is called "historicism."[10] In cultural and historical relativism, the idea is that there are no objective ethical truths transcending culture or history, respectively. Humans are bound to the ethical opinions of their individual cultures or historical periods.

Evaluation of Ethical Relativism

Gilbert Harman, a professional analytic philosopher, is a leading advocate of ethical relativism. In a 2015 paper, he wrote:

> Moral relativism is not a claim about the grammar of moral judgments. It is a claim about reality. It is a version of moral realism. It is the [fact] that there are many moralities or moral frames of reference and whether something is morally right or wrong, good or bad, just or unjust, virtuous or not is always a relative matter. Something can be right or good or just only in relation to one moral framework and wrong or bad or unjust in relation to another. Nothing is simply right or good or unjust or virtuous.[11]

Nevertheless, Harman appeared to qualify this statement later in the article as follows:

> Moral relativism argues that there is no objective way to establish that a particular morality is the correct morality, and concludes that there is no reason to believe in a single true morality. *This is compatible with the possibility of certain moral universals just as there seem to be linguistic*

Chapter 1. What Is the Basis of Human Ethics?

universals even though there are very different kinds of language.[12]

Evidently, Harman thinks there may be implicit moral universals by analogy to implicit linguistic universals. But how could there be implicit moral universals when moral doctrines and practices on the ground, so to speak, can be and often are diametrically opposed to each other? What is the universal moral principle, implicit or otherwise, that unites Hitler with Jesus, Nietzsche with Tolstoy? If there are universal moral principles, they would not involve what is factually in common among all human beings but rather the ethical approach that most facilitates human life at its best (more on this later). Although linguistics may be tainted in some instances with good or bad ethical values, linguistics is not ethics.

Harman also uses analogy to try to prove the first of the above-quoted two statements. He claims that moral relativity is proven by way of analogies to relativity in physics and "the relativity of grammar and meaning to a language . . . ."[13] But again he is comparing apples to oranges. Physics is notoriously value free, and grammatical relativity, as remarked above, has little to do with ethics. We discuss the test for a correct analogy in Chapter 2. Harman's analogies of ethics to physics and linguistics fail to meet that test.

If ethical relativism is true, the Holocaust was just as ethical as the beneficent practices of an ideal democratic republic, and slavery is just another cultural practice that we are forbidden to judge. It is a wonder that anyone has ever advocated such moral equivalencies. Relativism is simply refuted by a reductio ad absurdum.[14]

Chapter 1. What Is the Basis of Human Ethics?

Moreover, relativism is a self-contradiction. The argument that all ethical values are relative necessarily entails the conclusion that the relativist premise itself is relative to an individual or to a particular culture or historical period and therefore cannot be stated as an objective universal truth.[15] Leo Strauss made the same point regarding historicism: "Historicism thrives on the fact that it inconsistently exempts itself from its own verdict about all human thought. The historicist thesis is self-contradictory or absurd."[16]

Many people defend the doctrine of ethical relativism on the ground that it promotes tolerance. However, the examples of the Holocaust and of American slavery before and during the Civil War show that "tolerance" can be a two-edged sword: tolerance of genocide and slavery gives aid and comfort to intolerance. Moreover, if all values are relative, tolerance is itself relative. If relativism is true, there are no objective ethical principles, including tolerance.

Although different cultures and different eras have different customs, there are some ethical truths that apply to all people in all cultures and all times. This book explores what those concepts are. We next consider what the philosophers Plato and Aristotle wrote on this subject.

CLASSICAL REASON

The classical Greek philosophers Plato and Aristotle elaborated ethical teachings in which human reason was the ultimate architectonic principle. Plato articulated a tripartite division of the human soul, with reason in command, guiding spiritedness and desire. Note that Plato did not dream of eliminating the spirited and

Chapter 1. What Is the Basis of Human Ethics?

desiring parts of the soul. Rather, he argued that those impulses should remain under the intelligent supervision of reason.[17]

Similarly, Aristotle taught that living in accordance with reason—as distinguished from a life in which passion is dominant—is the kind of life that fulfills the unique *ergon* (work or function) of human beings and is the essential component of happiness.[18] Aristotle defined *phronēsis* (variously translated as active wisdom, prudence, practical judgment, practical intelligence, or practical wisdom) as "a true characteristic that is bound up with action, accompanied by reason, and concerned with things good and bad for a human being."[19] For Plato and Aristotle, life in accordance with reason is an end in itself; it is not a means to another end. As explained later, Aristotle regarded reason as having a decisive role in ascertaining correct ethical conduct.

Plato and Aristotle postulated the principle of contradiction (which contemporary philosophy professors often call the principle or law of noncontradiction). Plato wrote: "It's plain that the same thing won't be willing at the same time to do or suffer opposites with respect to the same part and in relation to the same thing."[20] In an endnote to this passage, the translator/editor remarked: "This is the earliest-known explicit statement of the principle of contradiction—the premise of philosophy and the foundation of rational discourse."[21]

Similarly, Aristotle stated: "There is a certain principle in beings about which it is not possible to be mistaken, but always necessary to do the opposite, and I mean to attain the truth, and it is of this sort: that it is

Chapter 1. What Is the Basis of Human Ethics?

impossible for the same thing at one and the same time to be and not to be, and for the other things that are opposite to each other in that way to belong to it."[22] He also wrote: "It is not possible for the same thing at the same time both to belong and not belong to the same thing in the same respect (and as many other things as we ought to specify in addition for the sake of logical difficulties, let them have been specified in addition). And this is the most certain of all principles . . . ."[23]

Some present-day scholars question the universal applicability of the principle of contradiction.[24] It is true that this principle appears to break down at the frontiers of physics. Our understandings of quantum physics and perhaps relativity physics do not seem amenable to the principle of contradiction—not to mention the long-standing metaphysical perplexities of a first cause, the beginning of time, and the infinity of space. But it is my strong conviction that the principle of contradiction applies, and should apply, to ethical and political matters. When individual persons and political leaders violate the principle of contradiction in their individual or our collective lives, the result is insanity and chaos. We see examples of this throughout history, including (and perhaps especially) in our own time. We will discuss this and other types of fallacious thinking in later chapters of this book.

Plato proceeded in his dialogues by way of rational dialectic, ascending from the contradictions of opinion to the noncontradictory plane of knowledge. Aristotle developed a complex system of logic. Plato and Aristotle recognized the importance of both inductive and deductive reasoning,[25] though medieval Scholasticism focused on Aristotle's deductive logic.

Chapter 1. What Is the Basis of Human Ethics?

Needless to say, the problem with deductive logic is that it starts with unquestioned premises. Such a procedure was, of course, compatible with medieval theology, but the formulation and questioning of premises by way of inductive reasoning was part of the philosophical approaches of both Plato and Aristotle and is also characteristic of modern science.

Aristotle made it clear that ethical philosophy is not subject to the same kind of precision and exactitude as are mathematics and natural science. In his *Nicomachean Ethics*, he observed:

> The inquiry [regarding ethics] would be adequately made if it should attain the clarity that accords with the subject matter. For one should not seek out precision in *all* arguments alike . . . .
>
> It would certainly be desirable enough, then, if one who speaks about and on the basis of such things demonstrate the truth roughly and in outline, and if, in speaking about and on the basis of things that are for the most part so, one draw conclusions of that sort as well. Indeed, in the same manner one must also accept each of the points being made. For it belongs to an educated person to seek out precision in each genus to the extent that the nature of the matter allows: to accept persuasive speech from a skilled mathematician appears comparable to demanding demonstrations from a skilled rhetorician.[26]

He later stated that to be very precise about ethical issues "would be more appropriate to another philosophy."[27] "[E]very argument concerned with what ought to be done is bound to be stated in outline only and not precisely—just as we said at the beginning as well, that the demands made of given arguments should accord with the subject matter in question."[28]

Plato and Aristotle both had a teleological view of human nature—that human beings could only be properly understood in light of their potential for rational and ethical thought and conduct. This approach, as we will now see, has been rejected by much of religion as well as by certain dominant strains of modern philosophy.

RELIGION

Ethics based on religion can be of two kinds: tradition alone and tradition predicated upon an alleged divine revelation. Confucianism and Buddhism, which may be more philosophical than religious, are permeated with ethical thinking but do not claim to be informed by divine revelation. In contrast, many other religious traditions teach that their ethical precepts are based on supernatural revelation.

Ethics based on tradition alone may or may not be salutary, depending on the tradition. Confucian ethics are generally sensible and, in important respects, rational. But religious or quasi-religious traditions glorifying militarism and violence are a different story.

Systems of morality based on alleged divine revelation face the problem that there are many conflicting claims to revelation. Examples include Hinduism, the oracle of the ancient Egyptian god Amon, Ikhnaton's religion of Aton based on his alleged personal revelation from the god Re, Judaism,

Chapter 1. What Is the Basis of Human Ethics?

Zoroastrianism, the ancient Greek Homeric gods and associated Delphic oracle, Norse mythology, Christianity, Gnosticism, Manicheism, Islam, Sikhism, Swedenborgism, the Shakers (alleged revelation to Mother Anne Lee), the Bahá'í faith, the Latter-day Saints (alleged revelation to Joseph Smith), the alleged revelation to the Paiute Native American prophet Wovoka (Jack Wilson), Thelema (alleged revelation to Aleister Crowley), televangelists Oral Roberts and Pat Robertson (who both claimed to speak with God), and the prophetic utterances of people who claim that God told them that Donald Trump would and did win a second term as U.S. president in 2020. The appendix to this book discusses some of the conflicting claims to religion in depth. Chapters 2 and 5 analyze, among other things, the claims to revelation by some Trump supporters.

The various claimed revelations often have different ethical teachings. For example, ancient Greek ethics differs from Norse (Viking) ethics, and both of them differ significantly from Christian ethics. Under such circumstances, it is impossible to rationally choose among the various religions. Moreover, many religions reject reason. For them, the key is faith. But this merely begs the question: faith in what? In practice, faith usually means acceptance, without questioning, of the religious tradition in which one was brought up.

By definition, then, reason is not essential to religion. It is nevertheless interesting that, during the later medieval and early modern periods, the western Christian (Roman Catholic) church superimposed its moral and other theological doctrines on the rational philosophy of Aristotle. Thomas Aquinas was the most important figure in this attempted reconciliation of philosophy and theology. But Martin Luther, the founder of Protestantism, opposed such Aristotelian and Catholic perspectives. Luther decried reason, claiming that individual salvation is only by faith and that faith is given as a matter of God's grace as part as a predestinarian order that antedates the life of the individual. John Calvin agreed. "Reason," according to Luther, "is the fountain and headspring of all mischiefs." "[E]very Christian is a true priest: for first he offereth up and killeth his own reason . . . ." As part and parcel of the combined theological and philosophical/scientific attack on medieval Scholasticism, reason suffered a demotion: it now was concerned only with means, not ends. "Teleology" (the concern with ends) became a dirty word, which remains the case today—centuries after Martin Luther, John Calvin, Francis Bacon, and Thomas Hobbes consigned that concept to oblivion.[29] Chapter 2 discusses the concepts of reason and teleology in greater depth.

Religion's claim to be the exclusive arbiter of ethics encounters another problem. The scriptures of many religions contain some ethical teachings that are at odds with our contemporary understanding of what is right. For example, the Christian Bible commands or condones imperialistic genocide (Deuteronomy 7:1–2, 20:16–17),[30] stoning of those who curse (Leviticus 24:10–16), stoning of those who worship false gods (Leviticus 20:1–27, Numbers 25:5, Deuteronomy 13:6–10, 17:2–7), stoning of rebellious children (Leviticus 20:9, 21:17; Deuteronomy 21:18–21), stoning of adulterers (Leviticus 20:10, Deuteronomy 22:23–24; but see John 8:3–11), execution of male homosexuals

Chapter 1. What Is the Basis of Human Ethics?

(Leviticus 20:13); stoning of mediums (Leviticus 20:27), stoning of those who work on the Sabbath (Exodus 31:15, Numbers 15:32–36); predestinarianism (Romans 8:29–30, 33, 9:11–18, 11:5–6; Ephesians 2:8–10), female subservience (1 Corinthians 11:3, 15, 14:34–35; 2 Corinthians 11:15; Ephesians 5:22–24; 1 Colossians 3:18; 1 Timothy 2:11–14; 1 Peter 3:1); and slavery (Ephesians 6:5–7, Colossians 3:22). It is well known that the southern states before and during the U.S. Civil War explicitly and repeatedly invoked the Bible in support of their argument that slavery was divinely ordained. Finally, an ox that gored a man or woman to death was to be stoned (Exodus 21:28). (As an interesting aside, it is noted that such criminal prosecutions and punishments against an offending animal or inanimate object were also part of ancient Greek, Roman, and early English law.)[31]

Harmful religious teachings and practices have not been confined to antiquity. Today's Christian Reconstructionists advocate literal compliance with Old Testament stoning commands as well as establishment of a strict Calvinist theocracy.[32] Calvin's sixteenth-century theocracy in Geneva executed, whipped, banished, and otherwise persecuted those who deviated from Calvin's narrow doctrinal positions, including burning one scholar at the stake.[33] The theocracy of Massachusetts Bay in seventeenth-century colonial America hanged and whipped Quakers, imprisoned and whipped Baptists, and banished others who disagreed with their religious laws.[34] England and continental Europe engaged in religious persecutions and wars throughout the medieval and early modern periods. As I write this book, the Taliban have reconquered Afghanistan, restored their theocracy, and subjected everyone in that country, especially women, to their strict, fundamentalist Islamic beliefs. Daily reading or watching of reliable news sources reveals many other religious persecutions and conflicts throughout the world. See the appendix for additional details.

Religions often have some ethical teachings that are consistent with reason. Both the Hebrew scriptures and the Christian Gospels, for example, contain some admirable moral precepts that are consistent with a rational, philosophical outlook. But religious people must, if they are honest, pick and choose among their faith's collection of commandments. Whether or not they are consciously aware of it, they are, in such cases, exercising their reason to separate the good from the bad or, to use a religious metaphor, the wheat from the chaff.

MODERN MORAL SENTIMENT/EMOTION

One of the themes of modern ethical philosophy is that human reason serves a subsidiary function to what was originally called "moral sentiment," which included such mental states as feeling, emotion, instinct, impulse, affection, sympathy, and empathy. The following discussion considers the development of this theory in the writings of Francis Hutcheson, David Hume, Adam Smith, and Jonathan Haidt.

Francis Hutcheson (1694–1746)

Francis Hutcheson, who is often considered to be the founder of the Scottish Enlightenment, wrote in his *Short Introduction to Moral Philosophy* that "[w]hatever is ultimately desirable is either

Chapter 1. What Is the Basis of Human Ethics?

recommended by some immediate sense or some natural instinct or impulse, prior to all reasoning. 'Tis the business of reason to find out the *means* of obtaining what we desire: or if various objects of desire interfere, to inquire which of them is of most importance to happiness, and what the best means of obtaining such objects."[35]

Similarly, in his *System of Moral Philosophy*, Hutcheson stated:

> In general, all descriptions of moral goodness by conformity to reason if we examine them well, must lead us to some immediate original sense or determination of our nature. All reasons exciting to an action will lead us to some original affection or instinct of will; and all justifying reasons, or such as shew an action to be good, will at last lead us to some original sense or power of perception....
>
> ... And 'tis pretty plain that *reason* is only a subservient power to our ultimate determinations either of perception or will. The ultimate end is set[t]led by some sense, and some determination of will: by some sense we enjoy happiness, and self-love determines to it without reasoning. Reason can only direct to the means; or compare two ends previously constituted by some other immediate powers.[36]

Hutcheson taught that God implanted certain feelings in the human soul, from which we acquire the first notions of good and evil. These divinely implanted feelings govern not only our ethical disposition toward ourselves but also our feelings of sympathy toward others. Human reason exists for the purpose of understanding, organizing, and devising means to satisfy those feelings. The implanted moral feelings establish the ethical ends; the main function of reason is to ascertain the best means of achieving those ends. It is true that moral disorders are prevalent in human beings, but "a full and certain account" of them "will never be given by any mortal without a divine revelation." Divine law and providence ultimately govern morality, and "both our social and our selfish affections will harmoniously recommend to us one and the same course of life and conduct."[37] With regard to the latter point, it should be noted that Adam Smith, the author of *The Wealth of Nations* and *The Theory of Moral Sentiments*, was one of Hutcheson's devoted students at the University of Glasgow.

David Hume (1711–1776)

Another, more rebellious student of Hutcheson was David Hume, who also happened to be Adam Smith's best friend. Hume disliked Hutcheson's theological bent and, as a young man, complained of such tendencies in letters to his former professor. For example, in a letter to Hutcheson dated March 16, 1740, Hume argued that "since Morality, according to your Opinion as well as mine, is determin'd merely by Sentiment, it regards only human Nature and human Life." Hume was objecting to the notion that morality was determined by the common reason of rational, superior beings: "[N]othing but Experience can assure us, that the Sentiments are the same. What Experience have we with regard to superior Beings? How can we ascribe to

Chapter 1. What Is the Basis of Human Ethics?

them any Sentiments at all? They have implanted those Sentiments in us for the Conduct of Life like our bodily Sensations, which they possess not themselves."[38]

At the time of his correspondence with Hutcheson, Hume was writing and arranging for publication of his first major work, *A Treatise of Human Nature*. He was in his late twenties. The *Treatise* is famous or infamous for two controversial statements. The first was that "[r]eason is, and ought only to be the slave of the passions, and can never pretend to any other office than to serve and obey them."[39] In making this assertion, Hume defined reason very narrowly to mean pure abstract reasoning as in mathematics. This was, however, a false dichotomy, as Hume failed to address the concept of reason described in the works of Plato and Aristotle as well as in the present book (see especially Chapter 2). His second quite famous passage objected to the derivation of an "ought" from an "is."[40] We will address the "is-ought" issue in the final section of this chapter and in subsequent chapters.

Hume's *An Enquiry Concerning Human Understanding* appeared several years later in 1748. In an "Advertisement" prefaced to the *Enquiry*, he called the *Treatise of Human Nature* a "juvenile work, which the author never acknowledged" (it was published anonymously). He concluded the "Advertisement" by requesting that the *Enquiry Concerning Human Understanding* "alone be regarded as containing his philosophical sentiments and principles."[41] He expressed similar disparaging sentiments regarding the *Treatise* in a February 1754 letter to John Stewart.[42]

Hume presented his definitive, mature work on ethics in *An Enquiry Concerning the Principles of*

Chapter 1. What Is the Basis of Human Ethics?

Morals, published in 1751.[43] In this book, Hume emphasized the importance of a utilitarian approach to promote justice and societal happiness. He now even extolled reason, "since nothing but that faculty can instruct us in the tendency of qualities and actions, and point out their beneficial consequences to society and to their possessor." But only "sentiment," not reason, provides the end, for which reason is the means. "This sentiment can be no other than a feeling for the happiness of mankind, and a resentment of their misery . . . ." He continued to insist that reason does not apply to moral judgments. Rather, "[t]he hypothesis which we embrace is plain. It maintains, that morality is determined by sentiment. It defines virtue to be *whatever mental action or quality gives to a spectator the pleasing sentiment of approbation*; and vice the contrary." He concluded that "the ultimate ends of human actions can never, in any case, be accounted for by *reason*, but recommend themselves entirely to the sentiments and affections of mankind, without any dependance on the intellectual faculties." Indeed, "[r]eason, being cool and disengaged, is no motive to action, and directs only the impulse received from appetite or inclination, by showing us the means of attaining happiness or avoiding misery."[44]

Hume's rejection of reason for the evaluation of ends cannot be correct. If ends are determined solely by "sentiment" or emotion, then one cannot distinguish the ends of tyrants, criminals, and others who have no "sentiment" that they are doing wrong from the ends of beneficent human beings. We have witnessed, in the twentieth and twenty-first centuries, dictators and nonstate actors who use rational means to achieve irrational and (for most, but not all, of us) evil ends. The present book explains how reason can and should be used to evaluate ends as well as means.

Adam Smith (1723–1790)

Adam Smith's *The Theory of Moral Sentiments*[45] is a very long and complicated work, for which only a book-length analysis would be adequate.[46] It is sufficient for present purposes to observe that Smith continued the "moral sentiments" tradition of his professor, Francis Hutcheson, and his friend, David Hume. But Smith went beyond and, to an extent, disagreed with each of them regarding certain particulars. *The Theory of Moral Sentiments* emphasized the moral sentiment of sympathy and thereby anticipated the emphasis on sympathy and empathy in twentieth- and twenty-first-century scholarship. But that book also reflected Smith's view of providence (the "invisible hand") and the role of self-interest in economic matters, which he elaborated further in his later work *The Wealth of Nations*.

Jonathan Haidt (1963–)

Jonathan Haidt, a social psychologist, is one of many twenty-first-century scholars to argue that emotions dictate our moral judgments and that reasoning about them is normally after the fact and confabulatory. His most famous paper espousing this thesis is aptly titled "The Emotional Dog and Its Rational Tail."[47]

Haidt loves Hume and dislikes Plato. He wholeheartedly accepts Hume's youthful dictum, discussed above, that "[r]eason is, and ought only to be the slave of the passions, and can never pretend to any

Chapter 1. What Is the Basis of Human Ethics?

other office than to serve and obey them." He rejects Plato's contrary teaching that reason ought to supervise the passions.[48] He cites with approval the moral sentiment school of Hutcheson, Hume, and Smith.[49]

Haidt bases his conclusion that emotion is dominant in human life on numerous social science studies, many of which were conducted by him and his team. One of the dissenters from his views is Hanno Sauer, a philosophy professor, who has published an extensive and intensive critique of Haidt's studies, methods, and conclusions.[50]

From my perspective, the most important thing to understand about Haidt's work is that he analyzes how people often *do* think instead of considering how they *should* think. As Horatio said to Hamlet, "There needs no Ghost my lord, come from the Grave / To tell us this."[51] The fact that many or most people are irrational is not news. If there were ever any doubt about that "fact," the extreme irrationality of at least some portion of the populace became quite evident in the United States on January 6, 2021, when emotion prevailed over reason in a mob assault on the Capitol building, resulting in several deaths, many injuries, and substantial property damage. The question is whether we are going to sit idly by, fiddling while Rome burns, and let emotionalism ruin our individual and collective lives. Social scientists accepting as gospel the Humean is–ought and Weberian fact-value distinctions may take a nonjudgmental view of such developments, as will relativists of every stripe. But such quiescence enables and encourages demagogues and authoritarians and is destroying our social and political life.

Chapter 1. What Is the Basis of Human Ethics?

KANT'S CATEGORICAL IMPERATIVE

Immanuel Kant (1724–1804)[52] postulated that what he called the "categorical imperative" is the fundamental law of all morality: "There is, therefore, only a single categorical imperative and it is this: *act only in accordance with that maxim through which you can at the same time will that it become a universal law.*"[53] "For the purpose of achieving this it is of the utmost importance to take warning that we must not let ourselves think of wanting to derive the reality of this principle from the *special property of human nature.* For, duty is to be practical unconditional necessity of action and it must therefore hold for all rational beings (to which alone an imperative can apply at all) and *only because of this* be also a law for all human wills."[54] Nonhuman "rational beings," for Kant, included rational beings on other planets, God, and, possibly, angels.[55]

According to Kant, "we do not indeed comprehend the practical unconditional necessity of the moral imperative, but we nevertheless comprehend its *incomprehensibility*; and this is all that can fairly be required of a philosophy that strives in its principles to the very boundary of human reason."[56] In his later *Metaphysics of Morals*, he concluded that "these laws [the categorical imperative and freedom of choice], like mathematical postulates, are *incapable of being proved* and yet *apodictic* . . . ."[57]

Kant's categorical imperative is one way of thinking about ethics, and, indeed, it can often be helpful as a check against erroneous ethical conclusions. But I do not agree that it should be an absolute rule. Kant himself inadvertently showed its

Chapter 1. What Is the Basis of Human Ethics?

limitations when he argued that, given the categorical imperative against lying, one should not lie to a person at one's door who is intent on murdering a person hiding in one's house.[58] Unlike many armchair "thought experiments," this scenario actually occurred in Nazi Germany when individuals were hiding Jews whom the police were trying to apprehend and send to concentration camps. It is unlikely that any of the persons answering the door, imbued with the categorical imperative, told the truth about the situation.

Kant also claimed it was just for a woman to kill an illegitimate child (after birth) and for a junior officer to kill in a duel someone who had insulted his honor. Evidently, these situations involve applications of the categorical imperative, though Kant's discussion of them is less than clear.[59]

Kant believed that ethics or morality could be reduced to absolute rules formulated by philosophical reflection. He argued in the above-quoted passages that ethics should be based on rules designed for all rational beings (including God, angels, and rational beings on other planets)—without reference to human nature or experience. Yet, like other human beings, he could not know the mind of God or even the minds of angels or rational beings on other planets. His own examples were "human, all too human."

Kant wrote that the categorical imperative was the equivalent of a mathematical postulate. In contrast, Aristotle taught that ethical philosophy is not subject to the same precision and exactitude as are mathematics and natural science. See the section "Classical Reason" earlier in this chapter for Aristotle's discussion of this question. I agree with Aristotle on this issue.

Chapter 1. What Is the Basis of Human Ethics?

UTILITARIANISM

Different writers have different formulations of the basic principles of utilitarianism. The present discussion focuses on the views of John Stuart Mill as set forth in his essay titled "Utilitarianism."[60]

Mill wrote that "[t]he creed which accepts as the foundation of morals, Utility, or the Greatest Happiness Principle, holds that actions are right in proportion as they tend to promote happiness, wrong as they tend to produce the reverse of happiness. By happiness is intended pleasure, and the absence of pain; by unhappiness, pain, and the privation of pleasure" (II.2).

But what did Mill mean by pleasure? Although he distinguished between higher and lower pleasures (II.4–8), Mill included such things as power, fame, and money for their own sakes as legitimate forms of happiness if that is what people really wanted (IV.6): "the utilitarian standard . . . tolerates and approves [such] desires, up to the point beyond which they would be more injurious to the general happiness than promotive of it" (IV.7).

Mill argued that "questions of ultimate ends do not admit of proof, in the ordinary acceptation of the term. To be incapable of proof by reasoning is common to all first principles . . . ." (IV.1). To Mill, "the sole evidence it is possible to produce that anything is desirable, is that people do actually desire it" (IV.3). Accordingly,

> No reason can be given why the general happiness is desirable, except that each person, so far as he believes it to be attainable, desires his own happiness. This, however, being a fact, we have not only all the proof which the case admits of, but all

> which it is possible to require, that happiness is a good: that each person's happiness is a good to that person, and the general happiness, therefore, a good to the aggregate of all persons. (IV.3)

Mill considered, but did not affirmatively accept, the notion that utilitarian feelings are innate or embedded by God or nature in human beings. Although he took no absolute position on the issue, he stated that "I see no reason why the feeling which is innate should not be that of regard to the pleasures and pains of others. If there is any principle of morals which is intuitively obligatory, I should say it must be that" (III.7). Mill then remarked:

> On the other hand, if, as is my own belief, the moral feelings are not innate, but acquired, they are not for that reason the less natural. It is natural to man to speak, to reason, to build cities, to cultivate the ground, though these are acquired faculties. The moral feelings are not indeed a part of our nature, in the sense of being in any perceptible degree present in all of us; but this, unhappily, is a fact admitted by those who believe the most strenuously in their transcendental origin. Like the other acquired capacities above referred to, the moral faculty, if not a part of our nature, is a natural outgrowth from it; capable, like them, in a certain small degree, of springing up spontaneously; and susceptible of being brought by cultivation to a high degree of development. Unhappily it is also

Chapter 1. What Is the Basis of Human Ethics?

> susceptible, by a sufficient use of the external sanctions and of the force of early impressions, of being cultivated in almost any direction: so that there is hardly anything so absurd or so mischievous that it may not, by means of these influences, be made to act on the human mind with all the authority of conscience. To doubt that the same potency might be given by the same means to the principle of utility, even if it had no foundation in human nature, would be flying in the face of all experience. (III.8)

Mill followed this passage with an elaboration of how the utilitarian (greatest) happiness principle could and should gradually replace the selfish passions as the lodestar of ethical thought and conduct; he regarded the development of such social feelings as a matter of historical progress, of which his own era witnessed only a rudimentary form (III.9–11).

Mill had a kind of utopian dedication to the general good, defined as the greatest happiness, but his utilitarian theory is vague on how the general good is to be determined. Like Rousseau's General Will, the utilitarian doctrine raises the prospect of majority tyranny. During several centuries of American history, European settlers pushed Indigenous people off their lands, occasionally enslaved them, and sometimes tried to forcibly convert them to Christianity. This probably made the European immigrants, who sooner or later became the majority in America, happy in the utilitarian sense of the concept. Many other examples could be cited: American slavery before and during the Civil War, "Manifest Destiny" during the nineteenth century, racial segregation and Jim Crow laws during the twentieth century, and countless other such instances in American and world history. The utilitarian doctrine does not clearly prohibit such majoritarian happiness at the expense of minorities. Individual rights must apparently give way when they conflict with the happiness of the majority.

In my view, the doctrine of utilitarianism is defective for the reasons indicated above. In practice, it could lead to what might have been the opposite of Mill's intention. Mill was focused on the future, not the past. But the danger of ignoring the historical realities of the past is that they, or their like, will be repeated in the future. Progress is not inevitable, especially when one does not learn from history what could go wrong with utopian impulses.

VIRTUE ETHICS

A philosophical movement called "virtue ethics" emerged in the last half of the twentieth century and has continued into the present century. This school of thought has been mostly neo-Aristotelian (see the section "Classical Reason" earlier in this chapter). However, some of its votaries have looked to Hutcheson, Hume, Nietzsche, Heidegger, Confucianism, Buddhism, and Hinduism for inspiration.[61]

The following discussion focuses on one approach to virtue ethics—that of Philippa Foot (1920–2010) in her book *Natural Goodness*.[62]

Foot's thesis is that "moral judgement of human actions and dispositions is one aspect of a genre of evaluation itself actually characterized by the fact that

Chapter 1. What Is the Basis of Human Ethics?

its objects are living things" (4). The standard fact-value (is-ought) dichotomy ignores the difference between biological and inorganic life (24–37). Biological teleology, far from being a religious concept, distinguishes living beings (30–33, 40–43), but "the teleological story [for human beings] goes beyond a reference to survival itself" (43). "[T]he grounding of a moral argument is ultimately in facts about human life.... [M]oral action is rational action, and... human beings are creatures with the power to recognize reasons for action and to act on them." Nevertheless, Foot explicitly bows to Hume in acknowledging that sentiments such as shame, revulsion, sympathy, self-respect, and pride can play a role in motivating human virtue (24).

Foot observes, citing John Stuart Mill as an example, that "[m]any if not most moral philosophers in modern times see their subject as having to do exclusively with relations between individuals or between an individual and society, and so with such things as obligations, duties, and charitable acts." Foot argues (along with virtue ethicists generally) that "self-regarding" virtues such as courage, temperance (moderation), and wisdom should also, as they were for Plato and Aristotle, be an essential component of ethics (68–69). I agree, as will become clear in the course of the present book.

Philippa Foot's *Natural Goodness* goes into considerable detail in her application of these basic principles to human ethics. I do not always agree with those details, and my general theoretical approach takes another step beyond virtue ethics as normally understood. However, we can thank Foot and other virtue ethicists for carving out a promising niche in academia that was earlier barred due to the pervasive influence of analytic philosophy and other modern philosophical dogmas.

EVOLUTIONARY BIOLOGY

Since the time of Charles Darwin, scientists and others have studied the concept of evolution by natural selection with a view, among other things, toward evaluating what implications, if any, such evolution has for human ethical and political life.[63] One early doctrine was Social Darwinism—the idea that life is, and should be, the survival of the fittest, especially in the economic field, and that government should permit that struggle to reach its allegedly natural conclusion without any interference to mitigate its harshness. During the twentieth century, however, biologists, ethologists, neurologists, psychologists, and other experts discovered that patterns of cooperation, empathy, and reason also evolved among nonhuman and human mammals.[64]

Human cerebral evolution culminates in the development of the frontal lobes, specifically the prefrontal cortex. Neuroscientist Elkhonon Goldberg writes: "The frontal lobes perform the most advanced and complex functions in all of the brain, the so-called executive functions. They are linked to intentionality, purposefulness, and complex decision-making. They reach significant development only in humans; arguably, they make us human."[65] "At a very late stage of cortical evolution, two major developments took place: the emergence of language and a rapid ascent of the executive functions. [L]anguage acquired its place

Chapter 1. What Is the Basis of Human Ethics?

in the neocortex by attaching itself to various cortical areas in a highly distributed way. And the executive functions emerged as the brain's command post in the front portion of the frontal lobe, the *prefrontal cortex*. The frontal lobes underwent an explosive expansion at the late stage of evolution."[66]

In describing the frontal lobes, Goldberg could not resist resorting to figures of speech:

> Like a large corporation, a large orchestra, or a large army, the brain consists of distinct components serving distinct functions. And like these large-scale human organizations, the brain has its CEO, its conductor, its general: the frontal lobes. To be precise, this role is vested in but one part of the frontal lobes, the prefrontal cortex. It is a common shorthand, however, to use the term *frontal lobes*.
>
> Like the exalted leadership roles in human society, the frontal lobes were late in coming. In evolution their development began to accelerate only with the great apes. As the seat of intentionality, foresight, and planning, the frontal lobes are the most uniquely "human" of all the components of the human brain.[67]

Whatever the logical validity of such analogies, the functions of the human prefrontal cortex, as described in part by Goldberg, are well known. Reasoning, including ethical reasoning, also activates the prefrontal cortex.[68]

It is undisputed that the frontal lobes are interconnected with many other parts of the brain and that, accordingly, reason and emotion interact, for good or for ill, in human life.[69] The remainder of this book discusses the role of reason in human life and ethics.

A SECULAR TELEOLOGICAL VIEW OF HUMAN NATURE

As indicated above (see the subsections "Evaluation of ethical relativism" and "Jonathan Haidt"), a characteristic premise of twentieth- and twenty-first-century experimental psychology and similar academic disciplines is the assumption that the study of ethical matters should be limited to how ethics manifests itself in the lowest common denominator. This leads to the fallacy of hasty generalization: if, for example, some people confabulate about some things, then it is incorrectly concluded that all people confabulate about all things. A similar fallacious thought process occurs among many thinkers who reject the concept of free will: some human behavior at some times is the result of unconscious or subconscious emotional impulses, ergo no human conduct is the result of a rational exercise of free will.[70]

We have mentioned David Hume's is-ought distinction and the similar fact-value dichotomy of modern social science. Both doctrines assume that ethical "values" are not "facts" that can be scientifically and rationally analyzed. Rather, they assert that values are subjective preferences or feelings not subject to scientific and rational proof.

However, biological life (unlike physics, for example) is teleological (end-seeking).[71] "Unlike a mentally conceived purpose, a biological function lacks an explicit representation of the end with respect to

Chapter 1. What Is the Basis of Human Ethics?

which it operates. Nevertheless, it exists because of the consequences it tends to produce."[72]

In considering "facts," we must consider all the facts, not just the facts recognized by physics. The teleological nature of biological life is simply a fact that is unscientific to ignore. Human beings possess a reasoning faculty by nature.[73] They also possess some degree of free will.[74] This is how ethical "values" arise out of "facts"—or, to use Humean terminology, how the "ought" arises from the "is." Humans use their reasoning powers to identify and fulfill their individual, social, and political potentials. This is simply a biological "fact" of human nature. It is not a fact of physics or mathematics, nor does it have anything to do with religion.

The following chapters elaborate on these basic principles.

Chapter 2

Human Reason

> Reason did not, in earlier centuries, mean simply logical calculation but rather the whole process of discovering sound first principles and *then* reasoning from them to sound conclusions. What seems distinctive in our time is the widespread conviction that our choice of first principles is itself irrational or capricious.
>
> —Wayne C. Booth, *Now Don't Try to Reason with Me: Essays and Ironies for a Credulous Age*[1]

Human Reason and Teleology

Chapter 1 discussed the meaning of human teleology. The English word "teleology" derives from the ancient Greek words *telos* (which means "end," "completion," "fulfillment," or "purpose") and *logos* (meaning, in this context, "an account of"). *Logos* is the classical Greek word for "account," "word," "speech," and "reason." Accordingly, "account," "speech," and "reason" were intimately connected in the language of classical Greece, and all of these concepts were important in understanding the *telos* of human beings. Plato's dialogues and Aristotle's treatises were all about giving an account (*logos*) in speech (*logos*) based on reason (*logos*).[2]

Aristotle had an account (*logos*) of the meaning of cause. By what came to be known as "material cause," Aristotle meant "that out of which something comes into being, still being present in it, as the bronze of a statue or the silver of a bowl, or the kinds of these." He described what we call "formal cause" as "the form [*eidos*] or pattern [*paradeigma*], and this is the gathering in speech [*logos*] of what it is for something to be, or again the kinds of this (as of the octave, the two-to-one ratio, or generally number) and the parts that are in its articulation." What we call "efficient cause" is "that from which the first beginning of change or rest is, as the legislator is a cause, or the father of a child, or generally the maker of what is made, or whatever makes a changing thing change." The "final cause" is "the end [*telos*]. This is that for the sake of which, as health is of walking around. Why is he walking around? We say 'in order to be healthy,' and in so saying think that we have completely given the cause."[3]

Modern philosophy, starting with Francis Bacon and Thomas Hobbes, suppressed Aristotle's formal and final causes in favor of material and efficient causes.[4] The motivation was opposition to the medieval mindset wherein final cause (teleology) was construed in theological terms. As one scholar has observed, "Hobbes's doctrine of causes may be seen as a systematic attempt to discard the scholastic view on causality and replace it with strict mechanistic explanatory principles."[5] This prejudice remains today, with teleology continuing to be characterized as medieval Scholasticism and theological design.[6] As

Chapter 2. Human Reason

shown by the above quotation from Aristotle's *Metaphysics*, however, this is not what Aristotle (who died long before the advent of Christianity and whose writings contain no concept of a creator god) meant by final cause.

Modern science has ardently desired to reduce everything to physical (material and efficient) causes. However, this project has proved to be impossible, because living organisms and their constituent parts obviously have external ends and internal functions as well as evolving species-defined forms. Biological beings, with self-preserving, self-fulfilling, and reproductive needs and strategies, are not rocks.[7]

Moreover, even physics cannot be reduced to efficient and material causes, understood in the conventional billiard-ball account of Isaac Newton's laws of motion. Newton himself realized that gravitation did not fit the efficient-cause paradigm. One could add other examples from physics: electromagnetism, general relativity, and quantum entanglement.

Modern science and philosophy often dismiss teleology as a theological concept. However apt that description might have been for medieval thought, it is a straw person when applied to contemporary science and philosophy.[8] The present book discusses teleology in a strictly biological context. It is a principle of biological life, not a religious notion. It is a scientific fact, not a matter of supernatural design.

REASONING ABOUT ENDS AND MEANS

Human ethics, understood in a teleological, secular, biological sense, has three goals, ends, purposes: (1) to identify and promote the best possible state of being for each individual human being (the subject of Chapter 3), (2) to identify and promote the best possible relations between individual human beings and other human and nonhuman beings (the subject of Chapter 4), and (3) to identify and promote the best possible political order for human beings. The third purpose involves a transition between ethical and political philosophy. Chapters 5 and 6 of the present book address political philosophy in the context of citizen, media, and political ethics. My next book, provisionally titled *Reason and Human Government*, will discuss additional issues regarding political philosophy.[9]

Of course, the above-listed goals depend on what we mean by "best possible." To ascertain the character of these ends, we must use reason. Feelings, "sentiments," and passions—Hume and other modern philosophers to the contrary notwithstanding—do not suffice.[10] Various human beings have different, often contradictory feelings, sentiments, and passions. Although empathy and sympathy properly play a role in reasoning about ends, human reason must be the ultimate guide. But what, you might ask, is reason?

As explained in the preceding chapter, modernity has trained us to believe that reason has only to do with means, not ends. Reason is, in this view, purely instrumental. The assumption is that ends are postulated by feelings, sentiments, and passions.

A typical contemporary paradigm is that ends depend on subjective individual preferences and that reason exists only to find the most rational means of achieving these ends. It follows from this view that reason is merely a tool of whatever ends an individual may come up with.[11] For example, Hitler had a very rational war machine that assisted him in his irrational goal of imposing his brand of tyranny over continental Europe and eventually the world—*heute Deutschland, morgen die Welt* ("today Germany, tomorrow the world"), as the Nazi slogan went. Hitler was eventually—at great cost of blood and treasure—defeated, but only (or substantially) because his irrationality was so pervasive that it ultimately affected the means, as well as the end, of his life work. We will explore the tyrannical personality in the final chapter of the present book.

CASE STUDY: REASONING ABOUT ENDS

Plato's *Republic* and other of his dialogues provide examples of reasoning about ends. The question in the *Republic* is "what is justice?" Plato depicts Socrates as being the narrator of discussions between himself (Socrates) and others about the meaning of justice. We focus here on Socrates's dialectical exchanges with Thrasymachus, a famous Greek sophist, at the end of Book I of the *Republic*. Socrates has just refuted, by way of his questions and Polemarchus's answers, the view that justice is giving help to one's friends and injury to one's enemies. Socrates, as narrator, then states: "Now Thrasymachus had many times started out to take over the argument in the midst of our discussion, but he had been restrained by the men sitting near him, who wanted to hear the argument out. But when we paused and I said this, he could no longer keep quiet; hunched up like a wild beast, he flung himself at us as if to tear us to pieces. . . . And he shouted out into our midst and said,

Chapter 2. Human Reason

'What is this nonsense that has possessed you for so long, Socrates?' "[12]

After a somewhat humorous procedural colloquy with Socrates, Thrasymachus seriously proposes that justice "is nothing other than the advantage of the stronger." When Socrates persists in asking him what he means by that assertion, Thrasymachus replies that some cities are ruled tyrannically, some democratically, and some aristocratically. In each city, the ruling group is master.

> And each ruling group sets down laws for its own advantage; a democracy sets down democratic laws; a tyranny, tyrannic laws; and the others do the same. And they declare that what they have set down—their own advantage—is just for the ruled, and the man who departs from it they punish as a breaker of the law and a doer of unjust deeds. This, best of men, is what I mean: in every city the same thing is just, the advantage of the established ruling body. It surely is master; so the man who reasons rightly concludes that everywhere justice is the same thing, the advantage of the stronger.

When one stops to think about it, Thrasymachus's view resembles that of contemporary postmodernism. The difference is that Thrasymachus thought that this was a good thing; the postmodernists think it is bad.[13] Like the "survival of the fittest" doctrine of Social Darwinism, Thrasymachus attempts to derive a perverse "ought" from a presumed "is." To this extent, we can agree with the modern criticism of attempting to derive an "ought" from an "is."

Chapter 2. Human Reason

Socrates gets Thrasymachus to agree to the proposition that it is just for the ruled to obey the rulers and, additionally, that the rulers, due to fallibility or lack of knowledge, sometimes command what is disadvantageous for themselves. This leads to the contradiction that the ruled, to be just, must obey a command that disadvantages the rulers.

But Thrasymachus wiggles out of the contradiction: He claims that "the ruler, insofar as he is a ruler, does not make mistakes; and not making mistakes, he sets down what is best for himself. And this must be done by the man who is ruled. So I say the just is exactly what I have been saying from the beginning, to do the advantage of the stronger."

However, in the course of the subsequent discussion Thrasymachus modifies the terminology of his position. What he earlier called "just," he later calls "unjust." Now he explicitly argues that injustice is to be preferred to justice. Socrates goes through an extended series of questions that, albeit illuminating, we need not elaborate here. He concludes with a demonstration that an unjust person, an unjust group of people (for example, a gang of robbers), and an unjust political regime are all self-defeating: they all can involve internal discord that leads to negative results. At the end of Book I, however, Socrates professes himself unsatisfied with this account, because the interlocutors have still not explained what justice is. It will take the remainder of the *Republic* to answer that question.

Accordingly, contrary to much of modern philosophy, reasoning about ends is not impossible. Plato's *Republic* is an example of how such reasoning can occur, whether or not one agrees with that dialogue's apparently final conclusion about what justice is.

GENERAL REMARKS ABOUT HUMAN REASON

Differences exist between reasoning about such abstract disciplines as mathematics and physics and reasoning about human decisions and actions. The question of human justice, addressed in Plato's *Republic*, is not a subject of mathematics or physics. Mathematics and the physical sciences ask what is *true* about matters *not* involving human decisions and actions. Biology, unlike mathematics and physics, involves ends and means. Human decisions and actions involve *reasoning* about *both* ends and means. As Aristotle recognized in Book VI of his *Nicomachean Ethics*, correct reasoning should be applied both to the determination of ends and to the formulation of means.[14]

One common error is to identify reason solely with abstract rationality. We are familiar with child prodigies who are mathematical geniuses but lack the ability to reason properly regarding human ethical and political affairs. As Aristotle remarked long ago, young people are not good reasoners about ethical matters, because they lack experience in actions pertaining to life.[15] In our own time, Keith Stanovich, an applied psychologist, has demonstrated that many people—young and old—who score well on standard intelligence tests lack critical thinking skills, especially on matters pertaining to human decisions and actions.[16]

The discipline of "formal logic" involves abstract (symbolic) philosophical, mathematical, computational, or linguistic propositions that ignore questions about

Chapter 2. Human Reason

correct reasoning in ordinary human decisions and actions, whereas "informal logic" and "critical thinking" address the actual content of human thought and communication.

More precisely, formal logic is "the abstract study of propositions, statements, or assertively used sentences and of deductive arguments. The discipline abstracts from the content of these elements the structures or logical forms that they embody. The logician customarily uses a symbolic notation to express such structures clearly and unambiguously and to enable manipulations and tests of validity to be more easily applied."[17] "Formal" logic deals with "form."

In contrast, "informal" logic is not limited to "form." It includes inductive reasoning, evidence evaluation, and critical thinking as well as nonsymbolic deductive logic. Informal logic is greatly concerned with the correction of logical fallacies as they appear in human reasoning.[18] Informal logic and critical thinking are an important focus of the present book.

One aspect of the study of informal logic and critical thinking involves the distinction between quick, intuitive, heuristic human decisions, on the one hand, and more careful and deliberate human reasoning, on the other. People are sometimes confronted with situations in which fast thinking and reflexes are necessary and appropriate to respond to an immediate danger. In such cases, ancient emotional areas of the brain such as the amygdala are triggered, and fast reactions seem to be automatically generated. When, for example, an early human was confronted with a hungry lion, the situation called for immediate and drastic action. This kind of scenario is often called the "fight-or-flight" response. In modern times, we are not often confronted with large, hungry carnivores. However, these evolutionarily old aspects of our biology can be triggered by other situations. The fight-or-flight response could be activated by an encounter with a robber, for example. But this mechanism can be problematic when it is inappropriately actuated by events that do not involve immediate survival imperatives.[19]

Human thinking is often quick and heuristic (involving mental shortcuts) in order to address immediate issues that require decisions within a limited timeframe. Moreover, people sometimes make intuitive decisions based on their "gut" feelings, even when they could have taken more time to consider an issue in a rational and deliberate manner. Such rapid decisions are usually not of the same quality as conclusions formulated after explicit, thoughtful reasoning and deliberation. Careful, rational deliberation about ethical and other matters may, however, result in rough rules of thumb that become habitual, automatic, and immediately accessible when called upon in future situations.[20]

It is important for humans to think rationally about matters that concern them. We next examine some common fallacies that impede such reasoning.

SOME FAMOUS FALLACIES

Aristotle was evidently the first philosopher who made an elaborate attempt to classify and explain the various typical mental fallacies that human beings often commit.[21] From his treatises on logic, written in the fourth century BCE, to the present, philosophical thinkers have discussed the basic fallacies. Looking at fallacies could be compared with examining medical pathologies under a microscope. We will inspect a few of these interesting specimens here.[22]

The Post Hoc and Correlation Fallacies

Several types of fallacies have been assigned Latin names, because they became especially famous many centuries ago when Latin was the language of education and scholarship. One of the most common fallacies is called the post hoc fallacy, from the Latin phrase *post hoc, ergo propter hoc* ("after this, therefore because of this"). This fallacy occurs when one assumes that just because an event (Event 2) followed another event (Event 1), Event 2 was caused by Event 1. But no such conclusion is warranted on the basis of a temporal sequence of events alone.

For example, a student might eat oatmeal for breakfast one morning and take a test later in the day. If the student received a grade of "A" on the test, it would be fallacious for the student to conclude that the ingestion of the oatmeal caused the "A" grade. To determine whether the cereal had any causal effect on the grade, one would have to examine factors other than the fact that the ingestion of the cereal occurred before the administration of the test. One would have to look at the nutritional ingredients of the oatmeal as well as other facts. In this example, it is impossible to determine whether or not the oatmeal contributed in any way to the "A" grade. Perhaps it was a minor contributing cause with a more important cause being the student's preparation for the examination. However, one could rule out some clearly noncausal factors that occurred before the test, for example, the color of socks the student was wearing that day.

The point is this: A cause must occur before the effect of that cause, but the fact that Event 1 occurs before Event 2 does not necessarily mean that Event 1 caused (or had any contribution to the causation of) Event 2. To conclude that Event 1 caused Event 2, we must also examine factors other than the factor of what is called temporal priority (priority in time).[23]

The post hoc fallacy might seem so obvious that no one would ever commit it. In fact, however, it is committed all the time by people of all stations of life in many different contexts. Historians often commit this fallacy in attempting to explain the causation of events.[24]

The post hoc fallacy is closely related to the correlation fallacy (*cum hoc, ergo propter hoc*: "with this, therefore because of this"). Correlation does not, by itself, establish a causal relationship, because alternative antecedent causes may exist.[25]

There are three necessary elements in a causal relationship: temporal precedence, covariation of the cause and effect (correlation), and no plausible alternative explanations.[26] The post hoc and cum hoc fallacies account for some but not all of these requirements. Most importantly, they do not prove the absence of alternative explanations.

The post hoc and correlation fallacies are frequently committed by journalists and politicians who use statistical coincidence to suggest causation. The mere fact that Event 1 statistically occurs 90 percent of the time Event 2 occurs does not necessarily mean that one of these events caused the other. Other explanations include the possibility that the statistical correlation could be a coincidence or the possibility that both events could have been caused by another cause. Although high statistical correlations suggest that we might find a causal relationship upon further inquiry, we cannot conclude, on the basis of a statistical correlation alone, that one event caused the other event.[27]

A common example of these fallacies is when we experience coincidences in our lives that we interpret to be more than coincidences. In most cases, the coincidence has occurred purely by chance, given the huge multitude of possibilities that may happen to us at any given time. Our conclusion that a particular coincidence is more than a coincidence turns out to be an error in our statistical reasoning.[28]

Ambiguity or Equivocation

Another favorite fallacy is ambiguity, also known as equivocation. One manifestation of this fallacy is the implicit modification of the definition of a term in the middle of an argument so that the meaning of the term when used in the premise of the argument is different from the meaning of the term in the conclusion.[29]

There are many, many examples of the fallacy of ambiguity. In the nineteenth century John Stuart Mill discussed an example that could have been taken from the twenty-first-century rhetoric of people who deride evolution as being "just a theory":

> Another word which is often turned into an instrument of the fallacy of ambiguity, is Theory. In its most proper acceptation, theory means the completed result of philosophical induction from experience. In

that sense, there are erroneous as well as true theories, for induction may be incorrectly performed, but theory of some sort is the necessary result of knowing any thing of a subject, and having put one's knowledge into the form of general propositions for the guidance of practice. In this, the proper sense of the word, Theory is the explanation of practice. In another and a more vulgar sense, theory means any mere fiction of the imagination, endeavoring to conceive how a thing may possibly have been produced, instead of examining how it was produced. In this sense only are theory and theorists unsafe guides; but because of this, ridicule or discredit is attempted to be attached to theory in its proper sense, that is, to legitimate generalization, the end and aim of all philosophy; and a conclusion is represented as worthless, just because that has been done which, if done correctly, constitutes the highest worth that a principle for the guidance of practice can possess, namely, to comprehend in a few words the real law on which a phenomenon depends, or some property or relation which is universally true of it.[30]

In my observation (and Mill's), the fallacy of ambiguity is responsible for much confusion of thought—not only by ordinary people but also by philosophers.[31] This fallacy is committed all the time, but one can train one's mind to discern—and accordingly not be fooled by—it.

Circular Reasoning

Circular reasoning is often called "begging the question." This fallacy occurs when one attempts to prove a premise by using that very premise (often in disguise) in the course of the argument. For example, one could imagine a fictitious religion (call it "Truth") that has a holy book said to be based on revelation from certain gods (call them the Furies). In response to a question whether one should believe in the existence of the Furies, the defender of the religion says: "Because the holy book says so."[32]

Ad Hominem Arguments

This fallacy substitutes a personal attack on a person for rational argument. It may be perfectly true that a person is a scoundrel. That does not necessarily make that person's arguments untrue. To test those arguments, one must use reason, logic, and evidence, not emotional dislike of the source.[33]

Ad Populum Arguments

This form of irrational thinking assumes that just because many people think something to be true, that thing must be true. Throughout human history, popular opinion has often been wrong about many things. Accordingly, it is fallacious to base an argument on the numbers of people who believe it. Truth is not adjudicated by a popularity poll.[34]

Diversion; Straw Person

The fallacy of diversion is one of the most cherished mental tricks of lawyers and politicians. One of its most frequent manifestations is the "straw person" argument

Chapter 2. Human Reason

(formerly known as the "straw man" argument). This clever technique mischaracterizes another's position on an issue and then refutes the mischaracterized position. In other words, it constructs a "straw person" and then knocks it down. This methodology is often a last-ditch resort when the argument cannot otherwise be refuted or discredited. It is often used by attorneys in written briefs filed with courts on various legal and evidentiary issues. Instead of squarely responding to an opponent's arguments in an earlier filed brief, the subsequent briefwriter will mischaracterize the position of the opponent and then refute a position the other never took.[35] Another form of diversion is to ignore the other's argument and, instead, focus on irrelevant points, usually with a heavy emotional emphasis.

Politicians use the straw person diversion all the time. Usually, it takes the form of attributing an extreme position, espoused by some people in the politician's political party, to a particular politician even when that politician has expressly disavowed the extreme position taken by others in the party. This is a major reason for politicians losing elections through no fault of their own.

The straw person fallacy also operates when one answers a criticism that was not made instead of the criticism that was made.[36] This is also a common practice in political discourse. For example, in 2021, President Joe Biden was criticized for the manner in which he withdrew American troops from Afghanistan. Biden's initial response was to pretend that the criticisms were directed against his (and former president Donald Trump's) decision to withdraw from Afghanistan. That was not the precise issue, however.

Chapter 2. Human Reason

Many who favored withdrawing from Afghanistan, including members of Biden's own political party, nevertheless criticized the manner in which the withdrawal took place. On the other hand, most of the critics failed to explain how Biden, under the circumstances that he had recently inherited from the Trump administration, could have withdrawn the troops in a less disastrous way without prolonging the war indefinitely. And many of the critics did, in fact, disagree with the policy of withdrawing from Afghanistan. As Winston Churchill wrote, "It is always more easy to discover and proclaim general principles than to apply them."[37] The rational conduct of foreign policy requires attention not only to general principles but also to the concrete circumstances confronting the political leader—circumstances that could result in unintended or unwanted consequences. To the extent that Biden's critics complained about the manner of the withdrawal, it behooved them to show what specific alternative actions Biden could have taken that would have produced better results under the particular circumstances. Although I was closely following media reports of this controversy when it occurred, I did not see any such detailed alternative proposals. Instead, Biden's critics dwelled on generalized complaints suitable for popular media consumption—again committing the fallacy of diversion.

False Analogy

Analogies are sometimes useful as heuristic or educational devices to help hearers or readers understand a point that a speaker or writer is attempting to communicate. However, analogies can be problematic when they are used as alleged proof of an argument. Experts in logic, critical thinking, rhetoric, and science have long identified the fallacious uses of analogy in such circumstances.[38] Essentially, analogies can legitimately be used as proof of an argument only when the two alleged comparables share the same relevant characteristics. As one scholar has explained, "Whether or not an argument from analogy is strong depends on whether premise 1 is true–that is, are X and Y sufficiently and relevantly similar so that you can infer that P follows from Y just because P follows from X. The focus, therefore, should be on the reasons P follows from X and whether those reasons also apply to Y."[39]

False Equivalence

The fallacy of false equivalence is related to the fallacy of faulty analogy. It is similar to what is sometimes called the fallacy of "moral equivalence" and "whataboutism." A classic example is the way many Trump supporters reacted to the criticism of the violent Trumpian assault on the U.S. Capitol building on January 6, 2021. They argued that this attack was no different from the violence attending the Black Lives Matter protests earlier in 2020. Although many people (including myself) objected to the violence in both contexts, the Trumpian argument is a false equivalence. The January 6, 2021 insurrection was a deliberate attempt to violently stop an official governmental proceeding mandated by the Constitution of the United States, to hang the vice president of the United States for refusing to perpetrate an unconstitutional action, and to assassinate members of Congress, including the

Speaker of the House and the majority leader of the Senate. The attempted or actual violence by some extremists against buildings, private or public, during the 2020 Black Lives Matter demonstrations was deplorable, but it was not equivalent to the January 6, 2021 assault on the Capitol building, the initially successful interruption of a constitutional proceeding, and the attempted murder of the vice president and members of Congress.

Appeal to Authority

Appeal to authority is predominant in the fields of law, advertising, and religion. In law, it is part of the common-law heritage of judicial precedent. Since the courts can change precedent upon a proper showing of reasons for such change, the appeal to authority in law (called stare decisis) is not necessarily a bad thing and may be the only rule of thumb possible in a legal system in order to ensure some degree of consistency in judicial decisions.

Less lofty appeals to authority occur all the time, of course, in such matters as television commercials and other advertising, in which popular celebrities lend their name and credibility to commercial products and services that often have little to do with the reason for their fame. Strictly speaking, appeal to authority is never logical, because one thereby replaces one's own reasoning with mere faith that another person has arrived at a correct conclusion. Nevertheless, since it is impossible for an individual human being to be an expert on everything, it is often necessary, as a practical matter, to provisionally accept authoritative views on matters that one has not had time or knowledge to evaluate. One should, however, accept the expert's word only tentatively, keeping one's mind open to alternative conclusions on the basis of further evidence or expert opinion. Additionally, we should not rely on experts whose fields are different from the specific area of expertise relevant to our inquiry.

Reliance on authority is historically connected with religion. Chapter 1 briefly listed many of the various incompatible claims to revelation, and the appendix elaborates on some of the theological and violent conflicts among the claims to revelation. Historically, most Christian Protestants in the United States accepted the notion that revelation ceased with the accounts in the Christian New Testament. Nevertheless, some self-styled prophets of evangelical or charismatic Protestantism have claimed to receive revelation directly from God. During the 2010s and especially during the election controversies surrounding President Donald J. Trump's defeat in the 2020 presidential election, many of these "prophets" asserted that God had told them that God had appointed Trump—whose reputation for immorality, misogyny, and racism long preceded his rise to the presidency in January 2017—to be the authoritarian ruler of the United States and that God's will superseded any election or other laws to the contrary. Trump's loss in the 2020 election—confirmed by scores of judicial decisions, recounts, audits, and investigations[40]—was seen as a Satanic illusion, and the prophets (many of whom were praised by Trump himself) said that God would keep Trump in the presidency. This view was related to the QAnon belief that Trump would enlist the military to take over the United States Government by force and proceed to execute thousands of liberal Democrats who were accused (totally without evidence) of pedophilia and other sins. An autocratic theocracy would replace the United States democratic republic. The Constitution and laws of the United States would be trashed in the name of God. All of this went hand-in-hand with Trump's evidence-free mantra that the Democrats had stolen the 2020 election and that he had won by a massive landslide.[41]

This episode in American history illustrates quite clearly the extreme danger of the fallacy of appeal to authority. The "prophets" adduced no objective evidence to support their claims to revelation (indeed, no such evidence could ever exist). None of the many Trumpian lawsuits and investigations established any irregularities in the election that, if corrected, would have resulted in Trump's reelection. Trump's constant and continuing (to the time of this writing) claim that the election was stolen was a typical Big Lie perpetrated by an authoritarian or would-be authoritarian leader—a common tactic of such dictators as Stalin, Hitler, Putin, and many other autocrats.

All of these factors coalesced on January 6, 2021, when, pursuant to the Twelfth Amendment of the U.S. Constitution, the Congress met to count the electoral votes for president and to declare the winner of the electoral vote as the next president of the United States. While this proceeding was getting under way, Trump gave an inflammatory speech to his devoted supporters a few blocks away in which he intimated that they should "fight like hell" to maintain his presidency. Thousands of his supporters flocked to the U.S. Capitol Building, where Congress was meeting to count the electoral votes and declare the winner of the election. These supporters included militant right-wing militia members and White Supremacists as well as fanatical followers of the alleged Christian prophets and QAnon. They violently assaulted the Capitol, fighting with Capitol police officers and breaching the Capitol entryways. They expressed a desire to hang Vice President Mike Pence, who had incurred Trump's wrath by refusing, as president of the Senate, to change the electoral votes so as to ensure Trump's reelection. They also sought to murder Speaker of the House Nancy Pelosi and Senate Majority leader Chuck Schumer. Dozens of police officers were injured, many of them seriously, and several officers died as a direct or indirect result of their defense of the Capitol against the violent insurgents. Christian, QAnon, and White Supremacist signage and insignia permeated the mob attacking the Capitol. These facts are all well documented by video recordings of the event.[42]

This violent insurrection, which was intended to coerce the vice president and Congress either to change the electoral votes or to stop their proceedings entirely, was the direct result of the insurrectionists' commission of the fallacy of uncritically relying on authority. The authorities they blindly followed—Trump, the "prophets," the QAnon leaders, and others—had no evidence whatsoever to support their claims of a stolen election. They instigated thousands of people, all of whom suffered from a massive failure of critical thinking, to attempt to overthrow the U.S. Constitution and laws and assassinate high-level public officials.

Chapter 2. Human Reason

Jumping to Conclusions/Hasty Generalization

A common inductive fallacy, which we all have likely committed at one time or another, is the fallacy of jumping to conclusions. The fallacy of hasty generalization is one form of jumping to conclusions.

People often jump to conclusions because they do not wish to take the time to consider alternative possibilities. This is sometimes related to the fallacy of confirmation bias, in which the answer that we find acceptable reflects our previous experiences or preexisting biases, or the post hoc or cum hoc correlation fallacies, all of which are discussed in the present chapter.

Cognitive psychologist and neuroscientist Daniel J. Levitin gives an example how one can erroneously jump to a conclusion in everyday life:

> When evaluating a claim or argument, ask yourself if there is another reason—other than the one offered—that could account for the facts or observations that have been reported. There are always alternative explanations; our job is to weigh them against the one(s) offered and determine whether the person drawing the conclusion has drawn the most obvious or likely one.
>
> For example, if you pass a friend in the hall and they don't return your hello, you might conclude that they're mad at you. But alternative explanations are that they didn't see you, were late for a meeting, were preoccupied, were part of a psychology experiment, have taken a vow of silence for an hour, or were temporarily invaded by

bodysnatchers. (Or maybe permanently invaded.)[43]

The fallacy of hasty generalization involves the size of the sample from which one is generalizing: the smaller the sample size, the less likely the generalization. The traditional example is the question whether black swans exist. During the Middle Ages, a person living in a part of the world where all swans were white might have concluded that no black swans exist. However, black swans do exist, for example, in Australia. Accordingly, generalizations are often properly qualified by such language as "to the best of my knowledge" or "probably."[44]

False Dichotomy or False Dilemma

Another common error is the fallacy of false dichotomy or false dilemma, which is often committed by politicians and even scholars. The essence of this fallacy is that it implicitly or explicitly assumes that there are only two alternative explanations of something, ignoring the possibility that a third explanation is the legitimate one.[45] Although the fallacy is very common in political discourse, it is sometimes committed by famous scholars with high academic credentials, as I demonstrated in my book *Free Will and Human Life*.[46]

CRITICAL THINKING

What Is Critical Thinking?

Understanding and avoiding fallacies is a part of critical thinking. But critical thinking itself is a broader endeavor. It is a *habit of mind* in which one examines one's own thinking as well the statements of others in an attempt to ascertain whether specific propositions are consistent with reason and evidence. It involves, when appropriate, a careful appraisal of the reliability of the evidence allegedly supporting a particular statement.

Critical thinking does *not* mean that one *criticizes everything*. One should not start with the premise of sophomoric skepticism that everything is false and nothing is true. Critical thinking does not mean automatically taking an adversarial posture to every proposition or to the person espousing the proposition. Rather, a person should evaluate each argument with a properly skeptical attitude and question whether the assertions formulated by oneself or others are consistent with reason and evidence. The adjective "critical" in "critical thinking" means "exercising or involving careful judgment or judicious evaluation" rather than "inclined to criticize severely and unfavorably."[47]

Critical thinking is similar to the Socratic method—Socrates's questioning, through rational dialectic, of others' assertions, as depicted by Plato in his Socratic dialogues. Socrates's interrogation of others unfortunately led to youthful imitators who misused the method and gave Socrates a reputation in ancient Athens that he was corrupting the young with his skepticism and alleged heresy (not believing in the gods in which the city believed). Socrates was incorrectly conflated with the sophists of his day, even though the mature Socrates himself subjected the sophists to critical dialectical examination. As a result of the popular prejudice against him, Socrates was tried, convicted, and sentenced to death by the Athenian jury.[48]

Chapter 2. Human Reason

The experience of Socrates alerts us to the fact that critical thinking can be misused by people who do not properly understand it and, further, that critical thinking is not always welcome in society at large. Critical thinking is, first and foremost, an individual skill that we should acquire in order to free our own minds from irrationality. Additionally, we can use critical thinking to encourage other individuals and our society generally to become more rational. The latter objectives are, however, difficult and sometimes dangerous.

We now turn to a consideration of some of the principles and applications of critical thinking.

Principle of (Non)contradiction

The section "Classical Reason" in Chapter 1 discussed the principle of contradiction (often now called the principle or law of noncontradiction): the same thing cannot be and not be at the same time and in the same respect. With regard to individual, social, and political matters, this is a foundational axiom of critical thinking.

A contradiction is not the same thing as a paradox. A paradox appears on the surface to be a contradiction, but it is not a contradiction, because it involves a fact, not immediately evident, that accounts for the true reality behind the paradox. Once we understand the previously unknown fact, the matter no longer involves an apparent contradiction.

We do not know, and may never know, whether some of the apparent contradictions of physics and metaphysics (for example, the imponderables of quantum entanglement, a first cause, the beginning of time, and the infinity of space) are true contradictions or whether they are mere paradoxes. There may be a

Chapter 2. Human Reason

"logic," so to speak, that is currently or forever inaccessible to the human mind. However, such difficulties do not apply to normal human conduct. When, for example, a recent, twice-impeached president of the United States frequently contradicted himself on a daily basis, that was not a paradox. It was rather a deliberate obfuscation, meant to sow confusion and uncertainty in the minds of the general public. Governance by contradiction is a recipe for chaos.

What's the Source?

In evaluating a primary or secondary source, the first thing you should consider is whether the source is possibly biased. For example, is the source a well-known advocate for left-wing or right-wing causes? Is the source a careful historian or scientist or is the source a hack—perhaps a paid hack—for a particular ideological view? Knowing such facts about the source need not deter you from reading it, but you thereby become alert for possible omissions or biases in the source's treatment of factual or interpretive matters. Caveat emptor!

By the way, such care does not make you guilty of committing the ad hominem fallacy. The purpose of such source evaluation is to keep you on the lookout for possible problems, not for you to make a snap judgment.

Quotes out of Context

Many writers and speakers quote others out of context. If the quotation is important, look for the original place in which it was made, and consider the entire context of the remark.

Chapter 2. Human Reason

Anecdotal Evidence: the Good and the Bad

Sometimes a claim is supported by anecdotal evidence. Statistical evidence would seem to be more reliable, but, as discussed below, statistical evidence can be and often is misused. Additionally, statistical evidence is not always available. Anecdotal evidence has its benefits but should not be mistaken for a more thorough approach. Careful consideration of anecdotal as well as statistical evidence is part of the endeavor to avoid hasty generalization.

Critical Thinking about Statistics

Statistics are often misused by advertisers, journalists, politicians, and others. Sometimes the trickery is deliberate; on other occasions, it is inadvertent or negligent.

One of the clearest expositions of statistical deception is in part 1 of Daniel J. Levitin's book *A Field Guide to Lies: Critical Thinking with Statistics and the Scientific Method*. Levitin is a cognitive psychologist and neuroscientist. Here are some of his pointers regarding the evaluation of statistics (page references are to the Kindle version of the 2019 edition of his book):

- Initially, consider whether the statistical or numerical information is plausible (3–10). "[I]f someone says they are two hundred years old, or that they can consistently beat the roulette wheel in Vegas, or that they can run forty miles an hour, these are not plausible claims" (4).
- Claims about averages can be misleading (11–25). Averages are calculated in three

different ways: (1) the *mean* average "is calculated by adding up all the observations or reports you have and dividing by the number of observations or reports," (2) the *median* "is the middle number in a set of numbers," and (3) the *mode* is "the number that appears more often than the others" (11–13). Those presenting statistical averages may not identify which of these averages they are using, and they accordingly can give a misleading impression. Life expectancy statistics are one example of confusion about averages. In earlier times, the mean average of lifespans was significantly lower than today as a result of the large number of infant deaths. But people who survived until age twenty often lived long lives (20–21).

- "There are many ways that graphs can be used to manipulate, distort, and misrepresent data" (26). Levitin discusses such methods at length (26–42).
- He also shows how statistical presentations often violate the principle (discussed above) that correlation does not prove causation (48–51).
- Levitin elaborates and provides examples of many other misleading statistical, numerical, and graphical representations (51–120).

In short, it is all too easy to be fooled by statistical data that do not actually demonstrate what they may appear to show. Levitin's book is one of many that discuss such matters in depth. Further elaboration of these principles is beyond the scope of the present book;

the interested reader can consult books and studies that specifically focus on these issues.

Confirmation Bias

Humans often look for information that supports their preexisting views and disregard contrary data or evidence. Critical thinking demands that we set aside confirmation bias and, instead, consider all relevant facts and arguments that pass a certain threshold of plausibility. Of course, it is not necessary to waste time on arguments that are ridiculous on their face (for example, the QAnon assertion that liberals are pedophiles who eat human children), except for the purpose, if required by the occasion, of refuting it.

Conspiracies—Actual, Probable, Possible, and Fictional: An Exercise in Critical Thinking

Historians have established the existence of some actual conspiracies throughout history.[49] Examples include the Cataline conspiracy (63 BCE), the successful conspiracy to assassinate Julius Caesar (44 BCE), the Pazzi conspiracy (1478), the 1605 Gunpowder Plot to blow up the British House of Lords at the official State opening of Parliament, the successful conspiracy to assassinate President Abraham Lincoln in 1865, the involvement of the U.S. Government's Central Intelligence Agency (CIA) in coups against foreign governments and assassinations and attempted assassinations of foreign political leaders, the Watergate conspiracy and coverup, and the conspiracy of militia and other groups to attack the U.S. Capitol on January 6, 2021.[50] No dispute about the reality of such historical facts exists among serious scholars.

Chapter 2. Human Reason

Some conspiracy theories have ample supporting evidence but are not yet universally accepted. These are "probable" or "possible" conspiracies, depending on the quantity and quality of evidence supporting them. For example, scholars, lawyers, journalists, other researchers, and witnesses have adduced substantial and even judicially admissible evidence that the 1964 Warren Commission's official version of the John F. Kennedy assassination—that Lee Harvey Oswald was the sole shooter and no conspiracy existed—is incorrect and that there was, in reality, a successful conspiracy of several (perhaps many) actors, inside and outside of the United States Government, who were involved in the planning, execution, and/or coverup of the assassination.[51] In 1979, the U.S. House of Representatives Select Committee on Assassinations concluded there was "a high probability that two gunmen fired at President John F. Kennedy" and that "President John F. Kennedy was probably assassinated as a result of a conspiracy."[52] In contrast, other analysts have attempted to debunk any and all such JFK assassination conspiracy theories.[53] In my view, it is probable, based on the overwhelming evidence cited in the endnote references, that a conspiracy to assassinate Kennedy did exist and that such conspiracy involved U.S. governmental officials as well as nongovernmental actors.

The JFK assassination documentation and literature is a treasure trove of evidence that begs for critical-thinking analysis in the sense we have elaborated it in this chapter. As referenced above, careful reasoners and researchers have already undertaken such analysis, and others are encouraged to evaluate their work. But unfortunately, to date, the Government has refused to produce all relevant documents in its possession and has substantially redacted many of the documents it has already produced. It is difficult to discern what national security secrets still lurk in documents that were generated almost six decades ago. Perhaps, eventually, all the relevant documents and their contents will be produced, and historians can reach a final consensus on the events of November 1963.

For every actual, probable, or possible conspiracy, there are countless conspiracy theories that are totally baseless. Recent examples of conspiracy theories that lack any supporting evidence but have rather been made up out of whole cloth include various false allegations about COVID vaccines, the Big Lie that the 2020 presidential election was stolen from Donald Trump,[54] and the related psychotic delusions of the QAnon fantasy world.

CONCLUDING REMARKS ABOUT HUMAN REASON

It is the thesis of this book that reason, rightly understood, and the rational evaluation of evidence are essential to human ethics. The present chapter has elaborated my concept of what human reason is. The remaining chapters address how reason properly applies to our individual, social, and political lives.

CHAPTER 3

INDIVIDUAL ETHICS

> From the emperor down to the mass of the people, all must consider the cultivation of the person the root of everything besides.
>
> It cannot be, when the root is neglected, that what should spring from it will be well ordered.
>
> —Confucius, *The Great Learning*[1]

The touchstone for individual ethics is what facilitates our individual mental and physical well-being, provided we do not violate our ethical duties to others. We address ethical duties to others in Chapters 4–6 of this book.

It is fairly easy to ascertain what is good for us physically. Good health is, of course, the primary desideratum for physical well-being. Accordingly, activities that facilitate good health are good; activities that are unhealthy—alcoholism, drug addiction, and so forth—should be avoided.

But what constitutes *mental* well-being? That is a question that preoccupied Plato and some other philosophers throughout the millennia. Plato spoke of the right order of the soul (*psyche*): reason should guide the spirted and desiring parts of the soul. What Plato meant by "soul" is a large question. To avoid

Chapter 3. Individual Ethics

theological issues, we can consider the term "mind" to be a synonym for "soul."[2]

WHY SHOULD WE WANT TO BE RATIONAL?

The preceding chapter discussed human reasoning about ends (noninstrumental reason) and human reasoning about means (instrumental reason). But why should we wish to be rational? What's in it for us?

Every thinking person asks important questions, often at a young age: How should I live? What are the attitudes I should hold about myself? How should I act? How should I conduct my life? What are my goals regarding work and family? How should I treat others? And so forth.

People who grow up in traditional cultures may not ask such questions. The answers may already have been decided for them by cultural conditioning or even by governmental laws. But many people today do not have to conform to any particular cultural way of doing things. Even if the culture in which they are born demands adherence to informal or formal norms, they can liberate themselves and become independent in both thought and action. They can decide for themselves what they will do—or try to do—with their lives, as long as they do not harm others.

Mature human beings are distinguished from other living things—at least in degree, if not in kind—by a fully developed prefrontal context, which enables them to exercise reason and planning regarding both ends and means.[3] Reason helps us ascertain the best ends as well as the most appropriate means to achieve those ends. Thus, the correct use of reason is of utmost importance to human beings. As discussed in the present chapter, the proper use of reason is necessary for individual human beings to reach their potentials.

NATURE AND NURTURE IN INDIVIDUAL HUMAN BRAIN DEVELOPMENT

The prefrontal cortex and other important regions of the human brain relevant to reasoning and self-control do not fully develop, on average, until age twenty-five or even later.[4] Thus, Aristotle was prescient when he wrote that young people are often incapable of adequately understanding ethics, though he attributed this to lack of experience in life.[5] It is only during the last few decades that we have acquired advanced neuroscientific knowledge regarding brain development, and Aristotle, of course, knew nothing of those developments. He was not, however, entirely wrong: it is quite likely that younger people often do not exercise good ethical judgment as a result of both biology and inexperience.

Accordingly, Aristotle was a strong advocate of ethical habituation of the young from early childhood through adolescence—a theme especially prominent in his *Nicomachean Ethics*. This is, of course, correct, especially regarding younger children. The problem is that habituation can be either good or bad, depending on the particular parents of the child or the culture in which the child is raised. For example, ancient Sparta trained its privileged children to steal from and terrorize the slave population.[6] Ancient Athens and Crete[7] accepted male pederasty. There are good habits, and there are bad habits.

Negative habituation can adversely affect a person's ability to be rational. People who have experienced psychological or physical abuse or other trauma in their environments may benefit from psychological counseling. Other impairments of reason may be traceable to biological rather than environmental factors. Although I have no training in clinical psychology or psychiatry, it is my understanding that many psychological problems can be effectively treated by cognitive behavioral therapy,[8] prescribed medicine, or psychoanalysis. Unfortunately, some individuals are born with irreparable brain damage, and others are victims of serious brain trauma as a result of war, crime, or accidents. Such people are not self-sufficient and require the care of others to survive.

The education and habituation of children and adolescents should encourage reason to the extent possible. Rational arguments, such as those offered in the present book, should be given to children and, especially, adolescents as grounds for ethical behavior. Although they may not yet be sufficiently mature to base their actions solely on such arguments, planting a rational seed in their minds will reap lifelong benefits. This is the experience component of the nature-nurture evolution of the ethical person.

A person may themselves develop bad habits, even after their physical brain has reached maturity. This often happens when adults associate with criminals or other bad actors. Continuing negative habituation of this sort makes it more and more difficult for such a person to become rational and ethical. Although Aristotle thought that some such individuals reached a point beyond hope, I am not quite so pessimistic.[9]

When a human's brain is fully developed and that person possesses an independent mind not under the grip of negative habituation, the individual is capable of reasoning about ethical behavior regardless of cultural conditioning. The present book can provide a guide for such persons.

THE LIFE OF REASON

Jesus is reported as saying: "You shall love your neighbor as yourself."[10] But what does it mean to love oneself? Jesus (as far as we know) did not clearly elaborate what he meant by such self-love.

Aristotle, however, did expressly discuss the concept of self-love. He observed that there are two kinds of self-love. The first is what we would now call "selfish":

> Now, then, those who bring self-love into reproach call "self-lovers" those people who allot to themselves the greater share of money, honors, and bodily pleasures, for the many long for these things and are serious about them on the grounds that they are what is best; hence too such things are fought over. Those who grasp for more of these things gratify their desires and, in general, their passions and the nonrational part of their soul. Such is the character of the many. Hence too this familiar term of reproach has arisen from the case that mostly prevails, which is indeed base. Those who are self-lovers in this way, therefore, are justly reproached.[11]

Chapter 3. Individual Ethics

Aristotle went on to discuss the second kind of self-love:

> For if someone should always take seriously that he himself do what is just, or moderate, or whatever else accords with the virtues, and, in general, if he should secure what is noble for himself, no one would say that he is a "self-lover" or even blame him. But this sort of person would seem to be *more* of a self-lover; at any rate, he allots to himself the noblest things and the greatest goods, he gratifies the most authoritative part of himself, and in all things he obeys this part. . . .
>
> A self-lover, therefore, is especially that person who is fond of and gratifies this authoritative part; and he is said to be either self-restrained or lacking in self-restraint depending on whether or not his intellect is in control, on the grounds that this part *is* the person himself. And those deeds that are accompanied by reason seem above all to be the ones done by people themselves, and done voluntarily. It is not unclear, then, that each person is this [rational] part, or is this above all, and that the decent person is fond of this especially. Hence he especially would be a self-lover, but in reference to a different form of it than the one subject to reproach. In fact it differs as much from this latter form as living in accord with reason differs from living in accord with passion, as much as longing for what is noble differs from

longing for what is held to be advantageous.[12]

These excerpts from Aristotle generally describe what the life of reason is and is not. To be human in the true sense means to commit oneself to a rational mode of life—to *think* rationally and to *apply* one's reason to the situations with which life confronts us. Such commitment to reason is not always easy. The following discussion examines some of the fundamental deviations from reason to which we human beings are exposed and to which we all too easily succumb.

GENERAL DEPARTURES FROM A RATIONAL LIFE

Mental Laziness

We are all familiar with the notion that to keep in shape physically we must eat right and exercise. The same is true of keeping the mind in shape. The mind, like the body, becomes flabby if it is not properly used. Moreover, irrational and illogical habits of thinking become the more ingrained the more one allows them to dominate one's mind. One must learn to examine one's own life, to question oneself about one's objectives, to think clearly about the issues with which one is confronted, and to exercise one's reason about the matters of both immediate and long-range concern. A person should always be on guard against sloppy, illogical thinking—particularly if that sloppy, illogical thinking is going on in one's own mind! Just as one should not abuse one's body with poison or with medically unnecessary narcotic drugs, so one should not allow one's mind to be poisoned or "doped" with stupidity. Although geniuses may be few, all who are not physically or psychologically brain damaged have the ability to improve, develop, and cultivate their minds. Since the human mind in general, and volitional reason in particular, is what distinguishes humanity from the rest of the universe known to us, we should take special care that our minds are not polluted with irrationality, dogmatism, or absurdity.

Conformism

One of the most tempting and perilous defects to which the human mind is prone is conformism. We all are familiar with the peer pressures that operate so blatantly among young people. However, peer pressure is not limited to the young. It is easy to adopt mental attitudes and habits not because we have rationally concluded that they are correct but because others tell us—explicitly or tacitly—that they are correct. We have a tendency to agree with others merely because we want them to like us. Such wish for social approval is the root of many evils.

The herd is not always right. Frequently, it can be dead wrong. Consider, for example, the fact that Hitler came to power not by taking over Germany with force but by being selected as a result of democratic procedures. Similarly, human sacrifice has been considered "normal" in some societies, and most people in those societies have assumed that such a practice is right because that is what they have been told. Human beings in advanced societies no longer need to accept abominations as morally right just because everyone thinks so. We need to learn to think for ourselves. This does not mean that we should play the iconoclast for the perverse pleasure of shocking other people. The goal of shocking other people is not rational.

One should be committed to reason as the highest principle of human life. If the crowd is irrational, one should not go along with it. It is not *always* necessary to *express* opposition to the irrationalism of others; indeed, doing so would be a full-time and dangerous job, as Socrates discovered. However, a fundamental requirement of morality is that one must refuse assent in one's own mind to irrationalism from any quarter. In that sense, even a person who is compelled to be a slave can be mentally free. One may be forced to live in the midst of irrationality, but one is never forced to agree in the privacy of one's own mind that irrationalism is right. Keeping one's own mind uncontaminated by irrationalism is a human being's most sacred commitment.

Materialism, Right and Wrong

Once we become adults, we must fend for ourselves economically. Very few are born into wealthy circumstances; most of us have to figure out some means of economic preservation. The goal of economic survival is a rational end. It is rational even insofar as one wishes to have a materially satisfactory life. But the vast accumulation of wealth in considerable excess of what one or one's family needs for preservation, even comfortable preservation, is not a rational end. An obsession with wealth for wealth's sake or money for money's sake is not rational. Money is properly understood as a means to other ends—material comfort and leisure for rational pursuits, for example. Money should not be an end in itself.

Chapter 3. Individual Ethics

Materialism is often merely a form of conformism. Many people like to impress others with their accumulations of material things. However, impressing others has nothing to do with rationality and true self-esteem. Thinking that one is liked or loved as a consequence of one's material possessions is the height of self-deception. The conspicuous consumer may think that they have many friends who are impressed by their "flash" (which, as the saying goes, may be greater than their actual "cash"). In reality, such "friends" are servile flatterers who would not stick around for a minute if one's fortunes were reversed. Materialism for the sake of impressing others is pure folly.

Nevertheless, the appreciation and enjoyment of material things for their usefulness or intrinsic aesthetic delight is not irrational. It is part of human nature to invent and manufacture tools, time-saving devices, and other technological conveniences that make our lives easier and in important respects happier. Technology has made feminism practicable and slavery obsolete. It has freed human women and men from lives that are nasty, brutish, and short, and, correspondingly, has opened up opportunities for human fulfillment that were far beyond the reach of most persons in earlier ages.

Yet even the legitimate use of material things can become mind numbing. Some people become so absorbed in their material possessions (even apart from any wish to impress others) that their minds become lazy, soft, and formless. Material things, properly considered, are a part of human life. They do not, in and of themselves, suffice for true human fulfillment. The ultimate aspirations of the human mind transcend human technology.

Chapter 3. Individual Ethics

Intemperance

The mind-numbing effects of conformism and thoughtless materialism are the "normal" deviations from reason of many people. Intemperance is an even more vicious departure from human reason. A way of life dominated by alcoholism, drug addiction, or similar behaviors is an irrational and inhuman way of life. It is also dangerous. For example, alcoholism and drug addiction can substantially injure a person's brain as well as lead to physical deterioration and even death.

Although intemperance is inhuman, rationalism does not imply or require the opposite extreme of asceticism. For example, sexual pleasure as part of a temperate life guided by reason is natural to human beings, no matter how much certain religions have attempted to instill guilt about it. But addictive drugs and similarly obsessive behaviors should be avoided by human beings who wish to preserve their humanity.

Anger

Anger is perhaps the most difficult human emotion to understand. Probably no human being who has ever lived has avoided experiencing the emotion of anger at one time or another in that person's life. Even Jesus is portrayed in the Gospels as exhibiting anger when the occasion appeared to justify such a posture. It is difficult to say whether the type of anger that affects one's internal state of mind is ever appropriate.[13] Certainly, it is not unethical to oppose injustice in a forthright and strong manner. But anger in and of itself tends to blind our ability to think rationally and clearly about the problem that provokes our anger. Accordingly, we should be slow to anger, and, when it nevertheless arrives, be quick to make every effort to substitute rational analysis and (if appropriate) thoughtful action for this emotion. Although anger (insofar as it does not incapacitate us) may have a legitimate use in strengthening our resolution to resist evil, anger is frequently used as a substitute for rational thinking in our contemporary society. The replacement of reason by anger is not consistent with our humanity and, moreover, often renders us unable to deal effectively with the source of our anger.[14]

Love of Power for Its Own Sake

Love of power for its own sake is, like conformism and conspicuous consumption, a substitute for true self-esteem. Although the most obvious manifestation of love of power is in politics, we also see love of power operating every day in nonpolitical human relationships. The person who is dominated by this vice imagines that it is possible to use physical, economic, or psychological coercion as a substitute for love. Like conformism and conspicuous consumption, love of power for the sake of power is a profound self-delusion.

Shakespeare deeply understood this dark side of some human beings. The result of his understanding was such masterpieces as *Macbeth*, *Richard III*, and his depiction of Claudius in *Hamlet*. However, love of power in this sense is not to be confused with the elevated state of mind of the rare public official whose knowledge, wisdom, and political objectives transcend petty political opportunism.

Chapter 3. Individual Ethics

THE ETHICAL MEAN

Both Confucius (551–479 BCE) in China and Aristotle (384–322 BCE) in Greece taught a doctrine of the ethical mean. Their respective versions of this doctrine are sufficiently similar that one wonders whether Aristotle had somehow heard of the Confucian teaching and been influenced by it. However, this doctrine makes so much sense that it is not all unreasonable to think that these two philosophers independently formulated it.

Although we have no proof of writings directly authored by Confucius, some Confucian works were prepared not long after his death and purport to quote him or accurately reflect his teachings.

In the Confucian *Analects*, the following statement is attributed to Confucius: "The moral power of the Middle Way is supreme, and yet it is not commonly found among the people."[15] Although the text at this point does not elucidate Confucius's meaning, it later sheds some light on it in an illustration:

> Zigong asked: "Which is the better: Zizhang or Zixia?" Confucius said: "Zizhang overshoots and Zixia falls short." Zigong said: "Then Zizhang must be the better?" Confucius said: Both miss the mark."[16]

Confucius also said: "If I cannot find people who steer a middle course to associate with, I shall be content with the crazy and the pure. The crazy dare do anything, whereas there are things the pure will never do."[17]

The Confucian work *The Doctrine of the Mean* was traditionally written by Tsze-sze, the grandson of Confucius, on the basis of oral tradition, including, possibly, his discussions with Confucius himself.[18] Although *The Doctrine of the Mean* praises the ethical mean in general terms, it does not provide specifics about what constitutes the mean in situations that are relevant to today's circumstances. For example, much of it involves matters of ritual and filial piety.[19]

Aristotle added content and context to the conception of the ethical mean. At the beginning of Book II of his *Nicomachean Ethics*, Aristotle distinguished between intellectual and moral virtue. Intellectual virtue includes reason, as discussed in Chapter 2 of the present book, as well as advanced theoretical studies. Moral virtue includes both individual and social virtues. The present chapter of this book discusses individual ethics; the remaining chapters address social and political ethics. This book is not the place for a critical scholarly analysis of the *Nicomachean Ethics* or for Aristotle's other major work on ethics, called the *Eudemian Ethics*. I disagree with Aristotle in some particulars; the following discussion focuses on areas in which I mostly agree with him.

Intellectual virtues are not evaluated by the ethical mean. However, what Aristotle called the moral virtues are. For present purposes, the individual moral virtues are courage and moderation.

Aristotle distinguished between the ethical mean and the arithmetic mean. The ethical mean is not the same as the arithmetic mean. Rather it is what is neither excessive nor deficient for an individual: "Thus every knower of the excess and the deficiency avoids them, but seeks out the middle term and chooses this—yet not a middle belonging to the thing in question but rather the one relative to us."[20]

He elaborated on the concept of the ethical mean as follows:

Chapter 3. Individual Ethics

> But I mean moral virtue, for it is concerned with passions and actions, and it is in these that excess, deficiency, and the middle term reside. For example, it is possible to be afraid, to be confident, to desire, to be angry, to feel pity, and, in general, to feel pleasure and pain to a greater or lesser degree than one ought, and in both cases this is not good. But to feel them when one ought and at the things one ought, in relation to those people whom one ought, for the sake of what and as one ought—all these constitute the middle as well as what is best, which is in fact what belongs to virtue. Similarly, in the case of actions too, there is an excess, a deficiency, and the middle term. Virtue is concerned with passions and actions, in which the excess is in error and the deficiency is blamed; but the middle term is praised and guides one correctly, and both [praise and correct guidance] belong to virtue. Virtue, therefore, is a certain mean, since it, at any rate, is skillful in aiming at the middle term.[21]

And, in a further passage, Aristotle beautifully summarizes his concept of the ethical mean:

> That moral virtue is a mean, then, and how it is such; that it is a mean between two vices, the one relating to excess, the other to deficiency; and that it is such on account of its being skilled in aiming at the middle term in matters of passion and action, have been stated adequately. Hence it is in fact a task to

be serious, for in each case it is a task to grasp what resides in the middle. For example, to grasp the middle of a circle belongs not to everyone but to a knower. And so too, to become angry belongs to everyone and is an easy thing, as is also giving and spending money; but to whom [one ought to do so], how much, when, for the sake of what, and how—these no longer belong to everyone nor are easy. Thus in fact acting well is rare, praiseworthy, and noble.[22]

Notice how similar Aristotle's views are to those of Confucius's brief statements, quoted above, regarding the ethical mean. Confucius and Aristotle apparently had the same conception, though some applications of it would have been different in their respective cultures.

We now turn to an application of these principles to the individual ethical virtues of courage and moderation.

Courage

Aristotle applied the ethical mean to courage in chapters 6–9 of Book 3 of the *Nicomachean Ethics*. Courage, he says, "is a mean with respect to fear and confidence...."[23] He discusses many aspects of courage. Some things, he says, are rightly feared, but the courageous person "will endure them in the way that he [or she] ought and as reason commands, for the sake of the noble, for this is the end of virtue."[24]

The person "who exceeds in confidence when it comes to frightening things is reckless, and the reckless person is held to be both a boaster and a pretender to courage; at any rate, as the courageous [person] actually is with respect to frightening things, so the reckless wishes to appear to be."[25]

Aristotle discusses courage in battle at some length. He observes that "[t]he reckless are also impetuous, and though prior to the dangers they are willing, in the midst of them they withdraw, whereas courageous [persons] are keen in the deeds but quiet beforehand."[26] Moreover, "[t]hose who fight on account of anger or revenge are fit for battle, but they are not courageous, since they fight not on account of the noble or as reason commands but on account of their passion."[27]

Aristotle's discussion of courage includes many other details, and the reader is encouraged, if interested, to consult it. The following are some of my own thoughts about courage.

Fear of death is one of the most common anxieties that humans experience. In many cases, this is due to theological doctrines that people who do not believe a particular dogma or who do not live a moral life will go to hell. First, any notion that a person will go to hell as a result of failure of belief is absurd. It would be an unjust deity indeed that would consign billions of people to hell for lack of belief in a particular dogma of which many of them had not even heard. As for the supposition that one's morality is determinative of one's post-life state, the solution is simple: live a rational and ethical life, and everything should be fine thereafter. However, one should be rational and ethical for the sake of a good life on earth, not for fear of hell.

Additionally, it is unclear whether anything follows death. These are things that fall within the Socratic dictum of not thinking one knows what one does not in fact know. Thus, Socrates faced death with complete equanimity when faced with execution for not believing in the gods in which the government of ancient Athens believed: "For to fear death, gentlemen, is nothing else than to think one is wise when one is not; for it is thinking one knows what one does not know."[28] "But now it is time to go away, I to die, and you to live; whether you or I go to a better circumstance is unclear to all except the god."[29]

If we understand and accept the foregoing reflections, death will not be something that frightens us. An obsession regarding death is pointless. We are here on earth to live human lives. What, if anything, happens after death will take care of itself.

Courage, then, begins with a philosophical attitude toward death. If one is not terrified about death, one is able to face necessary physical dangers without undue concern. This does not mean that we should take a cavalier attitude and expose ourselves needlessly to physical dangers. That would not be courage; it would be recklessness. Courage does mean, however, that if the occasion requires us to risk death or physical injury for a very important purpose—for example, justice, honor, the protection of our family, the defense of a free country against tyrannical aggressors—we can do so without succumbing to fear.

Courage to live truly as a human being requires that we be willing to face death if the alternative is injustice or dishonor. "Give me liberty or give me death" is an American slogan that we should admire, not disparage. When one is willing to become a slave without resistance, one has lost part of one's humanity. We may for a time escape death with such conduct, but we sacrifice, in the meantime, the possibility of a truly

Chapter 3. Individual Ethics

human existence. It is not unethical for a person to be unable to resist stronger force (except when one refused to take the preparations that were obviously necessary). It is unethical for a person to be willing to do injustice because that person fears death, physical injury, or other perceived unpleasantries. Thus, there was a huge moral difference between those who died fighting against Hitler's armies and those who collaborated with Hitler's puppet regimes after he had conquered their native land. The collaborators' bodies survived; their souls died a thousand deaths.

As I write this book in 2022, Russia, under the autocratic leadership of Vladimir Putin, has, without any legitimate justification, invaded Ukraine and wreaked untold death and destruction on its inhabitants and property in an attempt to conquer the nation and make it an appendage to Russia and its authoritarian regime. The world has stood in awe as Ukraine, under the inspirational leadership of Volodymyr Zelensky, has not only refused to surrender but has also obtained many battlefield victories against the Russian onslaught. The ultimate outcome is not at this time clear, but the courage of Ukrainians in resisting the tyrant has been exemplary. This is ethical courage at its best.

Courage is also morally necessary on more mundane occasions. For example, if we or our family are attacked by criminals, we must muster sufficient courage to deal with the situation. Physical self-defense (including defense of others) may be our only option. If we are confronted with such circumstances, we need to tap on that biological adrenaline that may make our defense somewhat effective against what are likely to be more experienced fighters. This may be the one occasion when anger is a serviceable emotion. It is probably the evolutionary reason why we have the emotion of anger. That emotion (to the extent it does not impede our ability to think rationally about tactics) may be helpful if hand-to-hand combat becomes necessary for the sake of defense of ourselves or others against aggressors. In addition, if we have an opportunity to escape, the adrenaline that may be generated by such a crisis may assist us in making a speedy exit. For courage does not mean that we have to fight every battle, no matter how useless that battle. Courage means that we fight when there is no just or honorable alternative. If we are individually confronted by a criminal and we can escape without a fight, there is no good reason not to escape. But if we are literally backed into a corner by a criminal or criminals who proceed to assault us, then we have no choice: we must fight or die. Thinking about such a possibility in advance can help us prepare mentally for it.

Physical courage without intelligence is not courage but stupidity. For example, people who dare all comers to test their physical prowess in a violent fight are foolhardy rather than courageous. But an ethical human being sometimes needs to summon the faculty of courage to defend what should be defended. When such defense is necessary, courage is a highly ethical attribute of a human being.

Courage also has nonphysical dimensions. As discussed in the subsection on "Conformism" earlier in this chapter, it is important not to sacrifice rationality for the sake of social approval. To refuse to give in to popular prejudices, notwithstanding the probability of consequent social disapproval, is an important

Chapter 3. Individual Ethics

manifestation of true courage. First, one must have the courage to think as rationally as one can without regard for the opinions of the crowd. Intellectual courage is the faculty of requiring ourselves to think in a strictly rational manner, even if our conclusions are different from those that are accepted by most people in our time and place. Second, one must be willing to risk social disapproval by maintaining one's rational conclusions and, if necessary, acting upon them. It is not always necessary to *express* opposition to the prevalent view. However, it is sometimes ethically necessary to refuse to go along with the group's program. We must refuse to go along with the group when the group is intent on doing injustice. We must be willing on such occasions to be the social outcast, to be unpopular. If the road to hell is paved with good intentions, the road to the deterioration of the human soul is paved with a desire for social approval. Modern society suffers greatly from this particular vice; indeed, it might be said to be the vice most common in modern democratic society.[30] Courage and its trustworthy companion, strength of character, are the resources upon which we must draw when the only ethical course is to walk alone in a sometimes insane world.

At one time or another, virtually every human being experiences serious misfortune. Such misfortune comes in many forms: physical illness, loss of loved ones, financial distress, an irrational work environment, and so forth. In such circumstances, one must learn to be courageous. Only through courage are we able in times of misfortune to retain our humanity. Indeed, courage helps us maintain our rationality in the face of bad times, and rationality can sometimes help us find a solution to our problems. But even when no solution is possible, for example in the case of a terminal illness, one can retain one's human dignity by drawing on one's courage. It does no good to wallow in self-pity and dwell on one's misfortunes. Rather, one must do the best one can in either dealing with one's problems or, when no solution is possible, keeping one's mind in a rational posture so that one does not betray one's humanity.

The philosopher Seneca wisely observed that misfortune can help strengthen the character of a human being and that the wise human being should therefore welcome the test of misfortune.[31] Although Seneca (who mistakenly believed that our respective lots are predestined) might have taken this thought a bit too far, there is undoubtedly an element of truth in it. However this may be, the truly human response to misfortune is rationality strengthened by courage.

Moderation

Aristotle applied the ethical mean to moderation in chapters 10–12 of Book 3 of the *Nicomachean Ethics*. He stated that "moderation is a mean with respect to pleasures...."[32] He wrote that moderation involves bodily not intellectual pleasures.[33]

Aristotle defined the subject matter of moderation differently from the way I understand it. For my own views, see the subsections "Materialism, Right and Wrong" and "Intemperance" earlier in this chapter.

Chapter 3. Individual Ethics

CONFUCIUS ON INDIVIDUAL ETHICAL WISDOM

Much of what Confucius reportedly said involved matters unique to the Chinese culture and government of his time. However, other of his pronouncements apply to all times and places, including our own. Here are some of them.[34]

- "To study without thinking is futile. To think without studying is dangerous" (*Analects* 2.15).

- "Self-control seldom leads astray" (*Analects* 4.23).

- "Ethical persons should be slow to speak and prompt to act" (*Analects* 4.24).

- Lord Ji Wen always thought thrice before acting. Hearing this, Confucius said: "Twice is enough" (*Analects* 5.20).

- "Glib talk, affection, and obsequiousness— Zuoqui Ming despised these, and I despise them too" (*Analects* 5.22).

- Confucius said to Zixia: "Be a noble scholar, not a vulgar pedant" (*Analects* 6.13).

- Confucius never talked of: miracles; violence; disorders; spirits (*Analects* 7.21).

- "Impetuous, yet insincere; ignorant, yet imprudent; naive, yet unreliable—such people are really beyond my understanding" (*Analects* 8.16).

- Confucius absolutely eschewed four things: capriciousness, dogmatism, willfulness, self-importance (*Analects* 9.4).

Chapter 3. Individual Ethics

- "One may rob an army of its commander-in-chief; one cannot deprive the humblest person of their free will" (*Analects* 9.26).
- "I cannot abide these people who are capable of spending a whole day together in a display of wits without ever hitting upon a single truth" (*Analects* 15.17).
- "Ethical persons resent their incompetence; they do not resent their obscurity" (*Analects* 15.19).
- "Ethical persons make demands on themselves; vulgar persons make demands on others" (*Analects* 15.21).
- "Ethical persons are principled but not rigid" (*Analects* 15.37).
- "My teaching is addressed to all indifferently" (*Analects* 15:39).

CONCLUDING REMARKS ABOUT INDIVIDUAL ETHICS

Individual ethics involves the ethical thought and conduct we direct to ourselves, as distinguished from others. First and foremost, we should strive to be rational about both ends and means (see Chapters 1 and 2). In human beings, this is difficult or impossible until about age twenty-five, when our prefrontal cortexes become fully developed and we have at least some experience in the "real world," as it is sometimes called. We should strive to avoid mental laziness, conformism, excessive materialism, intemperance, unqualified anger, and love of power for the sake of power.

Chapter 3. Individual Ethics

The concept of the ethical mean (as distinguished from the arithmetic mean) was discussed by both Confucius and Aristotle. Their idea was that humans should seek a middle way between excess and deficiency with regard to such things as courage and moderation. Life as we know it in the twenty-first century presents many circumstances in which application of the ethical mean is appropriate.

Individual ethics is guided by the quest for what humans can look to in order to fulfill the best possibilities of human nature. It is, in this sense, teleological.

We now turn to social ethics, which is the next step in our consideration of the secular teleology of human ethics.

CHAPTER 4

SOCIAL ETHICS

> Judge not that ye be not judged.
> —Jesus[1]

> Judge and be prepared to be judged.
> —Ayn Rand[2]

The preceding chapter addressed how individual human beings should think and conduct themselves with regard to their own mental and physical well-being. The present chapter considers how individuals should think and act regarding other human and nonhuman beings. Part of such ethical concern must be oriented toward the physical environment, since the environment affects all human and nonhuman life, including that not yet in existence. For convenient reference, we will call all such ethical thinking and action regarding others "social ethics."

EVALUATING OTHERS

The epigraphs at the beginning of this chapter epitomize contrasting views about judging others. They are, however, taken somewhat out of context.

Chapter 4. Social Ethics

Jesus's entire remark, according to the Gospel of Matthew, was as follows (verse numbers in parentheses):

> (1) Do not judge, so that you may not be judged. (2) For with the judgment you make you will be judged, and the measure you give will be the measure you get. (3) Why do you see the speck in your neighbor's eye, but do not notice the log in your own eye? (4) Or how can you say to your neighbor, "Let me take the speck out of your eye," while the log is in your own eye? (5) You hypocrite, first take the log out of your own eye, and then you will see clearly to take the speck out of your neighbor's eye. (NRSV)[3]

In context, Jesus apparently was focused on the commonplace judgmentalism that many people exhibit in ordinary life, then and now. Individuals often criticize others (usually behind their backs) over petty things without much knowledge of what is really going on in the others' heads and without consideration of their own faults.

This passage can, however, be interpreted in a larger sense as meaning that one should never make judgments about good or evil, even such evils as the Holocaust or aggressive wars. This is how Ayn Rand interpreted the passage. In answer to the title question of her essay "How Does One Lead a Rational Life in an Irrational Society?," she wrote:

> I will confine my answer to a single, fundamental aspect of this question. I will name only one principle, the opposite of the idea which is so prevalent today and which

is responsible for the spread of evil in the world. That principle is: *One must never fail to pronounce moral judgment.*

Nothing can corrupt and disintegrate a culture or a man's character as thoroughly as does the precept of *moral agnosticism,* the idea that one must never pass moral judgment on others, that one must be morally tolerant of anything, that the good consists of never distinguishing good from evil. . . .

But to pronounce moral judgment is an enormous responsibility. To be a judge, one must possess an unimpeachable character; one need not be omniscient or infallible, and it is not an issue of errors of knowledge; one needs an unbreached integrity, that is, the absence of any indulgence in conscious, willful evil. . . .

[The precept] "Judge not that ye be not judged" . . . is an abdication of moral responsibility: it is a moral blank check one gives to others in exchange for a moral blank check one expects for oneself. . . .

The moral principle to adopt in this issue, is *"Judge and be prepared to be judged."*[4]

The key sentence in this passage is the following: "To be a *judge,* one must possess an unimpeachable character; *one need not be omniscient or infallible, and it is not an issue of errors of knowledge*; one needs an unbreached integrity, that is, the absence of any indulgence in conscious, willful evil" (italics added).

Chapter 4. Social Ethics

Rand says "it is not an issue of errors of knowledge . . . ." But this is precisely the issue. Individuals should be sure they have sufficient, reliable evidence to make moral judgments. This is easier in some cases (evaluating Hitler, for example) than others. It involves using one's reason without distortion from fallacious thinking (see Chapter 2, above). Purity of heart is not enough; one must also be rational.

Jesus's injunction against judging others might also be interpreted as meaning that criminal law itself should be abolished. As discussed in my book *Free Will and Human Life*, some extreme predeterminists (opponents of free will) approach this position, arguing that everything any individual does is predetermined and therefore should not be subject to legal punishment or penalty. As discussed in that book, I reject this argument—both its premise and its conclusion.

Outside the courtroom, which is governed by strict legal standards of admissible evidence and substantive law, individuals may make tentative ethical judgments, in their own private minds, about others based on a rational evaluation of observable facts. But everyone is different, both in physiological and environmental influences. We cannot know all the circumstances involving other individuals, nor are we privy to others' innermost thought processes. A certain amount of tolerance is in order. Accordingly, one must be careful and rational in *expressing* moral judgment in the private sphere. It is appropriate to express opposition to individuals' *actions* when those actions are physically or mentally harmful to themselves or to others. The rational and civil expression of opposition to a person's *arguments* is also proper.

In public matters, it is always ethically correct to express, in a civil manner, reasoned and evidence-based arguments and conclusions about political and other general issues. For further discussion about such discourse, see Chapter 5, below, on citizen and media ethics.

THE GOLDEN RULE: A MODIFICATION

When asked "Is there any single word that could guide one's entire life," Confucius responded, "Should it not be *reciprocity*? What you do not wish for yourself, do not do to others."[5] The following statement is also attributed to Confucius: "When one cultivates to the utmost the principles of his nature, and exercises them on the principle of reciprocity, he is not far from the path. What you do not like, when done to yourself, do not do to others."[6]

Similarly, Jesus stated: "In everything do to others as you would have them do to you . . . ."[7]

Other philosophies and religions also have various formulations of the Golden Rule.

The Golden Rule may be a good general standard, but it has some drawbacks. Its literal application in all circumstances can lead to ethical quandaries. For example, if one killed another in self-defense, how would the Golden Rule apply? Plato addressed the situation of a criminal prosecution against someone who had committed a criminal act. His Socratic character concluded that punishment of an unjust person was actually good for that person because it could lead to a reformation of the latter's ethical state.[8] Of course, such is not always the case. We are familiar with a scenario in our own time when people who are imprisoned actually become ethically worse as a result of their incarceration and association with hardened criminals.

There may be other problems with a literal application of the Golden Rule. What one person wants, another may not, especially when they are from different cultures. Perhaps both people want something that is unethical. The Golden Rule may be a starting point for thinking about ethical obligations to others, but, like most rules, it does not necessarily always lead to a good end.

Nevertheless, the intent behind the Golden Rule is benign. What those who promulgated it probably meant was that one should normally treat others with respect and politeness. Here, another remark of Confucius is on point:

> Someone said: "To repay hatred with kindness—what do you think of that?"
> Confucius said: "And what will you repay kindness with? Rather repay hatred with justice, and kindness with kindness."[9]

Confucius's statement is consistent with a teleological view of human ethics. Social ethics involves cooperative conduct among human beings for just and good ends. When a person is unjust, however, that person's wrong actions should be opposed and, if possible, corrected.

PREJUDICE AND DISCRIMINATION

It is irrational and, accordingly, unethical to be prejudiced against another person on the basis of race, ethnicity, gender, sexual orientation, gender identity, disability, or similar personal characteristic. It is even more irrational and unethical to discriminate against others on such basis. We contribute to the improvement of ourselves and society by avoiding such thoughts and actions.

VERACITY

In Chapter 1 we discussed Immanuel Kant's absolute rule against lying, which extended even to answering truthfully a question by a murderer at one's door asking whether one is hiding someone that such person is intent on killing. It is clear that one does not have a moral obligation to tell the truth to the would-be murderer. But what about less extreme examples? How about so-called white lies undertaken to spare someone's feelings?

The default principle should be to tell the truth. As Kant recognized, society depends on it. However, there are rational exceptions. Parents do not always tell the entire truth to their young children, because youngsters would be incapable of understanding or mentally processing some truths at a tender age. Communications with mentally unbalanced people who appear to be an imminent physical threat to themselves or others may be conducted without full candor. The question of white lies arises in an infinite variety of circumstances and must be addressed on a case-by-case basis. As a general rule, one should tell the truth unless there is a very good reason to believe that the person being addressed cannot handle it or would misuse it. Lying in order to obtain a personal advantage (money, status, or power, for example) is wrong.

The television series *Seinfeld* illustrated, in almost every episode, how habitual lying for the purpose of obtaining a short-term advantage is futile as well as unethical. In most such cases in this situation comedy, the lie backfired, exposing the liar to embarrassment and shame. This makes for good comedy but not a good life, let alone a good society. In the end, the four main characters received their just deserts for their lying and related self-centered, unempathetic, reckless, and sometimes illegal behavior. The final episode sees them behind bars. Contrary to the popular consensus, I have always considered *Seinfeld* to be a morality tale.

FRIENDSHIP

Friendship is the voluntary association of compatible individuals without sexual conduct. As in other areas of human life, friendship has high and low forms and all the gradations between the high and the low. A criminal gang can be based on a sort of friendship, though it is susceptible to disintegration because the individuals cannot trust each other. "There is no honor among thieves," as the saying goes. There are many varieties of ethical friendships, since different persons have different kinds of interests. Friendships are a valuable part of human life when the friends are rational and ethical.[10]

ROMANTIC RELATIONSHIPS

Romantic love, at its best, is the mental, emotional, and sexual love between rational people who possess high ethical character. Of course, one need only read the news, watch television, see movies, read popular fiction, or listen to unenlightened popular music to know that there are many lesser forms of romantic love. Like other aspects of human life, romantic love has extremes of perfection, degradation, and everything in between.

Romantic love, in its true sense, requires ethical individuals. To the extent one or both of the individuals is not ethical, the relationship is unhappy. Thus, we see, in our time and in other times, marital and nonmarital relationships attended by physical brutality, petty bickering, stupidity, and other deviations from the essence of our human nature.[11] Romantic love in the proper sense is a great challenge because it requires that both individuals be of an advanced ethical character.

Romantic love is difficult to find and to obtain. In part, it depends on one's luck in finding a compatible, ethical mate. It may be, for one reason or another, that one never finds a person with whom one can share such intimacy. In such cases, one must refer to one's courage. Romantic love is part of human life. However, there are also other rewarding aspects of human life. Although a single person might wish to remain on the lookout for a compatible mate, such search should not become an obsession. True romantic love is a wonderful experience, but one can also achieve happiness in other ways. The person with true self-esteem will be able to live a fulfilling life with or without romantic love.

One must love oneself before one can truly love another person in a romantic relationship. A romantic relationship in which people lose their identity in the other is not love in the correct sense of the term; rather, it is a psychological problem. Romantic love requires intellectually self-sufficient individuals. One cannot mentally dominate the other. It is a relationship of equals, though the persons may not be equal in the same way. It is a well-known paradox of romantic love that opposites attract. This can be a healthy form of romantic love so long as the individuals are not opposite in ethical understanding and conduct. For example, a criminal and a person of high moral character are "opposite," but a true romantic relationship between them is impossible. In contrast, it is possible for a person who has one type of intellectual ability to have a successful romantic relationship with a person who possesses a different type of intellectual ability; such a romantic relationship may not be always easy, but it is not impossible, and in some cases it might even be great. For example, Voltaire, who was one of the most famous literary and philosophical writers in Western Civilization, had a lasting love affair with a woman who was a mathematical and scientific genius.[12] Such facts do not mean that lovers *must* have different types of abilities; the point is only that love can be bigger than superficial differences.

FAMILY

Romantic couples may or may not have children. Some people not in a lasting romantic relationship also have children. Those who have children have an ethical and legal obligation to take care of them. It is a fact of human nature that, unlike nonhuman animals, human offspring require a very long period of parental guidance before they mature into self-sufficient adult human beings.[13]

When children are part of the life of a couple, or when a person is in the situation of being a single parent, many questions involving the supervision, education, and training of the children arise. The question of the right way to raise children is quite difficult to answer.

Chapter 4. Social Ethics

Indeed, a huge number of books have been written on the subject. In general, a parent should not inculcate irrational notions in a young person's mind. A parent should rather help children develop their rational abilities. A child is born, so to speak, with an inquiring nature. A parent should learn how to assist the process of mental development by working with, rather than discouraging, the child's spirit of inquiry. These general principles, as well as other ethical principles set forth in this book, should be the basis of education; parents can learn through their own reflection, common sense, and experience how to apply these principles to particular situations.

The difficulty of knowing the specifics of the right way to raise children does not detract from the importance of parents making the best effort they can to educate their children to be rational and decent human beings. This parental duty is one of the most important obligations of human beings. Indeed, the future of civilization depends, in no small part, on parents fulfilling this duty.

WORK

Work and Human Preservation

Nonhuman animals are programmed by natural instinct (sometimes assisted by minor parental educative efforts) to provide for their own survival. Each animal species in the wild has a basic, inborn survival strategy. Human beings, in contrast, have a variety of options for maintaining their survival. Humans have to think out their options and, in some cases, formulate new methods to ensure their preservation. Moreover, human beings desire, by nature, not only to live but to live well.

Chapter 4. Social Ethics

Living well has both material and nonmaterial components. Human survival and well-being are connected, in the first instance, with issues regarding the acquisition and expenditure of money and property.

The first question facing adult human beings is whether they will acquire the goods they seek by rational and voluntary means or by physical force. The carnivorous (as distinguished from herbivorous) animal kingdom is characterized by the rule of brute force: the question is who is eating whom. Of course, human beings themselves cannot survive without eating other animals or plants.

Nonhuman animals fight even members of their own species for food, mates, territory, and so forth. Humans also fight wars and commit other violence against their own kind. It is, however, by nature possible for the relations between human beings within their own species to be different from the "law of the jungle" that typically applies to many nonhuman animals. When human beings initiate physical force against other humans for the sake of a perceived good, we call it crime or war. We do not blame nonhuman animals for their behavior, because that behavior is part of their nature. But we do blame human beings who initiate force against other humans, because we know that human beings are capable, by nature, of obtaining economic sustenance and other goods in a way that does not involve force. That other, exclusively human way is what we call work.

Work is the method by which human beings provide for their economic needs and desires. For millennia of human history, work mainly involved agriculture. Gradually, as civilizations grew, other kinds

Chapter 4. Social Ethics

of occupations evolved, and humans developed complicated divisions of labor and patterns of trade among themselves. Money became the medium of exchange and measure of value that facilitated such commerce. Money is the token of one's work. Human beings exchange these tokens for each other's products and services.

Such is the theory of laissez-faire capitalism. It is a beautiful theory on paper. Unfortunately, the implementation of the theory leaves some individuals behind, including some mentally or physically disabled people and those for whom remunerative work is not available. To the extent that family or private charity is not available to assist such persons, government steps in with various social welfare programs. This and other matters regarding the practice of capitalism are among the subjects of my next book, *Reason and Human Government*.

Sometimes couples with children decide that one parent will stay home to take care of the children while the other one works at gainful employment. In such cases, the person staying home is still doing valuable work, since raising children properly is an important human value. In the twenty-first century, both parents often work outside the home, with the children being occupied during work hours with child care and educational activities. These are highly variable individual choices, and I make no blanket judgment as to which is preferable. In many cases it is financially necessary for both parents to have gainful employment.

Business Enterprises

The corporation is a form of economic enterprise in which persons pool their financial resources in order to create an artificial legal entity licensed by a governmental entity (usually, in the United States, by a state government). The hallmark of the legal entity called a corporation is limited liability. This means that the owners (shareholders) of the corporation are not normally personally liable for the contract or tort liabilities of the corporation. If one purchases $5,000.00 of shares of Corporation Z, one's losses are limited to the $5,000.00 investment. No creditor of the corporation can recover from a shareholder more than the shareholder's investment in the corporation. Although there are some exceptions to this rule, a shareholder can usually invest in a corporation and know that the risk is limited to the amount of the investment.

The corporation has become the dominant form of business organization in modern societies. The corporation has been more fit than sole proprietorships or partnerships for survival in the economic arena. The investors in a corporation can be financial speculators with little or no connection with the actual operation of the corporation. Investment in corporations has indeed become a business in itself, which has developed quite sophisticated techniques of making short-term or long-term monetary gains in the public stock exchanges.

The modern corporation may never go away. It is perhaps the best solution to the complexities of large business enterprises and modern economic systems. The question is how we can retain an ethical orientation while working for and dealing with modern corporate and noncorporate business associations (hereafter collectively called "companies"). The following discussions of intercompany and intracompany ethics address that question.

Intercompany Ethics

In a market economy, the ethical implications of intercompany relations are simple. With regard to competitors, it is perfectly ethical to compete as well as one can by means of attempting to produce the best quality product or service at the lowest possible price. But quality and price may have a direct relationship: the greater the quality the higher the cost and thus the higher the price. It is ethical (though not always personally fulfilling) to compete in a lower-quality market on the basis of price. In such a market, consumers who cannot afford higher quality goods or services will nevertheless have access to what they can afford. In competing on price, the business is, in a sense, doing a public service to the less economically fortunate members of society. Of course, that is not usually the motive of the business. The motive is to make money, and it appears from economic history that huge profits can be made by servicing mass markets. At the same time, other companies (or other product or service lines within the same business entity) can focus on a market that can afford higher quality. All this is natural and consistent with common sense.

Laws prohibit, or should prohibit, any company from using force or fraud to gain an unfair advantage over another company. For example, a company may not hire goons to beat up the sales representatives of a competing company. Any such action changes the activity from that of free, voluntary exchange and competition to a relationship of physical force. One of the most important functions of government in a market

Chapter 4. Social Ethics

economy is to keep physical force and fraud out of economic and other relationships by means of the criminal law.

In a market economy, companies enter into contracts with other companies. These contracts provide terms and conditions for the exchange of goods and services. For example, a company that manufactures automobiles must contract with many other companies for steel, automobile components, and paint. If a dispute arises between the companies as to the meaning or application of a contractual term or provision, the dispute can be litigated in a governmental court or resolved by arbitration or mediation. Business contracts can and frequently do contain an arbitration clause whereby any contract disputes are to be referred to a private arbitration tribunal.

The foregoing is an oversimplification of the vast complexity of the modern market economy. Additionally, it does not address alternative forms of economic organization, for example, socialist economies in which government owns the means of production or heavily regulates them. Those kinds of issues are discussed in my work in progress, *Reason and Human Government*.

Intracompany Ethics

Intercompany ethics involves ethical questions regarding relations *between* separate companies. *Intracompany* ethics involves ethical issues *within* a company. Intracompany ethics normally involves relationships between employers (including supervisors) and employees. The following discussion regarding employers and employees addresses the ethical implications of these relationships.

Chapter 4. Social Ethics

Large for-profit corporations typically have a hierarchical organization that runs from the board of directors and chief executive officer (CEO) to the vice president responsible for personnel matters, to the division head, to the department manager, to the supervisor, to the nonsupervisory employee. For purposes of the following discussion, we will refer to all of the managerial personnel from the board of directors to the lowest supervisor as the "employer" insofar as they are acting in a supervisory capacity; "employees" are employees not acting in a supervisory capacity. We will use the same nomenclature for nonprofit and not-for-profit corporations as well as unincorporated business entities.

American corporations, whether profit or nonprofit, are governed by legislative statutes and administrative regulations. Unincorporated business associations are also subject to certain legislative and administrative regulations.

Employers in the United States have certain legal obligations to employees that are governed by various federal and state statutes and administrative regulations. Examples include wage and hour regulations, minimum wage laws, equal employment opportunity requirements, job safety standards, and legal frameworks for collective bargaining. Ethical employers will fulfill such legal obligations without any attempt to subvert their letter or spirit.

Employers should treat employees respectfully even apart from legal requirements. Employees should not be treated as mere tools. Traditionally, corporations considered themselves responsible custodians of three constituencies or stakeholders: shareholders, employees, and customers. In recent decades, however, corporations have tended to focus mostly on short-term shareholder benefit. Employees have suffered as labor unions have been "busted," resulting in reduced wages and worse working conditions. The owners of some of the biggest business enterprises wallow in billions of dollars of profits while their employees are paid amounts that hardly suffice for survival of themselves and their families. This is wrong.

Employees also have ethical obligations attached to their employment. They should do their jobs competently and honestly. A problem sometimes arises when the employer expects or requires an employee do something that is unethical or even illegal. Under no circumstances should an employee be required or permitted to do an illegal act. Legal but unethical conduct is more difficult to evaluate absent specific circumstances. In general, the employee will have to decide when an employer directive is so ethically egregious that the employee must take a stand that might result in the termination of employment.

Enlightened Capitalism

In recent years, a movement for socially conscious businesses has emerged and gained traction in the United States and some other countries. In his book *Rise Up: How to Build a Socially Conscious Business*, Ross Stoddard discusses in detail the purposes as well as the nuts and bolts of such enterprises. Socially conscious businesses consider not only *profits* but also *people* (workers and customers) and the *planet* (environment)—the three P's. Some states have created legal frameworks for socially conscious enterprises that permit them to pursue such multi-factored purposes without an exclusive focus on shareholder profits.[14]

For a historical example of enlightened capitalism, see the remarkable film documentary "Automat," directed by Lisa Hurwitz and starring Mel Brooks, Ruth Bader Ginsburg, Colin Powell, and Elliott Gould. This film shows that business owners and officers can succeed in creating a profit-making enterprise that focuses on the well-being (including diversity) of customers and employees, as well as profits. The documentary relates, through photographs and interviews of officers, employees, and customers, the history of the Horn & Hardart food services establishments in Philadelphia and New York. Founded by Joseph Horn (1861–1941) and Frank Hardart (1850–1918), this automat restaurant chain flourished from 1902 until the mid-1970s. It then gave way to social and economic developments of the late twentieth century.[15]

THE ETHICS OF PRESERVING OUR PLANET AND THE ETHICAL TREATMENT OF NONHUMAN ANIMALS

(Note: Most of the present section was written by my wife, Mimi Lindauer, who has graciously consented to my reproducing her thoughts, language, and references here. She is considerably more knowledgeable than I about the subject matters of this section.)

Human beings evolved along with other forms of life into a virtual Garden of Eden about 200,000 years ago. For hundreds of thousands of years, our ancestors lived in relative harmony with nature as hunter-gatherers, taking only what they needed from natural sources.

Chapter 4. Social Ethics

Survival was often challenging, but the environment was little touched by our species, which was just another form of life in nature. Approximately 10,000 years ago we developed agriculture, cities, technology, and the population increased. People drastically changed nature wherever they lived, but as late as the nineteenth century, it seemed as though nature would never stop giving. In the Americas and Africa particularly, vast expanses of forests and fields remained in a natural state. There seemed to be a balance that accommodated both human progress and the preservation of natural areas.

However, in the nineteenth and twentieth centuries this balance was destroyed. The expanded use of coal, oil, and gas to fuel transportation accelerated the spread of human habitation to the entire planet. Fossil fuels heated homes and factories, making life more comfortable for many of Earth's human inhabitants but discharging soot, carbon dioxide, and methane into the atmosphere which caused illness in humans and degradation of the natural environment. Corporations that benefited financially from dirty centralized energy production fought every effort to reduce pollution.

Despite waste disposal technology that hugely improved human health by preventing raw sewage from being dumped into waterways, people became careless about their other trash. The creation of plastic from fossil fuels provided convenience for consumers, more energy-efficient vehicles, and life-saving advances in medical equipment. But plastic, once created by compressing methane into nurdles in a highly polluting process, lasts forever. Discarded single-use plastic bags fill garbage repositories the world over, wreaking havoc

Chapter 4. Social Ethics

with land animals and humans. Vast "islands" of plastic float in certain eddies of the ocean, devastating sea life.

When humans travel the globe, we carry species of plants and animals with us, sometimes deliberately and sometimes due to carelessness. When alien species are introduced to an ecosystem, the native flora and fauna populations are often decimated.[16]

According to the World Wildlife Fund's Living Planet Index, nearly 70 percent of the world's animal, bird, and fish populations have gone extinct since 1970 due to deforestation, agricultural expansion, and other human activity.[17]

In agriculture, the use of pesticides such as DDT and herbicides such as glyphosate on farms and private lawns are contributing to the collapse of bee colonies[18] and other beneficial insects while increasing the risk of cancer in farmworkers who experience heavy exposure. Rachel Carson's 1962 book *Silent Spring*[19] sparked an environmental movement that resulted in a ban of DDT for agricultural uses in the U.S. and elsewhere.[20] In addition, runoff from applications of chemical fertilizers into rivers and lakes create algae blooms that foul the water, endangering humans, livestock, and wildlife.

In factory farming, the unnecessarily cruel treatment of animals by cramming them into small spaces filled with their own waste is unethical; it causes needless suffering to sentient creatures.[21] It also creates tons of livestock and chicken waste which foul the air for miles around and is sometimes released into streams and rivers, dirtying drinking water.

In *Silent Spring*, Rachel Carson called for us to act responsibly as stewards of the living earth. Other

Chapter 4. Social Ethics

scientists such as biologist Edward O. Wilson in *Half Earth*,[22] naturalist David Attenborough in his documentaries including "A Life on Our Planet,"[23] journalist David Wallace-Wells in *The Uninhabitable Earth*,[24] and Elizabeth Kolbert in *The Sixth Extinction*[25] explain our current dilemma and provide solutions.

It has become quite clear to every objective observer that climate change is real, that it is doing substantial damage to the environment, that it is already having serious effects on human health and welfare, and that much of it is anthropogenic (caused by humans). The human exploitation of fossil fuels is a main driver of climate change.[26] Some companies have recognized an obligation to reduce their reliance on fossil fuels even in the absence of governmental requirements. Many individuals have also taken steps to adjust their lives to a more climate-friendly way of doing things. These enlightened companies and individuals should be models to which all businesses and individuals should aspire. Additionally, governments should take appropriate action regarding environmental and climate change.

We have the knowledge and technical ability to slow global warming and to restore clean air and water. Now that we recognize the damage that humanity has done to the planet, the only ethical course of action is to restore the balance by cleaning up our mess.[27]

FORCE AND FRAUD

No one has a right to initiate physical force against another. Libertarians call this the nonaggression principle. Similarly, no one has a right to defraud another. These principles are embedded in most legal

Chapter 4. Social Ethics

systems and, as such, will be discussed in my next book, *Reason and Human Government*. As that book will explain, I do not agree with the unqualified libertarian extension of the nonaggression maxim to government, which would involve, for example, the abolition of all taxes and all preemptive governmental regulation of pollution.

In the present book we are concerned with private, not governmental, conduct. It is manifestly irrational and immoral for one person to kill another, except in self-defense or defense of others. It is also irrational and immoral to assault or rob someone. Theft is also wrong.[28]

If one initiates force against another, one forfeits the protection of the nonaggression principle by violating it. Of course, any defense of oneself or others must be proportionate (one cannot murder someone who merely taps one on the shoulder), and the law has elaborate rules for permissible and impermissible defense.

The question of abortion is very difficult from an ethical perspective: it pits the right, if any, of a nonviable fetus against the right of the mother to control her own body. Nature does not provide a clear answer to this issue. Even many of those who oppose abortion recognize exceptions for rape, incest, and risk to the life of the mother. To my mind, the ethical issue cannot be clearly resolved. I address the legal issue in my forthcoming book on political philosophy: it is my view that the law should recognize a woman's legal right to abortion of a nonviable fetus.

In the early 2020s, the nonaggression principle was triggered by the behavior of many people in the United States and around the world regarding the COVID-19 pandemic. Such individuals refused to wear protective masks or obtain vaccinations on the asserted ground of their individual freedom and personal choice. The science applicable to the pandemic demonstrated that, by refusing masks and vaccinations, people endangered not only themselves but also others around them in their families, workplaces, transportation facilities, and other indoor locations. The nonaggression principle holds that one's right to swing one's fist ends at another's nose. This is a very apt analogy to the pandemic situation. Those who refused to wear masks and obtain vaccinations initiated force against others in their environments. Such conduct was immoral, especially when extended to their own children going to school.[29]

SOME CONFUCIAN WISDOM REGARDING SOCIAL ETHICS

- "An ethical person seeks virtue; a small person seeks land. An ethical person seeks justice; a small person seeks favors" (*Analects* 4.11).[30]

- "To store up knowledge in silence, to remain forever hungry for learning, to teach others without tiring—all this comes to me naturally" (*Analects* 7.2).

- "Zigong asked how to treat friends. Confucius said: "Give them loyal advice and guide them tactfully. If that fails, stop: do not expose yourself to rebuff" (*Analects* 12.23).

- "An ethical person seeks harmony, but not conformity. A vulgar person seeks conformity but not harmony" (*Analects* 13.23).

- "An ethical person shows authority, but no arrogance. A vulgar person shows arrogance, but no authority" (*Analects* 13.26).
- "Clever talk ruins virtue. Small impatiences ruin great plans" (*Analects* 15.27).
- "Words are merely for communication" (*Analects* 15.41).
- "Those who make virtue their profession are the ruin of virtue" (*Analects* 17.13).
- "Peddlers of hearsay are virtue's derelicts" (*Analects* 17.14).

CONCLUDING REMARKS ABOUT SOCIAL ETHICS

This chapter has discussed social ethics, which involve our thoughts and actions toward other human and nonhuman beings, including matters pertaining to the physical environment.

We have concluded that there is an ethical mean between judging and not judging others. We have no direct knowledge concerning the operations of others' minds. Accordingly, it is wise not to make snap judgments about others' characters. However, it is proper to evaluate others' observable actions and to speak out when those actions threaten the well-being of themselves or others. Similarly, when others express arguments with which we disagree regarding public or perhaps even some private matters, it is ethically appropriate to counter with arguments based on reason and evidence (see Chapters 2 and 5).

Chapter 4. Social Ethics

The Golden Rule of Confucius, Jesus, and some others is not bad as a rule of thumb. However, there are exceptions that its proponents do not always perceive. As Confucius also said, we should be kind to people who are kind and just to people who are unjust. Injustice requires correction, not kindness.

Prejudice and discrimination on the grounds of race, ethnicity, gender, and so forth are always wrong.

The default rule for veracity is to tell the truth, There are, however, exceptions for unusual cases (the murderer at the door, people threatening imminent harm to themselves or others, children and some intellectually challenged adults, some "white lies" to sensitive people). Under no circumstance, however, is lying appropriate merely to obtain a personal advantage. It is not even practical: habitual liars from mundane *Seinfeld* characters to national or international leaders (I could name names) gain a reputation for lying to the point that no rational person believes anything they say.

Friendship and romantic love, to be happy and successful, require that all involved individuals have a high ethical character.

Parents have an ethical obligation to educate their children to be rational and ethical.

Work is the rational and ethical solution to the problem of human preservation. Work includes taking care of one's children when one's partner has gainful employment, if the parents jointly prefer this arrangement to that of both parents working outside the home. This chapter has discussed some of the ethical quandaries that can arise in work situations. Society should assist, through private charity or governmental programs, those who cannot work due to physical or intellectual disability or lack of employment opportunities. Businesses and other organizations should balance the need to make money with their social responsibilities.

The urgent worldwide climate and environmental crisis requires an all-hands-on-deck approach. This is a profoundly ethical obligation, since the future of the planet—and all living things on it—is at stake.

No individual or business entity has a right to initiate force or perpetrate fraud on anyone.

We have proceeded from individual ethics to social ethics. The next chapter discusses citizen and media ethics.

CHAPTER 5

CITIZEN AND MEDIA ETHICS

[T]here is ... something of ill-omen, amongst us. I mean the increasing disregard for law which pervades the country; the growing disposition to substitute the wild and furious passions, in lieu of the sober judgment of Courts; and the worse than savage mobs, for the executive ministers of justice. This disposition is awfully fearful in any community; .... Accounts of outrages committed by mobs, form the every-day news of the times. ...

[The living memories of the scenes of the American Revolution] were the pillars of the temple of liberty; and now, that they have crumbled away, that temple must fall, unless we, their descendants, supply their places with other pillars, hewn from the solid quarry of sober reason. Passion has helped us; but can do so no more. It will in future be our enemy. Reason, cold, calculating, unimpassioned reason, must furnish all the materials for our future support and defence.

—Abraham Lincoln, 1838[1]

All of the virtues depend upon truth, and truth depends upon them all. Final truth in this

> world is unattainable, but its pursuit leads the individual away from unfreedom. The temptation to believe what feels right assails us at all times from all directions. Authoritarianism begins when we can no longer tell the difference between the true and the appealing. At the same time, the cynic who decides that there is no truth at all is the citizen who welcomes the tyrant. Total doubt about all authority is naïveté about the particular authority that reads emotions and breeds cynicism. To seek the truth means finding a way between conformity and complacency, towards individuality.
>
> —Timothy Snyder, *The Road to Unfreedom: Russia, Europe, America*[2]

This chapter is primarily addressed to people in democratic republics whose governments recognize freedom of speech and voting rights. Those living under governments that do not recognize these rights will not be able to engage publicly in political discourse or exercise the electoral franchise. Nevertheless, the following discussion may be informative and useful to them in understanding their own situations.

THE U.S. FOUNDERS' CONCEPT OF PUBLIC VIRTUE

On June 20, 1788, in the Virginia Convention regarding the ratification of the U.S. Constitution, James Madison stated: "Is there no virtue among us? — If there be not, we are in a wretched situation. No theoretical checks — no form of Government, can render us secure. To suppose that any form of Government will secure liberty or happiness without any virtue in the people, is a chimerical idea."[3]

Madison's use of the word "virtue" may be confusing to us, because he meant something different from what we ordinarily understand today by the word. As journalist-historian Thomas E. Ricks explains,

> The best place to begin to understand the views of the Revolutionary generation is with a look at the word "virtue." This word was powerfully meaningful during the eighteenth century. Today it is a mere synonym for morality, and also, anachronistically, a signifier of female chastity or the lack of it, as in the euphemistic phrase "a woman of easy virtue." But for the Revolutionary generation, virtue was the essential element of public life. Back then, it actually was masculine. It meant putting the common good before one's own interests.[4]

The U.S. Founders thought that both public and private virtue were essential to the success of the new democratic republic. For example, John Adams stated:

> Public Virtue cannot exist in a Nation without private, and public Virtue is the only Foundation of Republics. There must be a possitive Passion for the public good, the public Interest, Honour, Power, and Glory, established in the Minds of the People, or there can be no Republican Government, nor any real Liberty. And this public Passion must be Superiour to all private Passions.[5]

George Washington[6] and Thomas Jefferson[7] had a similar understanding of public virtue as devotion to the public good, though Jefferson's political philosophy differed from that of Washington and Adams in some particulars.

A problem with John Adams's formulation is that he spoke of public "passion," as though reason had nothing to do with it. Today, our foremost problem is the prevalence of irrationality and emotionalism, culminating (at least as of the time of this writing) in the insurrection of January 6, 2021. With regard to the present situation, the quotation from Lincoln in the first epigraph to this chapter is especially relevant.

THE ETHICAL IMPERATIVE OF REASON IN PUBLIC DISCOURSE, POLITICAL ACTIVISM, AND VOTING

Reason, as elaborated in Chapter 2, is not only important for individual and social ethics. It is also of utmost importance in public discourse, political activism, and voting.

The decline of rational thinking in the United States and other countries is inducing transitions from democratic or semi-democratic governments to authoritarian or totalitarian regimes. At present, that transition is complete, or close to complete, in Russia (which only briefly had a rudimentary democracy), Hungary, Poland, Turkey, the Philippines, and several other countries. Authoritarian impulses have also begun to take root in the United States, and democracy as we know it will be doomed if Americans continue to abandon reason in favor of demagogic appeals to their emotions.[8]

Chapter 5. Citizen and Media Ethics

As explained in Chapter 2, reason is not a mere preference. It is not a mere option. It is an ethical imperative. Indeed, it is the most important component of ethics. Yes, empathy and sympathy are important. But reason, properly understood, must be in the driver's seat, especially in political affairs.

What happens when people let emotions overcome their reason in political matters? We don't need to speculate about this. History provides countless examples. The next section discusses some of these.

IDEOLOGY

The word "ideology" is susceptible to various definitions. It can denote, simply, a system of ideas. But it can also refer to a pattern of political beliefs that are based on emotion and quasi-religious or religious dogma rather than on reason and critical thinking. The latter is the meaning of "ideology" as used in this book.

Timothy Snyder, a history professor, described the emergence of fascist and communist ideologies in the twentieth century as follows:

> Both fascism and communism were responses to globalization: to the real and perceived inequalities it created, and the apparent helplessness of the democracies in addressing them. *Fascists rejected reason in the name of will, denying objective truth* in favor of a glorious myth articulated by leaders who claimed to give voice to the people. They put a face on globalization, arguing that its complex challenges were the result of a conspiracy against the nation. Fascists ruled for a decade or two, *leaving*

behind an intact intellectual legacy that grows more relevant by the day. Communists ruled for longer, for nearly seven decades in the Soviet Union, and more than four decades in much of eastern Europe. They proposed *rule by a disciplined party elite with a monopoly on reason* that would guide society toward a certain future according to supposedly fixed laws of history.[9]

Ideology is strongly correlated with demagoguery, whether of the political Right or the political Left.

Ideologies of the Right

Fascism and Nazism

During the twentieth century the ideologies of fascism and Nazism infected Germany, Italy, and other countries that were associated with the Axis alliance in World War II. These ideologies attracted masses of people as a result of their irrational nationalism, authoritarianism, and racism. Benito Mussolini and Adolph Hitler were classic demagogues, swaying people into supporting their respective dictatorships. Hitler himself initially came to power through constitutional and democratic processes. Thereafter, he proceeded to establish a totalitarian dictatorship.[10]

Contemporary Populist Authoritarianism

Globalization, xenophobia, racism, baseless conspiracy theories, the Covid-19 pandemic, and media and political disinformation and demagoguery have motivated recent populist authoritarian movements in several countries, including the United States.[11]

Chapter 5. Citizen and Media Ethics

The section "Appeal to Authority" in Chapter 2 of this book and Chapter 5 of the second edition of my book *The Electoral College* detail the ideology and actions of the populist authoritarian movement that led to the violent January 6, 2021 insurrection against the constitutionally mandated procedure of counting the Electoral College ballots in the January 6, 2021 Joint Session of Congress. See also the section "Transition to Authoritarianism?: The Presidency of Donald J. Trump (2017–21)" in Chapter 6 of the present book.

January 6, 2021 was the outcome of years, if not decades, of authoritarian demagoguery by far-right figures, both in and out of government. Certain very popular right-wing media sources trafficked in disinformation that resulted, directly and indirectly, in this attempt to overthrow the U.S. Constitution and government by force.

The January 6 attack on the Capitol was led by right-wing militia, White Supremacist, neo-Nazi, QAnon, and Christian nationalist groups, as evidenced by their signs, insignia, social media posts, and internal electronic communications before, during, and after the event. Although some of the people involved in the insurrection were followers, many of these were aware that they were entering the Capitol Building behind an illegal spearhead of violence. As of the time of this writing, many participants have pleaded or have been found guilty at trial of criminal offenses in connection with the insurrection, and others are still being prosecuted, some for the federal crime of seditious conspiracy.[12]

A related far-right ideology is the Great Replacement Theory, holding that elites are deliberately working to replace Whites with people of other races. This White nationalist trope, amplified by Fox News personality Tucker Carlson and other ultraconservative media and political figures, has been explicitly invoked by mass shooters in the United States and elsewhere as justification for their homicides. One version of this theory asserts that Jews are instigating the White replacement efforts. This may provide some context to the neo-Nazi "Jews will not replace us" and "blood and soil" chants at the 2017 Charlottesville riot, about which then President Donald J. Trump said there were "very fine people on both sides."[13]

Like the followers of Mussolini and Hitler in the twentieth century, the supporters of right-wing authoritarianism in the United States reject reason, evidence, and critical thinking. They worship a messianic strongman (currently Donald Trump), who they believe will institute their version of justice by demolishing democratic-republican laws, norms, and institutions and persecuting disfavored racial, ethnic, religious, and political groups.

Ideologies of the Left

Communism

Karl Marx (1818–83) and his colleague, Friedrich Engels (1820–95), formulated the modern doctrine of communism in their theoretical and polemical works. The basic idea was that history proceeds in certain inevitable stages, culminating in the successive dictatorship of the proletariat, the withering away of the state, and a vague, utopian fantasy of universal brotherhood and sisterhood after the destruction of private property.[14]

Chapter 5. Citizen and Media Ethics

On the ground, Marx's ideology never got beyond the dictatorship of the proletariat—or, more precisely, beyond Lenin's modification of Marx's dictum to mean the dictatorship of the "vanguard" (the Communist Party elite) of the proletariat. The most famous examples were the Soviet Union and the People's Republic of China during the twentieth century. After the breakup of the USSR in the late twentieth century, Russia eschewed its communist past and attempted to pursue a capitalist route under the tutelage of Western libertarian economists. This economic "shock therapy" had disastrous effects on the general populace, leading to the rise of populist authoritarian opinion that ultimately supported the right-wing dictator Vladimir Putin.[15]

Although China today is still officially a communist country, it has had a basically capitalist economy for many decades—some kind of hybrid of state capitalism and state socialism. It is also an authoritarian or totalitarian country that exerts considerable control over its huge population.

In the twenty-first century, only North Korea and Cuba could be said to have retained anything like the Marxist-Leninist doctrines of the erstwhile Soviet Union. These remain poor countries, though the North Korean totalitarian state is an emerging nuclear power.

In its heyday, the Soviet Union had considerable prestige in many places around the world. The egalitarian communist ideology was attractive to many, including a sizable portion of the population in the United States before the 1950s. It must be remembered that the USSR was an ally of the United States and the United Kingdom against the Axis powers during World

War II. It was not until the Cold War, starting in the late 1940s, that the Soviet Union and the Western nations became real adversaries.

Communist ideology explicitly opposed what it called "bourgeois" individual rights. Accordingly, wherever it has been adopted, the result has been some sort of totalitarian or authoritarian regime.

Postmodernism and Its Activist Offshoots

Postmodernism is an academic doctrine that arose in the second half of the twentieth century. It is a very complicated ideology, whose followers have different and sometimes inconsistent positions. As postmodern views have manifested themselves in the early twenty-first century, one of their principal teachings is that reason and evidence are inventions of the Western, White, straight, male patriarchy and, as such, are to be rejected or minimized. Helen Pluckrose and James Lindsay, two critics of theoretical and applied postmodern extremism, have observed:

> [Postmodernism] carries politically actionable consequences. If what we accept as true is only accepted as such because the discourses of straight, white, wealthy, Western men have been privileged, applied [postmodern] Theory indicates this can be challenged by empowering marginalized identity groups and insisting their voices take precedence. This belief increased the aggressiveness of identity politics to such an extent that it even led to concepts like "research justice." This alarming proposal demands that scholars preferentially cite women and minorities—and minimize

Chapter 5. Citizen and Media Ethics

citations of white Western men—because empirical research that values knowledge production rooted in evidence and reasoned argument is an unfairly privileged cultural construct of white Westerners. It is therefore, in this view, a moral obligation to share the prestige of rigorous research with "other forms of research," including superstition, spiritual beliefs, cultural traditions and beliefs, identity-based experiences, and emotional responses.[16]

An example of the postmodern style can be found in the following remarks in a book addressed to mathematics education professionals:

> On many levels, mathematics itself operates as Whiteness. Who gets credit for doing and developing mathematics, who is capable in mathematics, and who is seen as part of the mathematical community is generally viewed as White. School mathematics curricula emphasizing terms like Pythagorean theorem and pi perpetuate a perception that mathematics was largely developed by Greeks and other Europeans. Perhaps more importantly, mathematics operates with unearned privilege in society, just like Whiteness.[17]

Pluckrose and Lindsay's scholarly book *Cynical Theories* provides a detailed history and evaluation of postmodernism and its applications in postcolonial theory, critical race theory, queer theory, gender studies, disability studies, and fat studies. These authors express sympathy with many of the general objectives of postmodernism and its offshoots. They object, however, to the antiliberal doctrines of postmodernism—its attacks on reason and science, its cultural relativism, its replacement of individual with group identity, and its position that all disagreement with its doctrines should be suppressed.[18]

Postmodernism and its contemporary political manifestations have been popular in academia and in some private K–12 schools. Anecdotal evidence suggests that its concepts are filtering down to some K–12 public schools, but, as of the time of the present writing, no general study (to my knowledge) has assessed its prevalence at the K–12 public school level.[19]

THE ENVIRONMENT

Chapter 4 discussed the crisis of the environment, including but not limited to climate change. Citizens should encourage government to help ameliorate the problem rather than exacerbate it. Since this involves political philosophy and government policies, it will be discussed in my forthcoming book *Reason and Human Government*.

PANDEMIC MITIGATION

We discussed the ethics of obtaining vaccinations and wearing masks in indoor public places in Chapter 4. As will be discussed in my forthcoming book *Reason and Human Government*, it is my view that the government has an important role in such public health matters. Citizens should encourage rather than impede such governmental efforts.

MEDIA ETHICS

At the time of the U.S. Constitutional Convention in 1787, there were no national political parties, and the framers of the Constitution hoped and expected that there would never be such parties. Nevertheless, within a few short years after the new government went into operation in 1789, national political parties arose out of the conflict between what became known as Federalists and Democratic-Republicans.

The first president, George Washington, and the second president, John Adams, were Federalists, as was Alexander Hamilton, the first secretary of the treasury. Thomas Jefferson, the first secretary of state (under President Washington), and James Madison (a member of the first House of Representatives) were Democratic Republicans. The Federalists were in control of the presidency from 1789 until 1801, when Jefferson, who had won the election of 1800, became president.

By 1800, conflict between the political parties was in full display. Each party had its own newspaper, and each newspaper was highly partisan. Mudslinging was rampant, with personal ad hominem attacks being regularly featured in the newspapers' pages.

In their printed media, each party viciously attacked the other party's candidates and other leaders. For example, Federalist supporters accused Thomas Jefferson of being an atheist. There was, of course, an element of truth in this allegation. Jefferson did not accept conventional religion and even wrote a private version of the Gospels in which he expurgated all miracles and other supernatural happenings. He, like other votaries of the Enlightenment, was probably more of a deist than what we would now define as an atheist,

Chapter 5. Citizen and Media Ethics

but the epithet "atheist" was routinely hurled in that era at anyone who did not adhere to conventional Christianity.

Jefferson was also accused of keeping a Black slave as his mistress (Jefferson's wife had died some years earlier). During the late twentieth century, sufficient evidence was produced to convince almost everyone that this was a true fact. We now know a great deal about the genealogical line of Jefferson's offspring from this union.

So, personal attacks on political opponents are nothing new in U.S. history. Fast forward to the early twenty-first century. It is probably the case that no media source today is entirely rational and free from bias. However, some are better than others. The worst are the knowing purveyors of misinformation and disinformation. Some of these parrot propaganda from foreign governments: Russia, Iran, China, and other nations have conducted propaganda campaigns in the United States and elsewhere in recent times. Most of it, however, is home grown.

Today, social and other media traverse a vast ideological spectrum. The extremes traffic in deliberate misinformation and disinformation as well as personal attacks. At the present time, right-wing populist authoritarianism (including its mendacious propaganda) has captured one political party, while left-wing postmodernism has captured a portion of the other party. We have discussed such ideologies earlier in this chapter.

How do we protect ourselves from all these attempts to mislead us? The answer is to improve our reasoning and critical thinking skills. Chapter 2 of the present book explains how to immunize ourselves against falsehood. See also Andy Norman's recent book, (cited in Chapter 1 and in the bibliography) *Mental Immunity: Infectious Ideas, Mind-Parasites, and the Search for a Better Way to Think*, which discusses such matters in depth.

Furthermore, public media should strive to be as accurate as possible in reporting and commenting on public issues. In 2014, the Society of Professional Journalists (SPJ) adopted a Code of Ethics that, if followed by all media, would greatly improve public discourse. Here are a few of the SPJ's ethical principles:

SEEK TRUTH AND REPORT IT

Ethical journalism should be accurate and fair. Journalists should be honest and courageous in gathering, reporting and interpreting information.

Journalists should:
- Take responsibility for the accuracy of their work. Verify information before releasing it. Use original sources whenever possible.
- Remember that neither speed nor format excuses inaccuracy.
- Provide context. Take special care not to misrepresent or oversimplify in promoting, previewing or summarizing a story.
- Gather, update and correct information throughout the life of a news story . . . .

- Identify sources clearly. The public is entitled to as much information as possible to judge the reliability and motivations of sources. . . .
- Avoid stereotyping. Journalists should examine the ways their values and experiences may shape their reporting.
- Label advocacy and commentary.
- Never deliberately distort facts or context, including visual information. Clearly label illustrations and re-enactments.[20]

The survival and well-being of the U.S. democratic republic and of democratic republics all around the world require that media adhere to such principles and that citizens equip themselves with critical thinking to detect any departures from these standards.

CONCLUDING REMARKS REGARDING CITIZEN AND MEDIA ETHICS

We have proceeded from an analysis of the basis of human ethics (Chapter 1) to a study of what human reason is and is not (Chapter 2), to an examination of individual ethics (Chapter 3), to a discussion of social ethics (Chapter 4), to the present chapter on citizen and media ethics. All of these subjects are interrelated. In order to be good human beings and good citizens, we must resolve to think and act rationally with regard to both ends and means in our individual, social, and political lives.

Chapter 5. Citizen and Media Ethics

The final chapter of this book, to which we now turn, addresses political ethics, i.e., the proper ethical orientation of political leaders.

CHAPTER 6

POLITICAL ETHICS

And I was forced to say, in praise of the true love of wisdom, that it is through this that it is possible to understand all things just, both in politics and in the private sphere. As a result, humanity will not desist from evil until either those who truly and properly pursue philosophy come into power, or those who hold power in our cities . . . actually pursue philosophy.
—Plato[1]

It is in vain to say, that enlightened statesmen will be able to adjust these clashing interests, and render them all subservient to the public good. Enlightened statesmen will not always be at the helm: Nor, in many cases, can such an adjustment be made at all, without taking into view indirect and remote considerations, which will rarely prevail over the immediate interest which one party may find in disregarding the rights of another, or the good of the whole.
—James Madison[2]

The contrast between the political philosophies of Plato and James Madison, as reflected in the foregoing epigraphs, has often been noted. What has not so often been recalled is Madison's remark, quoted in Chapter 5, that "[t]o suppose that any form of Government will secure liberty or happiness without any virtue in the people, is a chimerical idea." The truth is that both public virtue and Madison's famous political checks and balances are necessary for the survival and well-being of a democratic republic. It is not either-or.

Madison's passing remark about "indirect and remote considerations" is also instructive. Political wisdom requires an understanding of the complicated circumstances that often confront a political society. This may be one of the things Socrates meant when he famously said that virtue is knowledge. As previous chapters of this book have observed, correct reasoning and critical thinking about facts are ethical imperatives. This is especially so in political matters.

POLITICAL RHETORIC

We have discussed the demagoguery that so often affects political society. This phenomenon is, of course, nothing new. Plato wrote an entire dialogue on rhetoric called the *Gorgias*. In that dialogue, rhetoric as it is so often practiced is justly given a bad name. However, Plato's character Socrates points out in this work that there is a kind of rhetoric his interlocutors have never seen—the rhetoric, based on knowledge, that encourages human rationality and moderation.[3]

In the preface to his translation of Plato's *Gorgias*, James H. Nichols Jr. states:

> [R]hetoric is the crucial link between philosophy and politics and must take an important place in education if political life

and intellectual activity are to be in the best shape possible. While it is easy to denigrate the art of persuasion, most obviously by contrasting its possible deceptiveness with the truth of genuine knowledge, science, or philosophy, one should never forget the fundamental political fact that human beings must coordinate their activities with other human beings in order to live well, and that the two most basic modes of such coordination are through persuasion and by force. Everyone knows the disadvantages of excessive reliance by a political community on force or violence. If the highest intellectual activities—science, philosophy—are to have much efficacy in practical political life, rhetoric must be the key intermediary.[4]

Political ethics and, indeed, the existence of decent government itself require that our political leaders understand and apply the foregoing principles. That most of them do not is, of course, a truism. We should keep these considerations in mind as we now discuss various kinds of political leadership.

AUTHORITARIAN, TYRANNICAL, AND TOTALITARIAN POLITICAL LEADERS

It is difficult to formulate clear distinctions between authoritarian, tyrannical, and totalitarian leaders. Often, the same ruler will exhibit a hybrid of two or all three of these types. This section discusses some examples.

Chapter 6. Political Ethics

Plato's Account of the Succession of Regimes Culminating in the Tyrannical Ruler

In the *Republic*, Plato's Socrates outlines a vision of the best political order—a political society based on reason and moderation with a guaranteed absence of graft and nepotism in the governing and guardian classes. However, this "beautiful city" (527c: *kallipolis*) in speech is impossible in practice. It commences with the expulsion by the philosopher-kings of everyone over ten years old (541a). It is based on a "noble lie" or myth (414b–17b). It requires, in the guardian class, a community of women and children: "all these women are to be shared among all these men, and none of the women is to live together privately with any of the men, and their children are to be shared too; a parent is not to know the offspring that are its own, or a child its parent."[5] The guardians are to live in common housing and to have only absolutely necessary private property (416c–e).

In reviewing such austere dictates, one scholar concluded: "The perfect city is revealed to be a perfect impossibility. What then was the use of spending so much time and effort on a city that is impossible? Precisely to show its impossibility. . . . [Socrates] shows what a regime would have to be in order to be just and why such a regime is impossible. Regimes can be improved but not perfected; injustice will always remain. The proper spirit of reform, then, is moderation."[6]

In the eighth and ninth books of the *Republic*, Socrates discusses the succession of inferior political regimes to the ideal city. He argues that each inferior regime arose out of defects of the immediately preceding polity. It is not necessary to evaluate the historicity of this claim here. However, Socrates's account of the various regimes suggests interesting parallels to our own time.

Timocracy or timarchy is the first successor to Socrates's best political order. In timocracy, the rulers love honor and victory more than reason and moderation. They focus on war, athletics, hunting, and (secretly) money (*Republic* 545b–50c). Translator Joe Sachs observes that the terms "timocracy" (*timokatria*) and "timarchy" (*timarchia*) were "[w]ords coined in this dialogue . . . for a polity like that of Sparta, animated by the love of honor, and in which those who earn the most honor also earn the right to rule."[7]

In an oligarchy, the moneymaking element becomes dominant. The wealthy rule: the poor have no political standing. Wealth replaces virtue in the governing class. Socrates emphasizes that wealth is not a substitute for political wisdom. He employs an analogy. If ship captains were chosen by their wealth, instead of by their knowledge and experience in the art of piloting ships, the result would be faulty sailing; sometimes a poor person knows more about this art than a wealthy one and would be a better captain. Similarly, if political leaders are chosen because of their wealth instead of their political knowledge, wisdom, experience, and competence, the result can be political malfeasance or misfeasance (see the subsection later in this chapter on President Donald J. Trump). People in an oligarchic political society wrongly assume that moneymaking prowess establishes a person's fitness for political office. As Plato's Socrates observed, the rich get richer

Chapter 6. Political Ethics

and the poor get poorer in an oligarchic polity, resulting in severe conflicts between rich and poor (550c–55b).

Socrates next considers democracy. By "democracy," he did not mean the kind of representative democracy present in today's United States and other democratic-republican countries. Socrates was referring to direct democracy as practiced in ancient Greek polities, especially that of Athens. In Athens, the enfranchised citizens (who were about 30 percent of the entire population) directly voted on legislation. Many, though not all, of the executive officials were appointed by lot from the citizenry. Unlike modern constitutional republics, there were no bills of rights limiting the power of the government and no checks and balances.

Plato's Socrates states that democracy involves freedom, especially free speech. He says it also entails the equality of desires, such that all ethical values are relative (compare the discussion of ethical relativism in Chapter 1, above). The typical democratic person is ethically nonjudgmental. Accordingly, in Athenian democracy, all things not criminalized were considered morally permissible, including the freedom of a philosopher to think, read, and communicate freely with others about philosophy (555b–62a). However, there were legal limitations to such freedom, as Socrates discovered when he was prosecuted, convicted, and executed for not believing in the gods in which the city believed and allegedly corrupting the young with philosophical skepticism. There was no separation of religion and government in the Athenian democracy.

A tyrant arises from democracy when the people rally behind a demagogic political figure to deliver them from perceived evils (565c–d). In the ensuing political struggles with others, this leader ends up consolidating power and ruling as a tyrant (565d–569c). The tyrannical personality gives reign to all kinds of irrational desires (571a–73d). "[A] man becomes precisely tyrannic . . . when, by his nature or pursuits or both, he becomes drunken, lustful, and crazy" (573c). The tyrannical person pursues "feasts, revelry, celebrations, prostitutes, and everything of the sort" (573d, Sachs translation).

Plato had personal experience of tyranny when he visited Sicily on three occasions during the tyrannical leadership of Dionysius I and his son, Dionysius II. Plato described the characters of these rulers in his *Seventh Letter*, which most scholars now regard as authentic.[8] The Sicilian regimes of Dionysius I and II were simple tyrannies. They did not have the immense power over the minds and lives of people as have totalitarian regimes of the past hundred years equipped with modern technology. The rulers were not ideological and moralistic "big brothers" determined to brainwash their subjects in a comprehensive system of ideology, government, and life patterned after a vulgarized understanding of a great thinker. Rather, these dictatorships constituted an old and cowardly world in which both rulers and subjects primarily sought power, wealth, and indulgence in corporeal pleasures. Dionysius II was, according to Plato, a child in his desires, lacking sound education and good friends (332c–d). The arbitrary will of the tyrant was supported by an armed force strong enough to deter for a time foreign invasion and domestic subversion. No tradition of constitutional and civil law existed. The people did

Chapter 6. Political Ethics

not care about politics. They were happy if their desires could be satisfied, and this was possible under either a tyrant or a democratic leader. The similarities between tyranny and extreme democracy find historic proof in the Sicilian regime.

In a remarkable passage, Plato described in the *Seventh Letter* what he observed during his visits to Sicily:

> I was not at all pleased with what the Italians and Sicilians call the blessed life, one laden with feasts, spent stuffing oneself twice a day, never going to bed alone at night, and all the other things that go hand-in-hand with this lifestyle. With such habits, nobody under the sun who had followed this path since childhood could ever develop any sense—no one is tempered by so admirable a nature—nor would anyone ever be likely to become moderate. Of course, the same reasoning would apply to every other kind of virtue, and no city would find peace under laws of any kind, as long as men thought it necessary to squander everything to the extreme, and believed that they should be lazy about everything except feasting, drinking, and the avid pursuit of sexual pleasure. On the contrary, it is inevitable that such cities constantly rotate between tyranny, oligarchy, and democracy, and that those ruling such cities are unable to bear the very mention of a just government based on equality under the law.[9]

Chapter 6. Political Ethics

Accordingly, Plato understood that the various kinds of political regimes were supported by people who reflected the character of those regimes. This is especially true in the extreme case of tyranny. We now turn from the distant past to some twentieth- and twenty-first-century examples of tyrants.

Joseph Stalin (1878–1953)

Joseph Stalin rose to power in the Soviet Union after the death of Vladimir Lenin in 1924, eliminating his political opponents during and after the transitional period. Among other things, he arranged for the expulsion (1929) and later assassination (1940) of his principal rival, Leon Trotsky.[10]

Lenin had compromised with capitalism, but Stalin had other ideas. His first five-year plan required rapid industrialization and the collectivization of agriculture. Farmers were forced to give up their private land and join state farms. This scheme and other governmental measures resulted in substantial famine, especially in Ukraine.[11] Many farmers resisted, resulting in mass arrests followed by executions, exile, or imprisonment in concentration camps. Historian Stephen Kotkin observes that "[c]ollectivization involved the arrest, execution, internal deportation, or incarceration of 4 to 5 million peasants; the effective enslavement of another 100 million; and the loss of tens of millions of head of livestock."[12]

Although Stalin's industrialization policy was successful in rapidly bringing the Soviet Union to the status of an industrial power, it also had failures. When things did not go Stalin's way, he subjected industrial managers to show trials in which the defendants were compelled to confess guilt to crimes they did not

Chapter 6. Political Ethics

commit in order to provide public scapegoats for Stalin's own errors.

Stalin also executed, by way of show trials or otherwise, many other figures in the Communist Party, the military, and other walks of life. Untold numbers of people were "liquidated" or sent to the gulag (the system of concentration camps), where they often died. Stalin's decimation of the Soviet military leadership came back to haunt him when Hitler's Wehrmacht invaded the Soviet Union in 1941.

As the Constitutional Rights Foundation has observed:

> While the new Soviet Constitution of 1936 provided for due process guarantees such as the right to defend oneself in a public trial, Stalin took steps to "simplify" the judicial system. He eliminated the right of defense. He sped up trials and often held them in secret. He suppressed the right of appeal. He expanded the death penalty to cover hundreds of offenses and extended it to children as young as age 13.
>
> The use of terror by Stalin and his henchmen ensnared thousands and then millions of Soviet citizens, most of whom were innocent of any wrongdoing.[13]

In his *Memoirs*, Nikita Khrushchev, a member of Stalin's inner circle who later became the Soviet leader, detailed his personal observations of Stalin. He wrote that "Stalin's character was harsh and abrupt, and his habits were coarse and rude. But his rudeness was not at all a reflection of his anger about a particular situation or his attitude toward a specific individual. It was a kind

Chapter 6. Political Ethics

of generalized anger, an inborn rudeness and crudeness, although it was most likely exacerbated by his upbringing and the influence of his environment."[14] "He would vent his anger by taking it out on the people he had worked with, who had traveled the long road together with him, and who unfortunately were witnesses to the undeserved deaths of many honest people."[15] "He behaved toward people as though he were God and had created them; his attitude was at once patronizing and contemptuous.... He showed his strength by destroying everything that might give nourishment to a true understanding of events, to sensible reasoning that might contradict his point of view."[16] "Stalin's admission that he didn't trust anyone, including himself, raises the curtain on some of the reasons for the tragedy that raged during his time as leader of the party and the country. And the Stalin era lasted a very long time. Heads flew, the heads of honest people who were guilty of absolutely nothing."[17] Khrushchev's *Memoirs*, edited by his son Sergei, were based on secret tape recordings that Nikita made after his expulsion from Soviet leadership. They provide many other fascinating details regarding Stalin's tyranny.

    Svetlana Alliluyeva, Stalin's daughter, related additional information about the personality of her father in her own memoirs, published after she left the Soviet Union. In the concluding chapter, she wrote: "It was as though my father were at the center of a black circle and anyone who ventured inside vanished or perished or was destroyed in one way or another." Her final words in that chapter were: "The Good triumphs over everything, though it frequently happens too late—

not before the very best people have perished unjustly, senselessly, without rhyme or reason."[18] In an epilogue, she summed up her father's reign of terror: "Millions were sacrificed senselessly, thousands of talented lives extinguished prematurely."[19]

Although Alliluyeva blamed secret police chief Lavrentiy Beria for having an Iago-like influence on Stalin, she did not absolve her father from guilt:

> I have already said that in a good many things Beria and my father were guilty together. I'm not trying to shift the blame from one to the other. At some point, unfortunately, they became spiritually inseparable. The spell cast on my father by this terrifying evil genius was extremely powerful, and it never failed to work.[20]

Alliluyeva was not, of course, present when Stalin and his henchmen planned their perfidious deeds, and she could not know whether or how their respective responsibility for them should be apportioned. Alliluyeva grew up under most bizarre circumstances, and it is clear throughout her memoir that she was torn between a child's natural love of her father and her rational appraisal that he was guilty of perpetrating unspeakable horrors. She was present when he died, and this remark appears to be her final judgment: "My father died a difficult and terrible death. It was the first and so far the only time I had seen somebody die. God grants an easy death only to the just."[21]

We now turn from the most infamous totalitarian dictator of the Left to the most infamous totalitarian dictator of the Right.

Chapter 6. Political Ethics

Adolph Hitler (1889–1945)

After becoming chancellor of Germany in 1933 through constitutional means, Adolph Hitler proceeded to establish what became a totalitarian state. He eliminated all non-Nazi parties, organizations, and labor unions. He directed the extrajudicial murder of political opponents in his own Nazi Party. After becoming president as well as chancellor in 1934, he required the armed services to swear an oath to himself personally. He had an expansionist foreign policy, and the story of his imperialistic actions in Europe, culminating in World War II, is well known.

He followed Benito Mussolini of Italy in creating a fascist police state in Germany. But Hitler developed and applied an extreme racist ideology on top of routine fascism. He taught that White Aryan people, specifically Germans, were the master race, and he ordered millions of allegedly inferior races to be incarcerated and murdered or worked to death in brutal concentration camps. He especially hated Jews, and about six million Jews died in his extermination camps.

Hitler has long been considered the personification of evil. His ideology was different from Stalin's, but his reign of terror was similar in its methodology.[22]

Vladimir Putin (1952–)

Stalin and Hitler created what might be called "hard" totalitarian systems. As of the time of this writing (June 2022), Russian President Vladimir Putin has not yet murdered as many people in his own country as did Stalin and Hitler, but his unjustified aggression in Ukraine and Syria, for example, has resulted in massive death and destruction in those countries. Moreover, Putin is in the process of creating an advanced

Chapter 6. Political Ethics

authoritarian or totalitarian system within Russia that is explicitly based on fascist ideology.[23]

To understand the background of Putin's character and actions, we must look at recent Russian history.

The Soviet Union imploded in 1991. Putin had been an intelligence operative for the Soviet government. He considered the breakup of the Soviet Union to be a catastrophic event, though his ideological views turned out to be fascist rather than communist.

The first post-Soviet leader was Boris Yeltsin, who encouraged capitalism while opening the door to so-called oligarchs, who made huge sums of money in the conversion of state-owned assets to private enterprise. Both Yeltsin and the oligarchs engaged in corruption. Yeltsin also had severe medical problems, including alcoholism.

On December 31, 1999, Yeltsin resigned, and Putin, then the Russian prime minister, became acting president. He immediately granted Yeltsin lifelong immunity from prosecution. After an election in which Putin won 53 percent of the vote, he was inaugurated as president on May 7, 2000. He was reelected to a second term as president in 2004. The Russian Constitution prohibited him from a third consecutive term, but he effectively retained power by becoming prime minister in 2008 after the preceding deputy prime minister, Dimitry Medvedev, won election to the presidency.

Putin returned to the presidency in 2012 and has continued as president to the present time (2022). As a result of constitutional amendments, he is eligible to have successive terms as president until 2036. Additionally, a law was passed giving Russian presidents lifetime immunity from prosecution.

Chapter 6. Political Ethics

As historian Timothy Snyder has observed,
> The decade of the 2000s was the lost opportunity for the creation of a Russian state that might have been seen as such. . . . What had been an oligarchy of contending clans in the 1990s was transformed into a kleptocracy, in which the state itself became the single oligarchical clan. Rather than monopolizing law, the Russian state under Putin monopolized corruption.[24]

To date, the Putin regime has committed many authoritarian or totalitarian acts, including but not limited to the following:

- Incarceration, murder, and attempted murder of political opponents.
- Show trials against disfavored persons that make a mockery of due process of law.
- Rigging of elections and abolishing regional and local elections (making governors and mayors appointable by the president).
- Criminalizing dissent, including mass arrests and prosecutions of peaceful protesters.
- Forcing dissenting media to shut down.
- Unwarranted military imperialism against other countries, especially Ukraine.
- Massive killing of populations and destruction of civilian homes, hospitals, schools, and other buildings in unjustified wars and military operations in Ukraine and Syria.
- Effective merger of the Russian government with religion such that the Russian Orthodox

Chapter 6. Political Ethics

Church has become a mouthpiece of Putin's propaganda.
- Incessant, mendacious propaganda inside and outside of Russia (including the United States) reflecting Putin's fascist ideology and short- and long-term goals.

Putin has repeatedly, explicitly, and publicly invoked the fascist ideology of Ivan Ilyin in support of his authoritarian or totalitarian objectives and schemes. Historian Timothy Snyder describes and quotes Ilyin's works at length in his book *The Road to Unfreedom*. He summarizes that ideology as follows:

> The fascism of the 1920s and 1930s, Ilyin's era, had three core features: it celebrated will and violence over reason and law; it proposed a leader with a mystical connection to his people; and it characterized globalization as a conspiracy rather than as a set of problems. Revived today in conditions of inequality as a politics of eternity, fascism serves oligarchs as a catalyst for transitions away from public discussion and towards political fiction; away from meaningful voting and towards fake democracy; away from the rule of law and towards personalist regimes.[25]

Today, there is, once again, an ideological conflict between Russia and constitutional democracy. But this time it is not between communism and capitalism. It is between fascist totalitarianism and the rule of law. This opposition has become so severe that, like the Cold War between the Soviet Union and constitutional democracies of the twentieth century, it is approaching the verge of nuclear war.

IRRATIONAL DEMOCRATIC-REPUBLICAN POLITICAL LEADERSHIP

History provides many examples of irrational democratic-republican leadership. The following are case studies of two of them.

The Presidency of George W. Bush (2001–9)

During the administration of U.S. President George W. Bush, some conservatives postulated a conflict between the "faith-based community" and the "reality-based community." President Bush and some in his political circle embraced faith-based thinking and eschewed reality-based reasoning. Bush himself often said that he made decisions based on his "gut" and "instinct." Reason and evidence were not of first importance to "the decider," as he called himself.[26]

Scott McClellan was Bush's press secretary from 2003 to 2006. In his 2008 book *What Happened*, McClellan wrote:

> President Bush has always been an instinctive leader more than an intellectual leader. He is not one to delve deeply into all the possible policy options—including sitting around engaging in extended debate about them—before making a choice. Rather, he chooses based on his gut and his most deeply held convictions. Such was the case with Iraq.[27]

Chapter 6. Political Ethics

Journalist Ron Suskind reported the following conversation he had with a senior adviser to the president in 2002:

> The aide said that guys like me were "in what we call the reality-based community," which he defined as people who "believe that solutions emerge from your judicious study of discernible reality." I nodded and murmured something about enlightenment principles and empiricism. He cut me off. "That's not the way the world really works anymore," he continued. "We're an empire now, and when we act, we create our own reality. And while you're studying that reality—judiciously, as you will—we'll act again, creating other new realities, which you can study too, and that's how things will sort out. We're history's actors . . . and you, all of you, will be left to just study what we do."[28]

The official's remark that "We're an empire now" referred to the great expansion—or attempted expansion—of American military power abroad after the events of September 11, 2001, when terrorists overpowered airline pilots and flew their airplanes into the World Trade Center and Pentagon, resulting in almost 3,000 deaths. Bush, supported by Congress, ordered an American invasion of Afghanistan to root out al-Qaeda, the terrorist group led by Osama bin Laden responsible for 9/11. Al-Qaeda had been sheltered in Afghanistan by the country's theocratic Taliban regime. This invasion resulted in America's longest war (2001–21). Al-Qaeda and the Taliban were initially defeated, but the Taliban immediately began an insurgency that lasted over many years, eventually resulting in the Taliban reconquering Afghanistan in 2021 and proceeding to reinstate a version of their old theocratic system.

In 2003, the Bush administration also invaded Iraq, claiming that the latter had "weapons of mass destruction," including nuclear weapons. However, the American invasion discovered no such weapons. Although Saddam Hussein's dictatorship was overthrown in 2003, American involvement in the Iraq War continued long after the end of Bush's presidency. At one point, there were more than 170,000 United States troops in Iraq.[29]

Journalist Suskind and many others reported on Bush's lack of curiosity about facts and his reliance on his faith and "gut." Suskind wrote in 2004:

> Every few months, a report surfaces of the president using strikingly Messianic language, only to be dismissed by the White House. Three months ago, for instance, in a private meeting with Amish farmers in Lancaster County, Pa., Bush was reported to have said, "I trust God speaks through me." In this ongoing game of winks and nods, a White House spokesman denied the president had specifically spoken those words, but noted that "his faith helps him in his service to people."[30]

As president, Bush's naive gut instincts led him to factually erroneous conclusions. For example, on June 16, 2001, following his meeting with Russian President Vladimir Putin, Bush stated that "I looked the man

Chapter 6. Political Ethics

[Putin] in the eye. I found him to be very straightforward and trustworthy. We had a very good dialogue. I was able to get a sense of his soul, a man deeply committed to his country and the best interests of his country."[31] By the end of his presidency, however, Bush realized that his initial impression was incorrect.[32]

President Bush substituted faith and feeling for reason and evidence in presidential decisionmaking. He relied on his instincts in trusting Vice President Dick Cheney and Secretary of Defense Donald Rumsfeld, while often failing to solicit and consider the contrary views of such knowledgeable and experienced officials as Secretary of State Colin Powell. Bush's irrationality extended to both ends and means. The results of his careless decisionmaking style were two long wars that cost the United States and others much blood and treasure. His "instinct" and "gut" led to disastrous scenarios in which his foreign policy objectives were not achieved.[33]

Transition to Authoritarianism?: The Presidency of Donald J. Trump (2017–21)

Donald J. Trump's presidency, like that of George W. Bush, was characterized by his self-advertised "gut instinct" rather than reasoned consideration of factual evidence and policy alternatives. Writing in January 2019, one journalist aptly observed that "to Trump, gut instinct has become a substitute for all expertise and all nuance. He doesn't need a multipage daily briefing to learn the intricacies of the world. He'll take some bullet points or diagrams. Or better yet, he'll watch Fox News."[34]

Chapter 6. Political Ethics

Trump's demagogic campaign of lies began before his presidency. For example, starting in 2011, he began suggesting that President Barack Obama (2009–17) was born in Kenya and thus could not legally be president under the U.S. Constitution. Trump finally admitted on September 16, 2016, that "President Barack Obama was born in the United States period."[35] In the meantime, millions of his supporters and others had come to believe that Obama was born in Kenya.

As I stated in the second edition (2021) of my book on the Electoral College:

> Trump has proved to be the most bizarre president in American history. He is a classic demagogue, starting at least as far back as the years of Barack Obama's presidency, when he repeatedly suggested that Obama was born in Kenya and demanded that Obama produce his birth certificate. During Trump's 2016 campaign and the years of his presidency, Trump continued his pattern of demagoguery, often asserting demonstrable untruths as "alternative facts." He is a master practitioner of the "Big Lie" technique of authoritarian leaders everywhere. His speech is often downright Orwellian. He frequently makes statements that implicitly or explicitly support racism and xenophobia. He contradicts himself daily, sometimes hourly. Some other presidents have been bad; none has appeared as overtly unbalanced, except perhaps when under the influence of alcohol (which Trump eschews). He has violated every norm of standard presidential conduct

Chapter 6. Political Ethics

since George Washington. He has a total ignorance of American history and of the principles of the U.S. Constitution and government. He has often expressed a desire to weaken libel laws so that he can sue his political opponents in a manner analogous to seditious libel laws that were abandoned in this country centuries ago. He has repeatedly expressed a desire to lock up his political opponents, especially Hillary Clinton. If he had his way, the country would become a banana republic. He has a deep affinity for authoritarian strongmen. While repulsing America's traditional democratic allies, he has frequently expressed admiration for blatant dictators like Russian President Vladimir Putin, Philippine President Rodrigo Duterte, Turkey's Recep Tayyip Erdoğan, and North Korea's Kim Jong-un. Contrary to the universal consensus of U.S. governmental intelligence agencies, Trump claimed that no evidence existed of Russian interference in the 2016 presidential election. In an infamous press conference with Putin, he explicitly sided with the Russian leader while rejecting the findings of the American intelligence community. At virtually every turn of his presidency, he praised and defended Putin and other authoritarian rulers while criticizing traditional Western European allies.[36]

Since leaving office on January 20, 2021, Trump has continued his admiration for Putin. In a February

Chapter 6. Political Ethics

2022 interview, Trump praised Putin's aggression toward Ukraine:

> I went in yesterday and there was a television screen, and I said, "This is genius." Putin declares a big portion of the Ukraine — of Ukraine. Putin declares it as independent. Oh, that's wonderful.
>
> So, Putin is now saying, "It's independent," a large section of Ukraine. I said, "How smart is that?" And he's gonna go in and be a peacekeeper.... That's the strongest peace force I've ever seen. There were more army tanks than I've ever seen. They're gonna keep peace all right. No, but think of it. Here's a guy who's very savvy.[37]

A sizable portion of the Republican base is, at the time of this writing, sympathetic to Putin and his authoritarian policies, including his invasion of Ukraine.[38]

According to Wikipedia, "During his term [2017–21] as President of the United States, Donald Trump made tens of thousands of false or misleading claims; one report gave the number as 30,573, an average of about 21 per day."[39] These deceptions culminated in the Big Lie that Trump had won the presidential election of 2020. There is absolutely no evidence to support this claim, but Trump once again convinced millions of his followers that it was true. Trump's falsehood that the 2020 election was stolen from him led to the January 6, 2021 insurrection in which massive numbers of Trump's followers violently attacked the Capitol Building in Washington, DC in an attempt to stop constitutionally mandated congressional proceedings

Chapter 6. Political Ethics

acknowledging the fact that Joe Biden had prevailed over Donald Trump in the election. This assault resulted in several deaths and a large number of serious injuries to defending police officers. The lives of Vice President Mike Pence (who was presiding over the Joint Session of Congress pursuant to the Twelfth Amendment to the U.S. Constitution) and of Speaker of the House Nancy Pelosi and Senate Majority Leader Chuck Schumer were threatened. A noose was erected outside the Capitol building amid chants of "Hang Mike Pence." The constitutional proceedings were, in fact, delayed for several hours, but early the next morning the Joint Session of Congress declared that Biden had won the election.[40]

As president, Trump attempted to subvert the Constitution and laws of the United States. At the end, he tried to prevent the peaceful transition of power on the basis of lies and demagoguery. Fifty years after Watergate, veteran journalists Bob Woodward and Carl Bernstein pointed out the similarities and differences between Trump and President Richard M. Nixon (1969–74):

> The heart of Nixon's criminality was his successful subversion of the electoral process—the most fundamental element of American democracy. He accomplished it through a massive campaign of political espionage, sabotage and disinformation that enabled him to literally determine who his opponent would be in the presidential election of 1972 [George McGovern rather than Edmund Muskie]. . . .

> Donald Trump not only sought to destroy the electoral system through false claims of voter fraud and unprecedented public intimidation of state election officials, but he also then attempted to prevent the peaceful transfer of power to his duly elected successor, for the first time in American history.[41]

From the time of President Bush to the time of President Trump, portions of the Christian nationalist movement had evolved into a messianic cult that believed Trump was chosen by God to be a theocratic authoritarian dictator who would, among other things, execute liberals. This was a core belief of QAnon as well as other segments of the Religious Right.[42]

Such is the result when reason and evidence are cast aside in favor of baseless fantasies and mindless acceptance of the mendacious propaganda of demagogues and dishonest media.

RATIONAL DEMOCRATIC-REPUBLICAN POLITICAL LEADERSHIP

Rational democratic-republican leadership would apply the lessons of this book, especially Chapter 2 ("Human Reason"), to carefully evaluate policy options and select that course of action which is most rational and ethical **under the circumstances**. A rational and ethical political leader recognizes the dangers of merely proceeding deductively from an assumed premise to a political conclusion. The premises, the means, and the possible outcomes (including unintended consequences) should be thoroughly vetted. The common wisdom that the road to hell is paved with good intentions ought to be remembered: historical examples include the French and Bolshevik revolutions. Purity of intention is not enough. The model political leader must also understand how a particular policy will play out on the ground.

Specifically, a president or prime minister of a democratic republic should consult and rationally evaluate expert and other advice from all sides before making a decision. Ideology should not be the driver of such decisions. Although the political leader will normally have an overall political perspective, opinions should never discount actual facts. Furthermore, "gut instinct" and blind faith should never determine political policies and actions.

Have we seen examples of such ethical and rational leadership in history? In all probability there has never been a perfect political leader, and voters should not expect perfection: the perfect is the enemy of the good. There is better and worse in human life and, especially, in human politics and governance. Voters should not discard a political leader for lack of perfection while voting in an alternative who is much worse.

President John F. Kennedy had his faults, most of them personal. But he tried to follow reason and evidence in policy matters, especially in foreign policy. His astute leadership in the 1962 Cuban Missile Crisis may have averted a hot war—possibly a nuclear war—with the Soviet Union. First-hand accounts of his deliberations during the Cuban Missile Crisis reveal a president who was considering all the factors mentioned in the preceding paragraphs.[43]

CONCLUDING REMARKS REGARDING POLITICAL ETHICS

Political leadership throughout human history has revealed a wide range of competence regarding the use of reason and evidence in policy decisions. At one extreme we have the evil of totalitarian and authoritarian dictatorships. At the other, we have the ethical, rational, and evidence-based decisionmaking exhibited by President John F. Kennedy in the 1962 Cuban Missile Crisis. Additional examples of good and bad political leadership could fill an entire book.

EPILOGUE

It is fashionable in some circles to assume that people in general are hopelessly irrational and that scholarly inquiry into human behavior should be limited to conducting social scientific and neuroscientific studies showing such irrationality or, even, that humans lack free will. Emotions, so they say, rule. Reason, like Nietzsche's God, is dead.[1]

Typically, conservatives and liberals proffer contrasting solutions to the problem of human irrationality. Prominent conservative intellectuals have argued for centuries that we should subsume such emotionalism into religion and thereby make it—contrary to bitter historical experience[2]—controllable. Some liberals argue for an intellectual elite that counterbalances the irrationality of the masses. Either of these procedures bespeaks an implicit or explicit condescension toward humankind.

Then there are the postmodern Left and the authoritarian Right, both of which reject reason, evidence, and science on principle. From their perspectives, only the votaries of the postmodernist or alt-right ideologies deserve to be heard.

I propose a different approach. If we start treating people on the hypothesis that they are capable of rational and ethical lives, maybe they will surprise us. It may not work, but what have we got to lose? Nothing else has worked. Call me a Pollyanna, but is it not worth a try?

The conception of secular human teleology, as adumbrated in this book, is something that should be attractive to all human beings. Who could object to a world in which people act in a rational and ethical manner, both with respect to themselves and others? Human life will improve to the extent people become more rational and ethical. If we stop disparaging human reason and instead begin promoting it, perhaps we will eventually see a world in which all people can be proud to call themselves human.

Of course, the ethical reformation of humankind will likely take centuries, if not millennia, to accomplish—if, indeed, it ever occurs at all. In the meantime, government is needed for the formulation and administration of criminal law, defense against foreign aggressors, and promotion of the common good. However, anarchocapitalists and anarchosocialists disagree with this conclusion. Assuming they are incorrect, what kind of government is appropriate for the foreseeable future? And would some kind of government be necessary even if all people were rational and ethical? Such are the questions to be addressed in the projected third volume—*Reason and Human Government*—of this philosophical trilogy on free will, ethics, and political philosophy.

Appendix

The Conflicts among the Claims to Revelation

Human history has known many claims by many different people to revelation. This appendix examines several of these claims, their inconsistencies with each other, and the persecutions and wars that have been waged in the names of these conflicting claims. We begin by describing various claims to revelation and their doctrinal incongruities with each other. We will then summarize the history of the violent strife occasioned by these conflicts.

Except as otherwise noted, the sources for the facts in this appendix are general history books and encyclopedias.

Theological Conflicts among the Claims to Revelation

The following discussion does not try to be exhaustive. Rather, I have selected a sampling of what I consider interesting examples of different claims to revelation. Some religions (for example, those conceived by Ikhnaton and Zoroaster) are treated more thoroughly than others, because the typical reader is not likely to be familiar with them and because these religions have, for one reason or another, an interest that transcends the limitations of their historical times and places.[1]

SOME EXPLICIT AND IMPLICIT CLAIMS TO REVELATION

The Ancient Egyptian Religions

Beginning more than five thousand years ago, a remarkable civilization appeared on the banks of the Nile River in what we now know as Egypt.[2] Although the ancient Egyptian civilization was advanced in many respects, its religion remained, for many centuries, simplistic and naturalistic, like the religions of many of its less civilized neighbors. The sun, the moon, the sky, the air, the earth, and other natural objects were each considered a divinity. However, a doctrine emerged that the ruler (called the pharaoh[3]) was divine. At first the pharaoh was identified with Horus (the falcon god) and Osiris (ruler of the dead). Later, sometime in the twenty-sixth or twenty-fifth centuries BCE, the pharaoh claimed to be the son and agent of Re, the sun god. Accordingly, the ancient Egyptians believed that the pharaoh ruled directly through divine revelation. Nevertheless, even the pharaoh was bound by the ancient customary law, which the Egyptians believed to be divinely ordained.

After a period of dominance of the sun god Re, other major deities began to usurp the worship of Re. Starting about the twenty-fourth century BCE, Osiris and his wife, Isis, and son, Horus, became especially popular. While Re was a kind of rational, abstract, objective god, Osiris was a more personal god who satisfied the emotional needs of the common people.

Appendix: Conflicts among the Claims to Revelation

Although at various times in Egyptian history the story of Osiris contributed to a conception of the difference between right and wrong,[4] irrationalism eventually won the day and Egyptian religion became a preserve of superstition and magic. An increasingly powerful priestly class sold magic charms and formulas for the purpose of insuring admittance into an afterlife that corresponded, vaguely, to the Christian concept of heaven; the priests taught that such artificial devices were much more important than ethical character for determining a person's post-life existence.

Another religious system emerged in about the twentieth century BCE. The god of this religion was Amon-Re or, as it became abbreviated, Amon. This god was a combination of the older god Re with the Theban god Amon. This synthetic religion continued to maintain the notion that the pharaoh was the divine representative of the god. At one point the oracle of Amon proclaimed that Hatshepsut, the wife of the deceased Pharaoh Thutmose II, should be pharaoh, and Hatshepsut became the effective ruler of Egypt for many years, being the more powerful of two titular leaders. Furthermore, over a period of centuries, a strong priestly class devoted to the worship of Amon developed.

During the fourteenth century BCE, a pharaoh appeared whose religious thought was revolutionary and forward looking. Pharaoh Amenhotep IV was disgusted with the prevailing religious doctrines and practices and with the powerful priestly class that perpetuated them. Soon after he came to power, he instituted a new, largely monotheistic religion based upon the worship of Aton, the disk of the sun. Aton was

Appendix: Conflicts among the Claims to Revelation

a more philosophical version of Re, the ancient sun god of the pharaohs. For example, Aton was not anthropomorphic like Re but was rather symbolized by the rays (disk) of the sun providing energy to the world. Ikhnaton claimed that Re himself ordered the new religion in a personal revelation experienced by Ikhnaton.[5]

To signify the revolution from the worship of Amon, the god of the dominant priests, to the worship of Aton, the pharaoh changed his name from Amenhotep ("He in whom Amon is content") to Ikhnaton ("Aton is satisfied" or "He in whom Aton is satisfied"). Ikhnaton (also spelled Akhnaton, Akhenaton, and Akhenaten) attempted to eliminate all vestiges of the older religions. For example, Ikhnaton caused the obliteration of all references to Amon (including the pharaoh's family name "Amenhotep") from monuments and statues. To achieve isolation from the physical memorials and from the vengeful priestly advocates of the past, Ikhnaton constructed a new capital, which he named Akhetaton ("Horizon of Aton"). He decreed that the land encompassing the new capital "belongs to my father, Aton . . . ."[6]

Ikhnaton composed two hymns to Aton, of which one bears striking resemblance to Psalm 104 of the Hebrew Bible, written centuries later.[7]

Ikhnaton's new conception of religion was revolutionary in several respects. First, it was, for the most part, monotheistic. Its only divergence from strict monotheism was in the idea that the pharaoh is divine, being the child of Aton. Such monotheism, especially when accompanied by Ikhnaton's attempted eradication of all other religions, was something of a heresy at this point in human history.

Second, unlike most religions during or before its time, the religion of Aton was universal. Aton was not merely the god of a particular locality or even of the larger Egyptian state. Ikhnaton conceived Aton to be the god of all human beings and the creator of the entire world. Historians have pointed out the fact that this universalist development in Egyptian religion corresponded to the expansion of the Egyptian empire. Ikhnaton expected all persons within his empire, which he had inherited from previous pharaohs, to worship Aton and recognize that god as the sole god.

Third, and perhaps most importantly, Ikhnaton's conception of Aton as a benevolent and rational god stood in sharp contrast to the superstitious, irrational, and dark religious ideas and thoughts of the immediate past.

Ikhnaton, who apparently died before reaching the age of thirty, was obsessed with thought, with ideas, with idealism. As an eminent scholar observed, "the modern world has yet adequately to value or even acquaint itself with this man, who in an age so remote and under conditions so adverse, became the world's first idealist and the world's first *individual*."[8] Unfortunately, Ikhnaton was far ahead of his time—perhaps, in some ways, far ahead of all times. Most people could not follow Ikhnaton's noble vision of his god and of the benevolence and beauty of the world created by his god. Superstition, magic, irrationalism, ignorance, and stupidity soon again became predominant.

Appendix: Conflicts among the Claims to Revelation

Ikhnaton was partly to blame for his own demise. In his youthful idealism, he was not sufficiently attentive to political and military considerations. He had no touch of Machiavelli's insights regarding the human condition. Consequently, Ikhnaton was a failure as a pharaoh. He lost the Egyptian empire and was overcome by the traditional forces hostile to him. We respect this incredible man not for his political acuity, which was nonexistent, but for his philosophical mind. Given time, Ikhnaton might have learned enough about political and military considerations to have withstood the powers of reaction and disintegration. But he was not given time. He is, perhaps, the earliest known example of the ancient Greek dictum that "the gods love those who die young." His life is, in a sense, a tragedy. In another sense, he is rightly honored as one of the few individuals, in remote antiquity, who possessed deep philosophical insight. For that great accomplishment, he will always be remembered by thinking human beings.

Zoroastrianism

Sometime between 1400 and 1200 BCE, in a pre-literate society somewhere in the steppes of central Asia, a giant of religious and philosophical thought inaugurated a great religion that has survived for more than thirty centuries.[9] We know his name as Zoroaster, which is the Greek and English form of the original name Zarathustra (or Zarathushtra).

Zoroaster composed a sacred work called the *Gathas*. The *Gathas* are in an ancient language known as Avestan. The Avestan word "Gathas" means "hymns" or "songs" or "chants." Although the *Gathas* were not written down until many centuries after Zoroaster's death, the text that has come down to us

Appendix: Conflicts among the Claims to Revelation

evidently reflects Zoroaster's own words because it is poetic in form, thus ensuring considerable accuracy in oral transmission similar to the career of Homer's *Iliad* and *Odyssey*. The fact that the *Gathas* are in a very ancient language is also a reflection of their authenticity. For many centuries, the priests of Zoroastrianism memorized the *Gathas* and transmitted this holy work, with meticulous exactitude, to succeeding generations until Zoroaster's words were finally written down.

Although the *Gathas* are a small part of the entire Zoroastrian sacred literature, we will focus here only on the *Gathas* in order to attempt to ascertain the ethical meaning of this religion as Zoroaster himself originally conceived it. In this endeavor, we are somewhat hampered not only by the language barrier but also by the fact that he designed these poetic hymns in an intricate manner such that much of their meaning could be gleaned only after considerable meditation and reflection. Furthermore, he sometimes utilized certain inherited myths or metaphors that were familiar to his immediate audience but are not familiar to the modern reader. Accordingly, we cannot hope to set forth a complete interpretation here. We can, however, indicate some of the main themes.[10]

In the *Gathas*, Zoroaster claimed to have received a revelation from Ahura Mazda ("Lord of Wisdom"), the creator of the world.[11] Ahura Mazda (abbreviated "Mazda") is the first and the last, the creator of right and of wisdom and the judge of the actions of life.[12] In the beginning, Mazda created the individual and individuality; Mazda gave each human being free will to choose between good and evil.[13] People are of three

Appendix: Conflicts among the Claims to Revelation

kinds: the true speaker, the false speaker, and the person who wavers back and forth between truth and falsity.[14] Mazda knows each person's merit or lack thereof.[15]

Each human being must choose between two basic forces in the world: good and evil.[16] The good created life; the bad created not-life.[17] Human beings must decide between good and evil in their thoughts, words, and actions.[18] Wise human beings will choose good; unwise human beings will choose evil.[19] Good and evil correspond to truth and untruth, and at the final reckoning the followers of the Lie will be consigned to the worst existence, while those who follow Right will have the best existence.[20] The final judgment will come with a fire of molten metal; the fire will separate the persons who follow Right from the persons who follow the Lie; the former will experience immortality (good mind through all time) and the latter torment.[21] Good action, good thought, and good speech are all essential and necessary for the reward of eternity, and those whose actions fail to reflect good thought will experience woe at the final judgment.[22]

Zoroaster was preoccupied with the problem of unjustified violence and, unlike Jesus, taught that such violence should be opposed and resisted.[23] Zoroaster lived in a rural area among pastoralists (raisers of livestock) who inhabited permanent settlements. During his lifetime this settled people was exposed to frequent attacks from nomadic raiders. Thus, Zoroaster focused much of his prophetic wrath against such plundering. But his thought was by no means limited to his immediate historical circumstances. His teaching regarding violence is just as relevant today as it was

Appendix: Conflicts among the Claims to Revelation

when he first spoke about this continuing problem of human life.

Zoroaster saw himself as a man with a mission. He considered himself an educator of humanity, a person who, on account of his unique understanding, could help advance humanity in the direction of good thought, good speech, and good action.[24] Yet he had doubts about his effectiveness and power against evil, and sometimes his poems reflect a Job-like questioning of the Almighty.[25]

Zoroaster did not ignore women in his religious vision; he regarded women equally as capable as men of ethical perfection.[26] And not a word authored by Zoroaster can be interpreted as an endorsement of asceticism; rather, he endorsed marriage and did not despise the body.[27] Far from being an ascetic, he taught that the best of all things, the life of Good Thought and Right, involves bliss and joy.[28]

Although Zoroaster was acutely conscious of the existence of evil as well as good, he did not promote any notion of original sin. Rather, as we have seen, he held that human beings have free will to choose between good and evil. He said that paradise is gained by right actions, good thought, and truth. Zoroaster emphasized right action to an extent not familiar to many Protestant Christians. Whereas Protestant Christianity emphasizes faith (which usually means belief in the historical narrative of the New Testament), Zoroaster taught that good action is the key to eternal life. Some people think that deathbed repentance is sufficient for salvation. Although Zoroaster does not appear to be on record as to this precise issue, the tenor of his teachings is that a person's actions throughout life constitute the most

Appendix: Conflicts among the Claims to Revelation

important criterion of whether that person will go to heaven or to hell.[29]

Unlike most religions of the ancient world, Zoroastrianism was not, in theory, limited to one nationality. Zoroaster wished to convert all human beings to his religion. However, in later centuries, Zoroastrianism was combined with elements of some of the religious practices that Zoroaster himself had opposed. Moreover, Zoroastrianism never became a religion that was accepted by large numbers of people throughout the world. During the Middle Ages, the predominance of Islam in Persia forced an emigration of a group of Zoroastrians to India, where they became known as Parsees. Today, the Parsees and a small group of Zoroastrians in Iran are the main contingents of the religion of Zoroastrianism, though there are Zoroastrians in other countries, including in the United States.

Organized Zoroastrianism, like all other organized religions, has its sets of dogmas and rituals. However, Zoroastrianism is, in its original conception, one of the most ethical religions that has arisen in human history. Zoroaster's ethical teaching is consistent with reason, with human nature, and with right philosophy. Like Ikhnaton, Zoroaster was a prophet of a philosophical kind. Thus, it is not surprising that Plato (427–347 BCE) referred respectfully to Zoroaster in one of his philosophical works.[30]

Mithraism

Zoroaster emphasized ethical principles over ritualism. However, ritualism eventually became more important, especially in an offshoot of Zoroastrianism called Mithraism. Although Zoroaster taught moderation rather than asceticism, Mithraism promoted severe asceticism (including laceration of the flesh) as a prerequisite to mystical union with the divine. Mithraism also utilized baptism and a sacred meal, and it considered Sundays and the twenty-fifth day of December as sacred days.

Mithraism became quite popular in the fourth century BCE at the time of the decline of the Persian Empire. Later, in the third and fourth centuries CE, Mithraism was the principal rival of Christianity in the Roman Empire. Some scholars think that Christianity borrowed some of its doctrines from Mithraism, which predated Christianity.

Gnosticism

A religion known as Gnosticism became popular in the second century CE. Its adherents claimed to have received a revelation from God. The Gnostics debunked reason, claiming that only an emotional, mystical attitude could establish contact with the divine. Gnosticism, like Mithraism and Manicheism, twisted the dualism of Zoroastrianism (the doctrine of two forces, good and evil) into an extreme rejection of the physical aspects of reality, including the human body. Zoroaster himself would have strongly condemned any such distortion of his much more moderate, humanistic teaching. As indicated above, the conflict between good and evil was not, for Zoroaster, a conflict between mind and matter. Unfortunately, Zoroaster had only one life to live and could not himself personally oppose all stupidity in all generations of human history.

Appendix: Conflicts among the Claims to Revelation

Manicheism

Mani, who lived in the last half of the third century CE, promulgated a religion known as Manicheism. Mani claimed that he was the last of a line of great prophets that had included Noah, Abraham, Zoroaster, Jesus, and Paul. Mani taught an extreme dualism of spirit and matter. According to Mani, all material things were evil. Human nature was evil because human beings had physical bodies; even marriage and procreation were the work of the devil. Because such doctrine was obviously incompatible with the survival of the human species, Mani distinguished between the "perfect," who were required to live extremely ascetic lives, and the "secular," who could depart from asceticism but who were nevertheless obligated to adhere to vegetarianism and to avoid fornication, idolatry, and other defined evils.

St. Augustine (354–430 CE) was a Manichean before he became a Christian. Accordingly, it is not surprising that Augustine was influential in implementing the Manichean distinction between the "perfect" and the "secular" in the institutions of the Christian Church. Christian monks and nuns were required to lead ascetic lives and were not permitted to procreate; most Christians, being incapable of such doctrinal perfection, could live a more normal existence.

Hinduism

Hinduism has been the dominant religion in India for several thousand years. Hinduism is a complicated religion with a complicated history. We cannot treat it adequately here, for such treatment would go far beyond our present purpose. Suffice it to say that Hinduism's

Appendix: Conflicts among the Claims to Revelation

doctrines of reincarnation and a caste system put it at odds with other religions, for example, Judaism, Christianity, and Islam. Although Hinduism is not as explicitly based upon a claim to revelation as is Zoroastrian, Judaism, Christianity, and Islam, Hinduism does have its holy books and implicitly asserts revelation as the basis of its religion.

Taoism

Taoism is a religion that began in China with Lao Tzu, born about 604 BCE Although not all Taoism is religious in nature, a religious form of Taoism developed in which Lao Tzu was considered one of three gods that composed its sacred texts. Religious Taoism emphasizes ritual and magic, and its doctrines are clearly not reconcilable with such religions as Judaism, Christianity, and Islam.

The Delphic Oracle

The ancient Greeks had a pantheon of gods of which one of the most important was Apollo. The Greeks believed that Apollo spoke to human beings through an oracle located at Apollo's temple in Delphi. The Greeks consulted the oracle about how they should conduct their political and other affairs. The oracle often spoke enigmatically, and the Greeks did not always understand the veiled meaning of the oracle until it was too late. Of course, the belief in the divinity of the Delphic oracle, along with the general polytheism of the ancient Greeks, is incompatible with such religions as Judaism, Christianity, and Islam.

Judaism

Judaism is one of the three religions which now dominate the Middle East, Europe, and the Americas.

Appendix: Conflicts among the Claims to Revelation

The other two major religions of these regions, discussed below, are Christianity and Islam.

Judaism holds that the Jews (also known earlier as the Israelites) were chosen by God to stand for monotheism and religious purity in opposition to such religious practices (widespread at the time of the origin of Judaism) as polytheism, idolatry, child sacrifice, temple prostitution, and debauchery. According to the Hebrew scriptures, the Israelites were commanded to destroy certain peoples, take their land, and establish a theocracy. Jewish history is complicated, and we will not attempt to detail it here. For the present purposes it suffices to observe that Judaism is based upon a belief that God spoke directly to Abraham, Moses, and other Jewish prophets. Christianity and Islam were offshoots of Judaism, but, as discussed below, these three religions are doctrinally incompatible with each other.

Christianity

Christians believe that Jesus, a Jew who lived in Israel, was the son of God, and most Christians believe that Jesus is part of a divine Trinity consisting of God the Father, God the Son (Jesus), and God the Holy Spirit (or Holy Ghost). Jesus opposed some of the practices of the Jewish priests and spoke of a direct relation between God and individual human beings, unmediated by the Jewish priesthood. Naturally, the Jewish priesthood did not agree with this view. After certain events set forth in the Christian Gospels, Jesus was crucified. Christians believe that Jesus rose from the dead (the Resurrection) and that Jesus will come again to rule the earth (the Second Coming). These doctrines are, of course, incompatible with Judaism, which has never accepted the doctrine of the divinity of Jesus. Many Christians

Appendix: Conflicts among the Claims to Revelation

believe that only those who accept the doctrine of the divinity of Jesus Christ will go to heaven.

The Christian Bible consists of the Old Testament, which is similar but not identical to the Hebrew Bible, and the New Testament, which consists of the four Gospels (*Matthew*, *Mark*, *Luke*, and *John*), the letters of Paul, and other scriptural writings. Differences exist among the Christian denominations about the canonicity of some religious writings. Many Christians believe that the Bible is literally the word of God, and fundamentalist Christians believe that everything in the Bible (including such miracles as Jonah having survived after being swallowed by a whale) is literally true. The Gospels contain many stories in which Jesus is alleged to have performed miracles. From a purely historical perspective it is virtually impossible to confirm or deny whether Jesus himself purported to perform miracles. In this connection, it needs to be observed that the Gospels were not written down until decades after Jesus's death. For example, a standard Christian fundamentalist edition of the Bible states that Jesus died in 30 CE, that *Matthew* was written two or three decades after Jesus's death, that *Mark* was written two or three decades after Jesus's death, that *Luke* was written about thirty years after Jesus's death, and that *John* was written about 55–60 years after Jesus's death.[31] According to this same conservative Christian source, the earliest writing in the New Testament is *James*, which was not written until 15-19 years after Jesus's death.[32] It must be remembered that Jesus lived in a society that did not have modern mass communications and in which people did not have a skeptical, scientific outlook.

Appendix: Conflicts among the Claims to Revelation

Accordingly, many scholars discount the miracle stories.[33]

Islam

The religion of Islam originated with Muhammad, who was born about 570 CE in Mecca in what is now Saudi Arabia. Muhammad lived in a society that was dominated by a primitive kind of polytheism replete with blood feuds and other unjustified violence. For many years Muhammad meditated on the evils he saw around him. He began to formulate his teaching of monotheism and ethical decency, but no one paid any attention to him. He was fortunate to marry a widow—a woman many years older than he—who provided intellectual and emotional support at a time when he himself doubted his ability to change the world around him. After many years of meditation in which Muhammad was developing and formulating his ideas, he received, according to Islamic tradition, a revelation from Allah (God), in which Muhammad was given the Qur'an (Koran), the Islamic scripture. The Qur'an teaches that Moses and Jesus were prophets in a continuing religious tradition that culminates in the prophecy of Muhammad. This is not the place to elaborate the specific doctrines of Islam or to comment on the history of Islamic theology.[34] It suffices for our present purposes to point out that Islam, Christianity, and Judaism are all doctrinally incompatible with each other. For example, both Islam and Judaism reject the doctrine of the divinity of Jesus, a doctrine that is fundamental to Christianity. The Qur'an also criticized the historical development of Judaism. Later in this chapter, we will consider the military conflicts that have attended these three conflicting claims to revelation.

Appendix: Conflicts among the Claims to Revelation

Latter-Day Saints

Joseph Smith (1805–1844) was the founder of the Church of Jesus Christ of Latter-day Saints, often referred to as the Mormon faith. At the age of fourteen, while living in western New York State, Smith claimed to experience his first revelation from God and Jesus Christ. When he was about twenty-one or twenty-two years old, according to Smith's account, an angel led him to buried golden plates. These golden plates, when translated by Smith, became the Book of Mormon. Three witnesses (Oliver Cowdery, David Whitmer, and Martin Harris) testified that an angel showed them the golden plates and the engravings on the plates, that the voice of the Lord told them that Joseph Smith had translated the golden plates, and that the voice of the Lord commanded them to bear witness of these events. Eight other witnesses testified further that Joseph Smith had shown them the golden plates and the engravings on them.

The Book of Mormon tells a story of some tribes of Israel that were led by the prophet Lehi from Jerusalem to America about 600 BCE. These people became the American Indians, and the religion set forth in the golden plates is the true religion.

Today, more than sixteen million people worldwide are Mormons. The Mormon religion criticizes Christianity on several points. The Christian churches do not, of course, believe that Joseph Smith received a genuine revelation, even though the three witnesses named above provided contemporaneous, written testimony of visitations by an angel and of the voice of the Lord, and eight other witnesses provided

Appendix: Conflicts among the Claims to Revelation

contemporaneous, written testimony that they had seen the golden plates.

VIOLENT CONFLICTS AMONG THE CLAIMS TO REVELATION

We have delineated some, though not all, of the conflicting claims to revelation in human history. Similarly, we will now describe some, but not all, of the violent conflicts between and among the various claims to revelation. We will focus on the main outlines of some of the historical conflicts. A thorough investigation of this subject would require a work of many volumes. However, such detail is not necessary for present purposes.

One of the first claims to revelation we investigated was that of the Egyptian pharaoh Ikhnaton. We indicated that Ikhnaton's life and teaching were short. No one knows why this noble theological philosopher died so young. But it is a good guess that the priests of Amon decided that a little regicide was better than a lot of heresy, and that getting rid of a pharaoh was preferable to their losing their long-established positions and perquisites. It was a dirty job, but somebody had to do it. To accomplish their objectives, the Amonite priests had to destroy not only Ikhnaton's life but also his reputation—they successfully labeled him "the criminal of Akhetaton"[35] and thereby foreclosed any attempt by subsequent pharaohs to revive Ikhnaton's religion.

Although Zoroastrianism has survived, in modified form, into our own age, Zoroastrians have not escaped hostility. When Arabic Muslims defeated the Sasanian Empire in the seventh and eighth centuries CE, they

Appendix: Conflicts among the Claims to Revelation

persecuted the Zoroastrians in Persia. To escape such religious persecution, some Zoroastrians later fled to India.

This brings us to the Abrahamic religions of Judaism, Christianity, and Islam. As indicated above, Judaism was virtually defined as a religion that rejected the beliefs and practices of its neighbors. Accordingly, the Israelites were ordered to kill every man, woman, and child of the cities they conquered for purposes of settlement.[36]

Much of the remainder of the history of the Jewish people has involved persecution by those who have considered Judaism as heretical or seditious. In 586 BCE, the Babylonians captured Jerusalem, burned its temple, and forced many Jewish people to leave their homeland and move to Babylonia. Some of the greatest scriptures of the Jewish prophets were written during this period (called the Babylonian Captivity). In 538 BCE the Jews were permitted to return to Jerusalem and rebuild their temple. However, in 70 CE, the Romans again destroyed the temple and later killed much of the Jewish peasantry. The Jewish theocracy disappeared, and many Jewish people were dispersed throughout Europe and other parts of the world. For many centuries, the Jews were often persecuted in the various places that they lived. This persecution culminated in what is known as the Holocaust, when Adolph Hitler, the leader of Nazi Germany, ordered the genocide of millions of Jews during the 1930s and 1940s.

As a result of the persecutions of Jewish people in other lands, many Jews committed themselves to Zionism—the doctrine that Jews should re-establish their homeland in the Middle East. This hope became a

Appendix: Conflicts among the Claims to Revelation

fact after World War II, when Jews formed the state of Israel. However, this development led to intermittent war between the Jewish inhabitants and their neighbors—the Palestinians who occupied the same land and the Arabic and Muslim countries surrounding Israel. Consequently, Israel has been involved in much warfare and bloodshed since its establishment as a nation after Second World War.

The conflict between Israel and the Palestinians remains intense, with progress in peace negotiations thwarted by the Jewish settler movement into the West Bank (the Palestinian area occupied by Israel as a result of the 1967 war) and Palestinian terror attacks. The basic problem appears to be that the more conservative Jews in Israel believe that Israel should extend to its biblically defined borders, while the Palestinians claim a right to their own Palestinian state within those borders, if not in Israel itself.

Christianity and Islam have also had bloody careers. Originally, the Christians were persecuted by the Romans, who delighted, for example, in using Christians as human torches at Roman festivities or as gladiators in fight-to-the-death contests. Similarly, the early Muslims had to fight for their lives against the forces of traditional religion in Arabia. The success of the Muslims in their early military conflicts eventually led them to take over northern Africa, the Middle East, and portions of southwestern Europe. During the Middle Ages, when Christianity was dominant in Western Europe, Christian kings led military crusades against Muslims in these regions.

In modern times, Christian militancy has focused mostly on violent conflict involving denominational

Appendix: Conflicts among the Claims to Revelation

splits within Christianity itself. After Martin Luther began the Protestant Reformation in the early sixteenth century, Europe was racked by wars between Roman Catholics and Protestants. In 1588, the Catholic Spanish Armada unsuccessfully attempted to invade England and depose the Protestant Queen Elizabeth. Within England, the established Church of England, in conjunction with the monarchy, persecuted Roman Catholics, Anabaptists, Puritans, Presbyterians, and Separatists, thus leading to several important migrations of dissident religionists to America. Scotland had an intolerant Presbyterian theocracy, which it attempted to export to England during the seventeenth-century English Civil Wars between Anglicans and other Protestants.

During the twentieth century, Protestants and Catholics battled each other in Northern Ireland, and Christians and Muslims made war against each other in areas earlier controlled with a heavy hand by the Soviet Union.

My book *The First American Founder: Roger Williams and Freedom of Conscience* details the history of religious persecution and wars among Christian sects in the modern era. Among other things, it discusses the sixteenth-century theocracy of John Calvin in Geneva, which executed and otherwise persecuted dissidents from Calvin's established church. It focuses especially on the religious persecutions of the seventeenth-century Massachusetts Bay Puritan theocracy, including its hanging, whipping, and imprisonment of Quakers, its imprisonment and whipping of Baptists, and its banishment of such religious dissidents as Roger Williams and Anne Hutchinson. In opposition to such

Appendix: Conflicts among the Claims to Revelation

theocratic doctrine and practice, Roger Williams founded the settlement of Providence in what later became Rhode Island. This new political society was based on total freedom of conscience and complete separation of church and state. Williams also authored several important books and pamphlets advocating church–state separation and freedom of conscience—writings that influenced both America and Europe, including the Establishment and Free Exercise Clauses of the First Amendment to the United States Constitution.

Murder and other persecution in the name of religion is alive and well even in the twenty-first century, for example, in the Islamist jihadi terrorist attacks in the United States and other countries on and after September 11, 2001, the Taliban wars and re-established theocracy in Afghanistan, the religiously motivated armed conflicts and terrorist attacks (against Shia Muslims, Sikhs, Yazidis, and Christians) by the theocratic Islamic State and similar Muslim extremist groups in the Middle East and Africa, the genocide by the Myanmar government against the Rohingya, and the discrimination against Muslims by the Hindu nationalist government of India.[37] Such practices are justified, in the minds of their perpetrators, by doctrinal and cultural differences between their religion and the religions and cultures of others. It is an irrationality that most modern human beings find difficult to understand. But it is a phenomenon that appears to be as old—or almost as old—as human history.

NOTES

Epigraph

[1] *The Analects of Confucius*, trans. and ed. Simon Leys (New York: W. W. Norton, 1997), 11.12 (I have changed "The Master" in this translation to "Confucius").

[2] Cicero, *The Tusculan Disputations*, bk. 5, § 4, in *Cicero's Tusculan Disputations*, trans. C. D. Yonge (New York: Harper & Brothers, 1899), 166.

Chapter 1. What Is the Basis of Human Ethics?

[1] *Analects of Confucius*, trans. Leys, 2.17.

[2] Plato, *Apology of Socrates* 21d (my translation).

[3] Leo Strauss, "Relativism," in *The Rebirth of Classical Political Rationalism: An Introduction to the Thought of Leo Strauss*, ed. Thomas L. Pangle (Chicago: University of Chicago Press, 1989), 15.

[4] Strauss, 18.

[5] Plato, *Theaetetus* 152a. This is a modification of Seth Benardete's translation in *Plato's Theaetetus* (Chicago: University of Chicago Press, 1986). Benardete's translation is: "Of all things (*khrêmata*) (a) human being is the measure, of the things which are, that (how) they are, and of the things which are not, that (how) they are not." The parenthetical language constitutes Benardete's attempt to convey the meaning of the original Greek in as literal a manner as possible. See also Plato, *Cratylus*, 385–86a.

[6] Mauro Bonazzi, "Protagoras," §§ 2.1, 2.2, in *The Stanford Encyclopedia of Philosophy*, fall 2020 ed., ed. Edward L. Zalta,

https://plato.stanford.edu/archives/fall2020/entries/protagoras/; Maria Baghramian and J. Adam Carter, "Relativism, § 3, in *The Stanford Encyclopedia of Philosophy*, spring 2021 ed., ed. Edward L. Zalta, https://plato.stanford.edu/archieves/spr2021/entries/relativism/; Maria Baghramian and Annalisa Coliva, *Relativism* (Oxford, UK: Routledge, 2020), 11, 27, Kindle. Cf. Lorraine Smith Pangle, *Reason and Character: The Moral Foundations of Aristotelian Political Philosophy* (Chicago: University of Chicago Press, 2020), 90, Kindle.

[7] Alasdair MacIntyre, *After Virtue*, 3rd ed. (Notre Dame, IN: University of Notre Dame Press, 2007), 11–12 (italics in the original), Kindle. See chapters 2 and 3 of MacIntyre's book for his elaboration and evaluation of various forms of emotivism. This view has faint terminological echoes in today's cognitive science. See Keith E. Stanovich, *The Bias That Divides Us: The Science and Politics of Myside Thinking* (Cambridge, MA: MIT Press, 2021), 48–51, Kindle.

[8] MacIntyre, *After Virtue*, 26–27; Leo Strauss, *Natural Right and History* (Chicago: University of Chicago Press, 1953), chap. 2.

[9] Baghramian and Coliva, *Relativism*, 274.

[10] Strauss, *Natural Right and History*, 12.

[11] Gilbert Harman, "Moral Relativism Is Moral Realism," *Philosophical Studies: An International Journal for Philosophy in the Analytic Tradition* 172, no. 4 (April 2015): 858, https://www.jstor.org/stable/24704141.

[12] Harman, 860 (italics added).

[13] Harman, 860–61.

[14] Properly used, *reductio ad absurdum* is a legitimate form of rational argument. Walter Sinnott-Armstrong, *Think Again: How to Reason and Argue* (New York Oxford University Press, 2018), 204–6 (distinguished from a straw person argument), Kindle; Gregory L. Block, "Appeal to Ridicule," in *Bad Arguments: 100 of the Most Important Fallacies in Western Philosophy*, ed. Robert Arp, Steven Barbone, and

Notes

Michael Bruce (Hoboken, NJ: Wiley–Walton, 2018), 119–20 (distinguished from ridicule), Kindle.

[15] Plato, *Theaetetus* 170a–71c; Baghramian and Coliva, *Relativism*, 27–28.

[16] Strauss, *Natural Right and History*, 25.

[17] Plato, *Republic*, bk. 9 (cf. *Republic* 438c–444d and Allan Bloom's endnote 27 on page 457 and his Interpretive Essay at page 376 in *The Republic of Plato*, 2nd ed., trans. and ed. Allan Bloom [New York: Basic Books, 1991]); Plato, *Gorgias* 504d, 506e –8a; Plato *Phaedrus* 246a–254e; Plato, *Seventh Letter* 326b–d, 330d–31a, 335a–e, 336a–c, 340d, 350d–e; Joe Sachs, introduction to Plato, *Republic*, trans. and ed. Joe Sachs (Newbury, MA: Focus, 2007), 3–5, 8–9.

[18] Aristotle, *Nicomachean Ethics* 1.3.1095a5–12, 1.7.1097b23–1098a18, 9.8.1168b33–1169a7.

[19] Aristotle, *Nicomachean Ethics* 6.5.1140b5–7, in *Aristotle's "Nicomachean Ethics"*, trans. and ed. Robert C. Bartlett and Susan D. Collins (Chicago: University of Chicago Press, 2011); cf. Aristotle, *Eudemian Ethics* 2.1.1219b25–30, 2.2.1220b3–6, 2.3.1220b26–33, 2.5.1222a6 –9, 1222b3–3. Lorraine Smith Pangle explains her choice of the translation "active wisdom" for *phronēsis* as follows: "*Phronēsis* is most commonly rendered into English as 'prudence' or 'practical wisdom.' In current usage, however, the terms 'prudence' and 'practical' both imply a focus on what is advantageous and especially materially advantageous; they thus have a narrowness that seems to set them in opposition to the concerns with beauty, eros, and nobility. *Phronēsis* for Aristotle is the form of wisdom that guides all intelligent choice and action, especially the choice of noble action in the moral and political sphere, but also the choice to pursue theoretical wisdom (NE 6.13). To better capture its full scope, I will translate it throughout as 'active wisdom.' " Pangle, *Reason and Character*, 279n2.

[20] Plato, *Republic* 436b, in *The Republic of Plato*, 2nd ed., trans. Allan Bloom.

[21] Bloom, in *The Republic of Plato*, 457n25.

Notes

[22] Aristotle, *Metaphysics* 11.5.1061b36–1062a3, in *Aristotle's "Metaphysics"*, trans. Joe Sachs (Santa Fe, NM: Green Lion Press, 2002).

[23] Aristotle, *Metaphysics* 4.3.1005b19–23, in *Aristotle's "Metaphysics"*, trans. Sachs.

[24] Graham Priest, *Beyond the Limits of Thought* (Oxford: Clarendon Press, 2002); Graham Priest, Francesco Berto, and Zach Weber, "Dialetheism," *The Stanford Encyclopedia of Philosophy*, fall 2018 ed., ed. Edward N. Zalta, https://plato.stanford.edu/archives/fall2018/entries/dialetheism/; Graham Priest, Koji Tanaka, and Zach Weber, "Paraconsistent Logic," *The Stanford Encyclopedia of Philosophy*, summer 2018 ed., ed. Edward N. Zalta, https://plato.stanford.edu/archives/sum2018/entries/logic-paraconsistent/.

[25] Aristotle, *Nicomachean Ethics* 1.4.1095a30–b4, 6.3.1039b25–35.

[26] Aristotle, *Nicomachean Ethics* 1.3.1094b20–29, trans. Bartlett and Collins (italics in the original).

[27] Aristotle, 1.6.1096b30–32.

[28] Aristotle, 2.2.1104a1–4 (editorial note omitted).

[29] Martin Luther, "A Commentary on St. Paul's Epistle to the Galatians," trans. Philip S. Watson, in *Martin Luther: Selections from His Writings*, ed. John Dillenberger (New York: Anchor Books, 1962), 128, 131 (quotations); Martin Luther, *The Bondage of the Will* (1525), trans. J. I. Packer and O. R. Johnston (Grand Rapids, MI: Fleming H. Revell, 1957); John Calvin, *Institutes of the Christian Religion*, trans. Henry Beveridge (1845; repr., Grand Rapids, MI: Wm. B. Eerdmans, 2001), bk. 3, chap. 21, § 4; John Calvin, "Articles concerning Predestination," in *Calvin: Theological Treatises*, trans. and ed. J. K. S. Reid (Philadelphia: Westminster, 1954), 179; Francis Bacon, *The Advancement of Learning*, bk. 2, § 7, ¶ 5 (1605), in *"The Advancement of Learning" and "New Atlantis"*, ed. Thomas Case (London: Oxford University Press, 1906), 110–11; Thomas Hobbes, *De Corpore*, pt. 2, chap. 9, ¶ 4, and chap 10, ¶ 7 (1656), in *Body, Man, and*

Citizen: Selections from Thomas Hobbes, ed. Richard S. Peters (New York: Collier Books, 1962), 116, 124; MacIntyre, *After Virtue*, 53–55, 81–84; Alan E. Johnson, *Free Will and Human Life* (Pittsburgh, PA: Philosophia, 2021), 7–17, 92–93.

[30] See also Exodus 23:23–24, 35, 34:13, 24; Leviticus 18:24, 20:23–24; Numbers 21:1–3, 21–35, 25:16–18, 31:1–18, 33:50–56; Deuteronomy 1:8, 2:24–25, 30–36, 3:1–10, 7:3–26, 11:23–25, 18:14, 31:3–8; Joshua, 3:10, 6:21, 8:21–29, 9:24, 10:1, 19–20, 26–42, 11:7–23; and Judges 1:1–20.

[31] Oliver Wendell Holmes, *The Common Law*, ed. Mark DeWolfe Howe (Boston, MA: Little, Brown, 1936), 10–12, 15–16, 17–21 (originally published in 1881).

[32] Walter Olson, "Reasonable Doubts: Invitation to a Stoning," *Reason*, November 1998, https://reason.com/1998/11/01/invitation-to-a-stoning/.

[33] Alan E. Johnson, *The First American Founder: Roger Williams and Freedom of Conscience* (Pittsburgh, PA: Philosophia, 2015), 326–31.

[34] Johnson, 331–35 and chapters 2–8 passim.

[35] Francis Hutcheson, *Philosophiae Moralis Institutio Compendiaria with A Short Introduction to Moral Philosophy*, 2nd ed., ed. Luigi Turco (Indianapolis: Liberty Fund, 2007), 1.2.2 (page 53 in the Turco edition) (italics in the original).

[36] Francis Hutcheson, *A System of Moral Philosophy*, vol. 1 (Glasgow, 1755), 57, 58 (italics in the original).

[37] Hutcheson, *Philosophiae Moralis*, 1.1 (quotations at 1.1.7, pages 49 and 51 in the Turco edition).

[38] David Hume to Francis Hutcheson, March 16, 1740, in *The Letters of David Hume*, ed. J. Y. T. Greig (Oxford: Clarendon, 1932), 1:40.

[39] David Hume, *A Treatise of Human Nature*, ed. L. A. Selby-Bigge (Oxford: Clarendon, 1896), 415 (2.3.3) (originally published 1740).

[40] Hume, 469 (3.1.1).

Notes

[41] David Hume, *An Enquiry Concerning Human Understanding*, in *Hume: An Enquiry Concerning Human Understanding and Other Writings*, ed. Stephen Buckle (Cambridge: Cambridge University Press, 2007), 2, Kindle.

[42] Hume, 210.

[43] David Hume, *An Enquiry Concerning the Principles of Morals*, ed. J. B. Schneewind (Indianapolis: Hackett, 1983).

[44] Hume, 82–88 (italics in the original of the quotations).

[45] Adam Smith, *The Theory of Moral Sentiments*, ed. E. G. West (Indianapolis: Liberty Classics, 1976) (originally published 1759).

[46] For such an analysis of this work and Smith's *Wealth of Nations*, see Joseph Cropsey, *Polity and Economy: With Further Thoughts on the Principles of Adam Smith* (South Bend, IN: St Augustine's Press, 2001).

[47] Jonathan Haidt, "The Emotional Dog and Its Rational Tail," *Psychological Review* 108, no. 4 (2001): 814–34, https://psycnet.apa.org/doiLanding?doi=10.1037%2F0033-295X.108.4.814. See also Jonathan Haidt, "Synthesis in Moral Psychology," *Science*, n.s., 316, no. 5827 (May 18, 2007): 998–1002, https://www.jstor.org/stable/20036276; and Jonathan Haidt, *The Righteous Mind: Why Good People Are Divided by Politics and Religion* (New York: Pantheon, 2012), Kindle.

[48] Haidt, *The Righteous Mind*, 27–29; Haidt, "The Emotional Dog and Its Rational Tail," 815–16.

[49] Haidt, "The Emotional Dog and Its Rational Tail," 815–16.

[50] Hanno Sauer. *Moral Judgments as Educated Intuitions* (Cambridge, MA: MIT Press, 2017), Kindle.

[51] William Shakespeare, "The Tragedie of Hamlet, Prince of Denmark," 1.3.816–17, in *The First Folio of Shakespeare: The Norton Facsimile*, 2nd ed., ed. Charles Hinman and Peter W. M. Blayney (New York: W.W. Norton & Co., 1996), 766.

[52] The first two paragraphs of this section are taken from Johnson, *Free Will and Human Life*, 61–62. Kant was the author of all writings cited in this section. All page citations to

Kant's writings are to the customary German Academy pagination.

[53] *Groundwork of the Metaphysics of Morals*, 4:421, in *Practical Philosophy*, trans. and ed. Mary J. Gregor (Cambridge: Cambridge University Press, 1996) (emphasis in the original). See also *Critique of Practical Reason*, 5:30, in *Practical Philosophy*; and *The Metaphysics of Morals*, 6:225, 376, 389, in *Practical Philosophy*.

[54] *Groundwork*, 4:425 (emphasis in the original).

[55] "Idea for a Universal History with a Cosmopolitan Aim," trans. Allen W. Wood, 8:23n (other planets), in *Anthropology, History, and Education,* ed. Günter Zöller et al. (New York: Cambridge University Press, 2007), Kindle; *Critique of Practical Reason*, 5:32 ("all finite beings that have reason and will and even includes the infinite being as the supreme intelligence"); *Anthropology from a Pragmatic Point of View*, trans. Robert B. Louden, 7:331–33 (other planets, angels), in *Anthropology, History, and Education*; *Metaphysics of Morals*, 6:405 ("holy (supernatural) being"), 6:435 ("seraph").

[56] *Groundwork*, 4:463 (emphasis in the original); cf. *Critique of Practical Reason*, 5:30–32.

[57] *Metaphysics of Morals*, 6:225 (emphasis in the original).

[58] "On a Supposed Right to Lie from Philanthropy," trans. Mary J. Gregor, in *Practical Philosophy*.

[59] *Metaphysics of Morals*, 6:335–36.

[60] John Stuart Mill, *Utilitarianism: With Related Remarks from Mill's Other Writings*, ed. Ben Eggleston (Indianapolis: Hackett, 2017). The citations in the text are to the sections and paragraphs of this edition. For utilitarianism and consequentialism generally, see Julia Driver, "The History of Utilitarianism," in *The Stanford Encyclopedia of Philosophy*, winter 2014 ed., ed. Edward L. Zalta, https://plato.stanford.edu/entries/utilitarianism-history/, and Walter Sinnott-Armstrong, "Consequentialism," in *The Stanford Encyclopedia of Philosophy*, fall 2021 ed., ed. Edward L. Zalta,

https://plato.stanford.edu/entries/consequentialism/. See also the subsection "David Hume," above.

[61] For a general description and discussion of virtue ethics, see Rosalind Hursthouse, "Virtue Ethics," in *The Stanford Encyclopedia of Philosophy*, winter 2018 ed., ed. Edward L. Zalta, https://plato.stanford.edu/entries/ethics-virtue/. Section 4 of Hursthouse's essay addresses the "New Directions" taken by some virtue ethicists, including the turn to philosophers other than Aristotle and Plato. See also Rosalind Hursthouse, *On Virtue Ethics* (Oxford: Oxford University Press, 1999), which contains a comprehensive account of Hursthouse's own approach to virtue ethics.

[62] Philippa Foot, *Natural Goodness* (Oxford: Clarendon, 2001). The textual page references in the remainder of the present section refer to this book.

[63] I wish to thank my wife, Miriam (Mimi) Lindauer, for introducing me to the scholarly literature on evolutionary biology. Her excellent essay, "The Biology of Morality: Why People Are More Often Good Than Bad," can be located at https://www.academia.edu/16610786/The_Biology_of_Morality_Why_People_Are_More_Often_Good_Than_Bad.

[64] Lindauer, "The Biology of Morality"; Jane Goodall, *In the Shadow of Man* (New York: Mariner Books, 2000) (originally published in 1971); Frans de Waal, *Primates and Philosophers: How Morality Evolved* (Princeton: Princeton University Press, 2006); Frans de Waal, *The Age of Empathy: Nature's Lessons for a Kinder Society* (New York: Three Rivers, 2009); Frans de Waal, *The Bonobo and the Atheist: In Search of Humanism among the Primates* (New York: W. W. Norton, 2014); Matt Ridley, *The Origins of Virtue: Human Instincts and the Evolution of Cooperation* (New York: Penguin Books, 1996); Richard E. Passingham and Steven P. Wise, *The Neurobiology of the Prefrontal Cortex: Anatomy, Evolution, and the Origin of Instinct* (Oxford: Oxford University Press, 2014); Leonard D. Katz, ed., *Evolutionary Origins of Morality: Cross-Disciplinary Perspectives* (Thorverton, UK: Imprint Academic, 2000); Walter Sinnott-

Armstrong, ed., *The Evolution of Morality: Adaptations and Innateness*, vol. 1, *Moral Psychology* (Cambridge, MA: MIT Press, 2008); William S. Cooper, *The Evolution of Reason: Logic as a Branch of Biology* (Cambridge: Cambridge University Press, 2001); Robert M. Sapolsky, *Behave: The Biology of Humans at Our Best and Worst* (New York: Penguin Books, 2017). Cf. Margaret Gruter and Roger D. Masters, "Balancing Altruism and Selfishness: Evolutionary Theory and the Foundation of Morality, *Jahrbuch für Recht und Ethik / Annual Review of Law and Ethics* 4 (1996): 561–73, https://www.jstor.org/stable/43593571.

[65] Elkhonon Goldberg, *The New Executive Brain: Frontal Lobes in a Complex World* (New York: Oxford University Press, 2009), 4.

[66] Goldberg, 31 (italics in the original).

[67] Goldberg, 21–22 (italics in the original).

[68] Passingham and Wise, *Neurobiology of the Prefrontal Cortex*, 298–303; Sapolsky, *Behave*, 479.

[69] Goldberg, *The New Executive Brain*, 33–34, 115–22.

[70] See the discussion in Johnson, *Free Will and Human Life*, 24–28, 30–34.

[71] Terrence W. Deacon, *Incomplete Nature: How Mind Emerged from Matter* (New York: W. W. Norton, 2013), Kindle; Robert Hanna, *Deep Freedom and Real Persons—A Study in Metaphysics* (New York: Nova Science, 2018), 15–16 and chap. 2 passim (vol. 2 of Hanna, *The Rational Human Condition*); Andrea Gambarotto and Auguste Nahras, "Teleology and the Organism: Kant's Controversial Legacy for Contemporary Biology," *Studies in History and Philosophy of Science* 93 (2022): 47–56, https://www.academia.edu/75441507/Teleology_and_the_Organism_Kants_Controversial_Legacy_for_Contemporary_Biology; James G. Lennox, "Darwin *Was* a Teleologist," *Biology and Philosophy* 8 (1993): 409–21, https://inters.org/files/lennox1993.pdf; Johnson, *Free Will and Human Life*, 92–93. Cf. Colin Allen and Jacob Neal, "Teleological Notions in Biology," in *The Stanford*

Notes

Encyclopedia of Philosophy, spring 2020 ed., ed. Edward L. Zalta, https://plato.stanford.edu/entries/teleology-biology/. See also the above section on "Virtue Ethics" in this chapter.

[72] Deacon, *Incomplete Nature*, 24–25.

[73] See the sections "Classical Reason" and "Evolutionary Biology," above.

[74] Johnson, *Free Will and Human Life*, 65–103.

Chapter 2. Human Reason

[1] Wayne C. Booth, *Now Don't Try to Reason with Me: Essays and Ironies for a Credulous Age* (Chicago: University of Chicago Press, 1970), 17–18 (italics in the original).

[2] Henry George Liddell and Robert Scott, comps., *A Greek-English Lexicon*, unabridged, rev. ed. (Oxford: Oxford University Press, 1996) s.v. "τελος" (*telos*) and "λογος" (*logos*).

[3] Aristotle, *Metaphysics* 5.2.1013a24–36, in *Aristotle's "Metaphysics"*, trans. Joe Sachs. Aristotle gives the same account in *Physics* 2.3.194b24–35: see *Aristotle's "Physics": A Guided Study*, trans. Joe Sachs (New Brunswick, NJ: Rutgers University Press, 1995), 54, 57–58. Sachs's literal translation of, and wise commentary on, these passages are excellent. *Note:* This and part of the following paragraph of the present book are drawn from Johnson, *Free Will and Human Life*, 92–93.

[4] Bacon, *The Advancement of Learning*, bk. 2, § 7, ¶ 5; Hobbes, *De Corpore*, pt. 2, chap. 9, ¶ 4, and chap 10, ¶ 7.

[5] Cees Leijenhors, "Hobbes's Theory of Causality and Its Aristotelian Background," *The Monist* 79, no. 3 (July 1996): 426, https://www.jstor.org/stable/27903492.

[6] E.g., David Robert Grimes, *Good Thinking: Why Flawed Logic Puts Us All at Risk and How Critical Thinking Can Save the World* (New York: The Experiment, 2019), 246, Kindle.

[7] Stuart A. Kauffman, *A World Beyond Physics: The Emergence and Evolution of Life* (New York: Oxford University Press, 1999), chaps. 2, 8, 11, Kindle; Deacon,

Notes

Incomplete Nature; Hanna, *Deep Freedom and Real Persons*, chap. 2 passim.

[8] See Kauffman, *A World Beyond Physics*; Deacon, *Incomplete Nature*; and Hanna, *Deep Freedom and Real Persons*.

[9] Both books also address human responsibility regarding the natural environment.

[10] See the section "Modern Moral Sentiment/Emotion" in Chapter 1.

[11] Steven Pinker agrees generally with the Humean principle that reason is only instrumental to ends that we individually and subjectively posit; however, he does (like Francis Hutcheson before him) see a role for reason when we have conflicting ends. Steven Pinker, *Rationality: What It Is, Why It Seems Scarce, Why It Matters* (New York: Viking, 2021), 45–56, 70, 175, 329, Kindle. "Pursuing our goals and desires is not the opposite of reason but ultimately the reason we have reason. We deploy reason to attain those goals, and also to prioritize them when they can't all be realized at once." Pinker, 70. In contrast, as the present book explains, I think reason can and should apply to ends as well as means regardless of whether we have conflicting ends.

[12] All quotations of Plato's *Republic* in this chapter are from *The Republic of Plato*, 2nd ed., trans. Allan Bloom. Socrates's dialogue with Thrasymachus is at 336b–54c of the standard Stephanus pagination (pages 13–34 of the Bloom edition). A new edition of this work, issued by the same publisher, was published in 2016. It appears to be identical to the second edition except for a new introduction by Adam Kirsch and the addition of Stephanus numbers to the Kindle edition (they were strangely absent in the Kindle edition of the second edition). Bloom's translation may be the most literally exact translation of the *Republic*. However, the translation by Joe Sachs is also very accurate and is based on a more recently published Greek textual edition: see Plato, *Republic*, trans. Joe Sachs. Sachs explains on page 13–16 of his introduction to this book the differences between his and Bloom's

translations. I have occasion to use Sachs's translation later in the present book.

[13] Although I independently noticed this similarity (and difference) between Thrasymachus and postmodernism, I later read a very similar analysis in Stephen R. C. Hicks, *Explaining Postmodernism: Skepticism and Socialism from Rousseau to Foucault*, expanded ed. (Roscoe, IL: Ockham's Razor, 2014), 108–9, Kindle. Postmodernism is discussed in Chapter 5, below.

[14] Aristotle, *Nicomachean Ethics* 6.1.1138b18–35, 6.2.1139a21–27, 6.5.1140b5–7, 6.13.1144b1–1145a11. Cf. Daniel C. Russell, *Practical Intelligence and the Virtues* (Oxford: Clarendon, 2009), pt. 1, Kindle.

[15] Aristotle, *Nicomachean Ethics* 1.4.1095a2–12, 6.8.1142a11–22.

[16] Keith E. Stanovich, *What Intelligence Tests Miss: The Psychology of Rational Thought* (New Haven: Yale University Press, 2009). See also Heather A. Butler, "Why Do Smart People Do Foolish Things? Intelligence Is Not the Same as Critical Thinking—and the Difference Matters," *Scientific American*, October 3, 2017, https://www.scientificamerican.com/article/why-do-smart-people-do-foolish-things/. I disagree with Stanovich on some matters, but I agree with him on this point.

[17] Morton L. Schagrin and G. E. Hughes, "Formal logic," *Encyclopedia Britannica*, November 2, 2018, https://www.britannica.com/topic/formal-logic.

[18] See Leo Groarke, "Informal Logic," in *The Stanford Encyclopedia of Philosophy*, fall 2021 ed., ed. Edward L. Zalta, https://plato.stanford.edu/entries/logic-informal/; David Hitchcock, "Critical Thinking," in *The Stanford Encyclopedia of Philosophy*, fall 2020 ed., ed. Edward L. Zalta, https://plato.stanford.edu/entries/critical-thinking/.

[19] Psychology Tools, "Fight or Flight Response," accessed June 17, 2022, https://www.psychologytools.com/resource/fight-or-flight-response/.

Notes

[20] For discussions of such matters, see, for example, Stanovich, *What Intelligence Tests Miss*; Daniel Kahneman, *Thinking, Fast and Slow* (New York: Farrar, Straus and Giroux, 2011); and Hanno Sauer, *Moral Thinking, Fast and Slow* (Oxford, UK: Routledge, 2019).

[21] See especially Aristotle's *On Sophistical Refutations*.

[22] The discussion in this section is not at all exhaustive of the subject of fallacies. For a historical overview, see Hans Hansen, "Fallacies," in *The Stanford Encyclopedia of Philosophy, summer 2020 ed.*, ed. Edward L. Zalta, https://plato.stanford.edu/cgi-bin/encyclopedia/archinfo.cgi?entry=fallacies. The many discussions of informal logic, fallacies, and critical thinking include Grimes, *Good Thinking*; Arp, Barbone, and Bruce, *Bad Arguments*; Daniel J. Levitin, *A Field Guide to Lies: Critical Thinking with Statistics and the Scientific Method* (New York: Dutton, 2016), Kindle; Jamie Carlin Watson and Robert Arp, *Critical Thinking: An Introduction to Reasoning Well*, 2nd ed. (London: Bloomsbury Academic, 2015), Kindle; Michael LaBossiere, *76 Fallacies* (n.p.: [Amazon Digital Services?], 2012), Kindle; Douglas Walton, *Informal Logic: A Pragmatic Approach* (New York: Oxford University Press, 2008), Kindle; Ralph H. Johnson and J. Anthony Blair, *Logical Self-Defense* (New York: IDEA Press, 2006); Marilyn vos Savant, *The Power of Logical Thinking: Easy Lessons in the Art of Reasoning . . . and Hard Facts About Its Absence in Our Lives* (New York: St. Martin's Griffin, 1996); Hans V. Hansen and Robert C. Pinto, *Fallacies: Classical and Contemporary Readings* (University Park, PA: Pennsylvania State University Press, 1995); Stephen Toulmin, *An Introduction to Reasoning*, 2nd ed. (New York: Macmillan, 1984); David Hackett Fischer, *Historians' Fallacies: Toward a Logic of Historical Thought* (New York: HarperPerennial, 1970); W. Ward Fearnside and William B. Holther, *Fallacy: The Counterfeit of Argument* (Englewood Cliffs, N.J.: Prentice-Hall, Inc., Spectrum Paperbacks, 1959); and John Stuart Mill, *A System of Logic, Ratiocinative and Inductive,*

Notes

Being a Connected View of the Principles of Evidence and the Methods of Scientific Investigation, 8th ed. (New York: Harper & Brothers, 1882). Although I disagree with Steven Pinker on some issues (including but not limited to his view that rationality is inapplicable to the ascertainment of ends except to the extent that ends conflict), his book *Rationality* provides some helpful discussions (many of them summarizing the existing literature): see, for example, his Index of Biases and Fallacies at 389–90. The following discussion draws on the foregoing and other references in describing some important fallacies that have been identified over the millennia.

[23] Mill, *A System of Logic*, 552–53.

[24] Fischer, *Historians' Fallacies*, 166–67.

[25] Mill, *A System of Logic*, 552–53.

[26] William M. K. Trochim, "Establishing a Cause-Effect Relationship," accessed June 17, 2022, https://conjointly.com/kb/establishing-cause-and-effect/.

[27] Mill, *A System of Logic*, 287–88; Levitin, *A Field Guide to Lies*, 48–51; Watson and Arp, *Critical Reasoning*, chap. 8 (section on "Causal Arguments").

[28] This phenomenon is discussed at some length in Levitin, *A Field Guide to Lies*, 198–201.

[29] Mill, *A System of Logic*, 561, 563–70.

[30] Mill, 565.

[31] For example, Mill considers Zeno's famous Achilles paradox as an example of fallacious ambiguity. Mill, 568–69. For background, see *Encyclopedia Britannica Online*, s.v. "Achilles Paradox," accessed June 17, 2022, https://www.britannica.com/topic/Achilles-paradox.

[32] Arp, Barbone, and Bruce, "Introduction," in *Bad Arguments*, ed. Arp, Barbone, and Bruce, 23–24.

[33] George Wrisley, "Ad Hominem: Bias," in *Bad Arguments*, ed. Arp, Barbone, and Bruce, chap. 8.

[34] Benjamin W. McCraw, "Appeal to the People," in *Bad Arguments*, ed. Arp, Barbone, and Bruce, chap. 16.

Notes

[35] I speak from personal experience during approximately three decades of practice as a litigation lawyer (now retired).

[36] Johnson and Blair, *Logical Self-Defense*, 94.

[37] Winston S. Churchill, *The Second World War*, vol. 1, *The Gathering Storm* (New York: Bantam Books, 1948), 188. Cf. Mill, *A System of Logic*, 562.

[38] Bertha Alvarez Manninen, "Weak Analogy," in *Bad Arguments*, ed. Arp, Barbone, and Bruce, chap. 50; Deacon, *Incomplete Nature*, 36–37 (fallacious analogy between the human mind and a machine); LaBossiere, *76 Fallacies*, 120–123; Walton, *Informal Logic*, 305–15 (§§ 9.4–9.6); Fearnside and Holther, *Fallacy*, 22–27; Mill, *A System of Logic*, 393–97, 553–58.

[39] Manninen, "Weak Analogy," 234; cf. Mill, *A System of Logic*, 557–58. See also Watson and Arp, *Critical Thinking*, chap. 8 (section on "Argument from analogy").

[40] See the massive evidence cited and discussed in Chapter 5 of Alan E. Johnson, *The Electoral College*, 2nd ed. (Pittsburgh: Philosophia, 2021).

[41] Johnson, *The Electoral College*, 2nd ed., chap. 5; Matthew Rowley, "Prophetic Populism and the Violent Rejection of Biden's Election: Mapping the Theology of the Capitol Insurrection," *International Journal of Religion* 12, no. 2 (December 2021): 145–164, https://www.academia.edu/67060884/Prophetic_Populism_and_the_Violent_Rejection_of_Joe_Bidens_Election_Mapping_the_Theology_of_the_Capitol_Insurrection; Sarah Posner, *Unholy: How Christian Nationalists Powered the Trump Presidency, and the Devastating Legacy They Left Behind* (New York: Random House, 2021), Kindle.

[42] See the discussion of these events and corresponding references cited in Chapters 5 and 6 of the present book.

[43] Levitin, *A Field Guide to Lies*, 152.

[44] See Michael J. Muniz, "Hasty Generalization," in *Bad Arguments*, ed. Arp, Barbone, and Bruce, chap. 84.

Notes

[45] Regarding the fallacy of false dichotomy or false dilemma, see, among other sources, Jennifer Culver, "False Dilemma," in *Bad Arguments*, ed. Arp, Barbone, and Bruce, chap. 81; Fearnside and Holther, *Fallacy*, 32–33; Walton, *Informal Logic*, 52–53, 259; and LaBossiere, *76 Fallacies*, 68–69.

[46] Johnson, *Free Will and Human Life*, 2, 64–103.

[47] Definitions 1c and 1a, respectively, in *Merriam-Webster Online* s.v. "critical," accessed January 5, 2022, https://www.merriam-webster.com/dictionary/critical.

[48] Plato, *Apology of Socrates*; Leo Strauss, "On Plato's *Apology of Socrates* and *Crito*," in *Leo Strauss: Studies in Platonic Political Philosophy*, ed. Thomas L. Pangle (Chicago: University of Chicago Press, 1983), chap. 2; Leo Strauss, *Socrates and Aristophanes* (New York: Basic Books, 1966), esp. 3–53, 313–14. Cf. Andy Norman, *Mental Immunity: Infectious Ideas, Mind-Parasites, and the Search for a Better Way to Think* (New York: Harper Wave, 2021), 20, 93–94, 99, 149, 262–68, Kindle.

[49] "6 Infamous Political Conspiracies," History.com, accessed December 31, 2021, https://www.history.com/news/6-infamous-political-conspiracies.

[50] "6 Infamous Political Conspiracies"; R. W. Pringle, "Central Intelligence Agency," *Encyclopedia Britannica*, January 28, 2020, https://www.britannica.com/topic/Central-Intelligence-Agency; Wikipedia s.v. "List of Assassinations by the United States," last modified, November 19, 2021, 21:30, https://en.wikipedia.org/wiki/List_of_assassinations_by_the_United_States. The facts about the Watergate conspiracy are now well known. See the relevant discussions in Chapters 5 and 6 of this book regarding the conspiracy behind January 6, 2021.

[51] The following books adduce substantial evidence that the JFK assassination was the result of a conspiracy by CIA, military, and possibly other governmental officials strongly opposed to JFK's foreign policy; Cuban exiles furious with JFK's handling of the 1961 Bay of Pigs invasion and the 1962

Notes

Cuban Missile Crisis; Mafia chieftains seeking revenge for Attorney General Robert Kennedy's prosecution of underworld figures; the FBI (perhaps only in the cover-up); and/or President Lyndon B. Johnson (perhaps only in the cover-up, though there is some evidence that he was also aware in advance of what was going to occur on November 22, 1963): James W. Douglass, *JFK and the Unspeakable: Why He Died and Why It Matters* (Maryknoll, NY: Orbis Books, 2008); Gaeton Fonzi, *The Last Investigation* (Ipswich, MA: Mary Ferrell Foundation Press, 2008); Bill Sloan with Jean Hill, *JFK: The Last Dissenting Witness* (Gretna, LA: Pelican, 1992); Robert D. Morrow, *First Hand Knowledge: How I Participated in the CIA–Mafia Murder of President Kennedy* (New York: S.P.I. Books, 1994); Casey J. Quinlan and Brian K. Edwards, *Beyond the Fence Line: The Eyewitness Account of Ed Hoffman and the Murder of President Kennedy* (Southlake, TX: JFK Lancer, 2008); Charles A. Crenshaw et al., *Trauma Room One: The JFK Medical Coverup Exposed* (New York: Paraview, 2001); James P. Johnston and Jon Roe, *Flight from Dallas: New Evidence of CIA Involvement in the Murder of President John F. Kennedy* (Victoria, BC: Trafford, 2005); Dick Russell, *On the Trail of the JFK Assassins: A Groundbreaking Look at America's Most Infamous Conspiracy* (New York: Skyhorse, 2008); Dick Russell, *The Man Who Knew Too Much* (New York: Carroll & Graf, 2003); John Newman, *Oswald and the CIA: The Documented Truth about the Unknown Relationship between the U.S. Government and the Alleged Killer of JFK* (New York: Skyhorse, 2008); L. Fletcher Prouty, *JFK: The CIA, Vietnam, and the Plot to Assassinate John F. Kennedy* (New York: Citadel, 1996); Abraham Bolden, *The Echo from Dealey Plaza: The True Story of the First African American on the White House Secret Service Detail and His Quest for Justice after the Assassination of JFK* (New York: Harmony Books, 2008); Phillip F. Nelson, *LBJ: The Mastermind of the JFK Assassination* (New York: Skyhorse, 2011), Kindle; Bill Sloan, *The Kennedy Conspiracy: 12 Startling Revelations about the JFK Assassination* (n.p.: n.p., 2012), Kindle; and

Notes

Jim Garrison, *On the Trail of the Assassins: My Investigation and Prosecution of the Murder of President John F. Kennedy* (New York: Paperless Publishing, 2012).

[52] *Final Report of the Select Committee on Assassinations, U.S. House of Representatives* January 2, 1979, page 3, in *The HSCA Final Assassinations Report*, introduced by Rex Bradford (Ipswich, MA: Mary Ferrell Foundation, 2007). For critiques of other conclusions of the Select Committee, see the above-referenced Introduction by Rex Bradford and the analysis of one of its investigators, Gaeton Fonzi, in Fonzi, *The Last Investigation*.

[53] The most comprehensive of such debunking attempts was Vincent Bugliosi's tome (in excess of 1500 pages) titled *Reclaiming History: The Assassination of President John F. Kennedy* (New York: W. W. Norton, 2007).

[54] See Johnson, *The Electoral College*, 2nd ed., Chapter 5.

Chapter 3. Individual Ethics

[1] Confucius, *The Great Learning*, ¶¶ 6 and 7, in *The Chinese Classics*, trans. and ed. James Legge, vol. 1, *The Life and Teachings of Confucius*, 2nd ed. (London: N. Trüber, 1869), 267 (italics in the Legge translation), https://babel.hathitrust.org/cgi/pt?id=uva.x000304472&view=1up&seq=7&skin=2021 (also available in a 2016 Owlfoot Kindle edition with Trüber print edition pagination in brackets, https://www.amazon.com/gp/product/B01MCUC6UD/ref=ppx_yo_dt_b_d_asin_title_o02?ie=UTF8&psc=1).

[2] The question whether the mind is identical to the brain is beyond the scope of the present book. See Johnson, *Free Will and Human Ethics*, which discusses some aspects of the mind–brain issue.

[3] See the sections "Classical Reason," "Virtue Ethics," "Evolutionary Biology," and "A Secular Teleological View of Human Nature" in Chapter 1; see also Chapter 2.

[4] Stephen Johnson, "Why Is 18 the Age of Adulthood If the Brain Can Take 30 Years to Mature?," Big Think:

Notes

Neuropsych, January 31, 2022, https://bigthink.com/neuropsych/adult-brain/; Mariam Arain et al., "Maturation of the Adolescent Brain," *Neuropsychiatric Disease and Treatment* 9 (2013): 449–61, doi:10.2147/NDT.S39776, https://www.ncbi.nlm.nih.gov/pmc/articles/PMC3621648/.

[5] Aristotle, *Nicomachean Ethics* 1.4.1095a2–12, 6.8.1142a11–22.

[6] Plato, *Laws* 633b.

[7] Plato, 636c–d.

[8] See, for example, Jeffrey M. Schwartz and Sharon Begley, *The Mind and the Brain: Neuroplasticity and the Power of Mental Force* (New York: HarperCollins, 2002), and Norman Doidge, *The Brain That Changes Itself: Stories of Personal Triumph from the Frontiers of Brain Science* (New York: Penguin, 2007).

[9] See the discussion on pages 49–54 of my book *Free Will and Human Life* for additional discussion of good and bad habituation and its interaction with free will.

[10] Matthew 22:39 (NRSV), in *HarperCollins Study Bible*, rev. ed., ed. Harold W. Attridge and Wayne A. Meeks (New York: HarperCollins, 2006), Kindle.

[11] Aristotle, *Nicomachean Ethics* 9.8.1168b15–23, in Bartlett and Collins, *Aristotle's "Nicomachean Ethics"*.

[12] Aristotle, 9.8.1168b24–1169a8 (italics and bracket in the Bartlett and Collins translation).

[13] The Roman philosopher Seneca took the position that anger is never proper for a human being. For a critical analysis of the Senecan view of anger, and a discussion of alternative philosophical perspectives on anger, see Anne Pippin Burnett, *Revenge in Attic and Later Tragedy* (Berkeley: University of California Press, 1998), especially pages 7-18.

[14] For a cogent illustration of this point, see William Shakespeare, *King Henry the Eighth*, 1.1.155–77, *The Folger Shakespeare* online,

Notes

https://shakespeare.folger.edu/shakespeares-works/henry-viii/act-1-scene-1/.

[15] *Analects of Confucius*, trans. Leys 6.29.

[16] *Analects* 11.16 (replacing "The Master" with "Confucius").

[17] *Analects* 13.21. Another translation is: "If one cannot find the company of temperate colleagues, one has no choice but to turn to the more rash and the more timid. The rash will forge ahead in their actions, and the timid will not do what they think is wrong." *The Analects of Confucius: A Philosophical Translation*, trans. and ed. Roger T. Ames and Henry Rosemont Jr. (New York: Ballantine Books, 1998), 168.

[18] Legge, *The Chinese Classics*, 1:36–38.

[19] Confucius and Tsze-tse, *The Doctrine of the Mean*, in Legge, *The Life and Teachings of Confucius*, 2nd ed., 282–320.

[20] Aristotle, *Nicomachean Ethics*, trans. Bartlett and Collins, 2.6.1106b5–8.

[21] Aristotle, 2.6.1106b17–28 (editorial note omitted, brackets in Bartlett-Collins translation).

[22] Aristotle, 2.9.1109a20–30 (brackets in Bartlett-Collins translation).

[23] Aristotle, 3.6.7–8.

[24] Aristotle 3.7.1115b12–14 (brackets added).

[25] Aristotle 3.7.1115b29–32 (brackets added).

[26] Aristotle 3.7.1116a7–9 (brackets added).

[27] Aristotle 3.8.1117a7–9.

[28] Plato, *Apology of Socrates*, trans. Harold North Fowler, Loeb Classical Library (Cambridge, MA.: Harvard University Press, 1914), 29a.

[29] Plato, *Apology of Socrates* 42a (my translation).

[30] See Alexis de Tocqueville, *Democracy in America*.

[31] Seneca, *On Providence*.

[32] Aristotle, *Nicomachean Ethics*, trans. Bartlett and Collins, 3.10.1.117b24–25.

[33] Aristotle, 3.10.1.117b28–1118b8.

[34] The following quotations are based on the Simon Leys translation of the Confucian *Analects*. Leys uses the term "gentleman" to translate the Chinese word *junzi*, which has otherwise been translated as "exemplary person" (Roger T. Ames and Henry Rosemont Jr.), "superior man" (James Legge), and "man-at-his best" (James D. Ware). Overall, I prefer the Leys translation (though I have no knowledge of the Chinese language). But Leys's employment of the terms "gentleman," "man," and associated male pronouns in his translation is dated and detracts from a contemporary understanding of the relevance of Confucius's thought to all human beings. Accordingly, I silently substitute "ethical persons" and gender-neutral language in the following quotations. I also silently replace "the Master" with "Confucius" for the sake of clarity. Quotation marks surround the words attributed to Confucius; the remaining language is in the *Analects* but is not attributed to Confucius.

Chapter 4. Social Ethics

[1] Matthew 7:1 (King James Version). I use the King James translation here because of its renowned stylistic quality. On other occasions, as below, I use the New Standard Revised Version.

[2] Ayn Rand, "How Does One Lead a Rational Life in an Irrational Society," in *The Virtue of Selfishness: A New Concept of Egoism* (New York: Signet, 1964), 72 (italics omitted).

[3] Matthew 7:1–5 (NRSV). The HarperCollins Study Bible notes that the Greek word translated here as "neighbor" actually means "brother." The New Revised Standard Version apparently thought that some readers might take the word "brother" too literally when Jesus meant a broader concept. However, Jesus's use of the word "brother" might have indicated that he was referring to private interpersonal relations rather than more public situations. Cf. the following paragraphs in the text of the present section.

Notes

[4] Rand, "Rational Life in an Irrational Society," 71–72 (italics in the original).

[5] *Analects of Confucius*, trans. Leys, 15.24 (italics in the Leys translation). Cf. *Analects* 5.12: "Zigong said: 'I would not want to do to others what I do not want them to do to me.' [Confucius] said: 'Oh, you have not come that far yet!' "

[6] Confucius and Tsze-tse, *The Doctrine of the Mean* 13:3, in Legge, *The Chinese Classics*, 1:290.

[7] Matthew 7:12 (NRSV).

[8] Plato, *Gorgias* 471b, 472e, 473b, 476a, 476d–77a, 478a–79e, 480a–c, 481a, 482a–b, 505b, 507c–d, 509b, 525b, 527b–c.

[9] *Analects* 14.34, trans. Leys.

[10] Aristotle discussed the different kinds of friendship at great length in Books 8 and 9 of his *Nicomachean Ethics*.

[11] For a memorable, fictional example of marital disharmony, see the twentieth-century television series *All in the Family* (Archie and Edith Bunker).

[12] Nancy Mitford, *Voltaire in Love* (Pleasantville, New York: Akadine, 1998).

[13] See the section "Nature and Nurture in Individual Human Brain Development" in Chapter 3, above.

[14] Ross Stoddard, *Rise Up: How to Build a Socially Conscious Business* (Boise, ID: Elevate, 2017).

[15] Lisa Hurwitz (director), "Automat" (film documentary), 2022, https://www.amazon.com/Automat-Mel-Brooks/dp/B0B1MDV2RB/ref=sr_1_1?crid=3MSRWHFGTNGLC&keywords=automat&qid=1655639140&s=instant-video&sprefix=Automat%2Cinstant-video%2C54&sr=1-1.

[16] World Wildlife Fund, "Why Some Species Are Unwelcome," accessed May 9, 2022, https://wwf.panda.org/discover/our_focus/wildlife_practice/problems/invasive_species/.

[17] World Wildlife Fund, "Nearly 70 Percent of Wildlife Lost since 1970," September 10, 2020,

https://www.trtworld.com/life/wwf-nearly-70-percent-of-wildlife-lost-since-1970-39628.

[18] Australian Academy of Science, "What's Killing the Bees?," accessed May 9, 2022, https://www.science.org.au/curious/earth-environment/whats-killing-bees.

[19] Rachel Carson, *Silent Spring* (New York: Houghton Mifflin Harcourt, 2002).

[20] Pesticide Action Network (PAN), "The DDT Story," accessed May 9, 2022, https://www.panna.org/resources/ddt-story#:~:text=Banned%20for%20agricultural%20uses%20worldwide%20by%20the%202001,the%20transition%20to%20safer%20and%20more%20effective%20alternatives.

[21] It is, of course, unethical for humans to mistreat sentient nonhuman animals. The question whether veganism (no meat or dairy) or vegetarianism (no meat), as distinguished from consumption of animal products, is the only ethical means of human sustenance is a difficult one. Most people now living were raised on a diet of meat and dairy, and it is difficult to liberate ourselves from that habituation. Good plant-based substitutes (for example, coconut and soy milk) currently exist for dairy products. Plant-based substitutes for animal meat are also being developed. Future generations may succeed in transitioning to a vegan (or vegetarian) diet. In the meantime, the production of meat and dairy products should be conducted in the most humane manner possible.

[22] Edward O. Wilson, *Half-Earth: Our Planet's Fight for Life* (New York: Liveright, 2016).

[23] David Attenborough, "A Life on Our Planet," 2002, https://www.imdb.com/title/tt11989890/.

[24] David Wallace-Wells, *The Uninhabitable Earth: Life after Warming* (New York: Tom Duggan Books, 2020).

[25] Elizabeth Kolbert, *The Sixth Extinction: An Unnatural History* (New York: Henry Holt, 2014).

[26] See the reports collected and linked on the website of the United Nations Intergovernmental Panel on Climate Change

Notes

(IPCC), https://www.ipcc.ch/. See also the references cited in the preceding four endnotes.

[27] See, for example, Patricia M. DeMarco, *Pathways to Our Sustainable Future: A Perspective from Pittsburgh* (Pittsburgh: University of Pittsburgh Press, 2017).

[28] There may be emergency situations of extreme need that complicate the issue of theft. These circumstances trigger ethical and legal considerations that are beyond the scope of the present book. My forthcoming work *Reason and Human Government* will address such issues as well as the issues of capital punishment and war.

[29] There may be very rare exceptions for the very small number of people who are medically endangered by wearing masks or obtaining vaccinations. Many people questioned the effectiveness of masks, and some concocted fantastical evidence-free conspiracy theories about masks and vaccinations. It is not possible here to detail the scientific evidence (which can be found in expert publications on the internet), but masks were the only protection against COVID-19 at the beginning of the pandemic when vaccination was not available. Geographical areas in which most people did not wear masks had higher incidences of infection than did those places in which mask wearing was prevalent or even required. As a result of the refusal of many people to wear masks and obtain vaccinations (when they became available), the original virus mutated again and again to the point that it was much more contagious than in the earlier stages. At that later stage, vaccinated people wearing masks sometimes contracted the virus in what were called "breakthrough infections." However, vaccination and mask wearing were always more protective of oneself and others than the alternative.

[30] *Analects of Confucius*, trans. Leys. See endnote 34 to Chapter 3.

Chapter 5. Citizen and Media Ethics

[1] Abraham Lincoln, "The Perpetuation of Our Political Institutions," Address Before the Young Men's Lyceum of

Notes

Springfield, Illinois, January 27, 1838 (italics in the original), http://www.abrahamlincolnonline.org/lincoln/speeches/lyceum.htm.

[2] Timothy Snyder, *The Road to Unfreedom: Russia, Europe, America* (New York: Tim Duggan Books, 2018), 180, Kindle.

[3] James Madison in the Virginia Ratifying Convention, June 20, 1788, *Documentary History of the Ratification of the Constitution, Digital Edition*, ed. John P. Kaminski and Gaspare J. Saladino (Charlottesville: University of Virginia Press, 2009), 10:1417, http://rotunda.upress.virginia.edu/founders/RNCN-02-10-02-0002-0009.

[4] Thomas E. Ricks, *First Principles: What America's Founders Learned from the Greeks and Romans and How That Shaped Our Country* (New York: Harper, 2020), 5, Kindle.

[5] John Adams to Mercy Otis Warren, April 16, 1776, in *Founders Online*, National Archives, https://founders.archives.gov/documents/Adams/06-04-02-0044 (capitalization and spelling as in original).

[6] Ricks, *First Principles*, 161–63, 234–35

[7] Garrett Ward Sheldon, *The Political Philosophy of Thomas Jefferson* (Baltimore: Johns Hopkins University Press, 1991), 60, 64.

[8] Anne Applebaum, *Twilight of Democracy: The Seductive Lure of Authoritarianism* (New York: Doubleday, 2020), Kindle; Ruth Ben-Ghiat, *Strongmen: Mussolini to the Present* (New York: W. W. Norton, 2020), Kindle; Masha Gessen, *The Future Is History: How Totalitarianism Reclaimed Russia* (New York: Riverhead Books, 2017), Kindle; Masha Gessen, *Surviving Autocracy* (New York: Riverhead Books, 2000), Kindle; Tom Ginsburg and Aziz Z. Huq, *How to Save a Constitutional Democracy* (Chicago: University of Chicago Press, 2018), Kindle; Shane Goldmacher, "Trump Endorses Viktor Orban, Hungary's Far-Right Prime Minister," *New York Times*, January 3, 2022, https://www.nytimes.com/2022/01/03/us/politics/trump-

Notes

endorses-viktor-orban-hungary.html; Adam Gopnik, "How to Build a Twenty-First-Century Tyrant: Autocracies Are Resurgent, and Today's Would-Be Strongmen Are Using a New Set of Tools," *New Yorker*, May 16, 2022, https://www.newyorker.com/magazine/2022/05/23/how-to-build-a-twenty-first-century-tyrant-the-revenge-of-power-spin-dictators; Kathleen Belew, *Bring the War Home: The White Power Movement and Paramilitary America* (Cambridge, MA: Harvard University Press, 2018); Fiona Hill, *There Is Nothing for You Here: Finding Opportunity in the Twenty-First Century* (New York: Mariner Books, 2021), Kindle; Steven Levitsky and Daniel Ziblatt, *How Democracies Die* (New York: Crown, 2018), Kindle; Moisés Naím, *The Revenge of Power: How Autocrats Are Reinventing Politics for the 21st Century* (New York: St. Martin's, 2022), Kindle; Pippa Norris and Robert Inglehart, *Cultural Backlash: Trump, Brexit, and Authoritarian Populism* (New York: Cambridge University Press, 2019), Kindle; Timothy Snyder, *On Tyranny: Twenty Lessons from the Twentieth Century* (New York: Tim Duggan Books, 2017), Kindle; Snyder, *Road to Unfreedom*; Timothy Snyder, "We Should Say It. Russia Is Fascist," *New York Times*, May 19, 2022, https://www.nytimes.com/2022/05/19/opinion/russia-fascism-ukraine-putin.html; Cass R. Sunstein, ed., *Can It Happen Here?: Authoritarianism in America* (New York: HarperCollins, 2018), Kindle.

[9] Snyder, *On Tyranny*, 12–16 (italics added).

[10] See, among many other studies, T. W. Adorno et al., *The Authoritarian Personality* (1950; repr. Brooklyn, New York: Verso, 2019), Kindle; Hannah Arendt, *The Origins of Totalitarianism*, new ed. (New York: Harvest Book, 1994), Kindle; Richard J. Evans, *The Coming of the Third Reich* (New York: Penguin, 2005), Kindle; and Nathanael Greene, ed., *Fascism: An Anthology* (New York: Thomas Y. Crowell, 1968).

[11] See the references cited in endnote 8, above.

Notes

[12] PBS NewsHour, "The Jan. 6 Insurrection, 1 Year Later" (video), https://www.youtube.com/watch?v=kvmasW_glUQ; David D. Kirkpatrick, Mike McIntire, and Christian Triebert, "Before the Capitol Riot, Calls for Cash and Talk of Revolution," *New York Times*, January 16, 2021, https://www.nytimes.com/2021/01/16/us/capitol-riot-funding.html; Sabrina Tavernese and Matthew Rosenberg, "These Are the Rioters Who Stormed the Nation's Capitol," *New York Times*, May 12, 2021, https://www.nytimes.com/2021/01/07/us/names-of-rioters-capitol.html?action=click&module=Spotlight&pgtype=Homepage; U.S. Department of Justice, "Leader of Oath Keepers and 10 Other Individuals Indicted in Federal Court for Seditious Conspiracy and Other Offenses Related to U.S. Capitol Breach," Press Release, January 13, 2022, https://www.justice.gov/opa/pr/leader-oath-keepers-and-10-other-individuals-indicted-federal-court-seditious-conspiracy-and; *United States of America v. Elmer Stewart Rhodes III, et al.*, Indictment, U.S. District Court for the District of Columbia, January 12, 2022, https://s3.documentcloud.org/documents/21178554/charges.pdf; Rachael Weiner and Spenser S. Hsu, "Guy Reffitt Guilty on All Counts in First Capitol Riot Trial," *Washington Post*, March 8, 2022, https://www.washingtonpost.com/dc-md-va/2022/03/08/guy-reffitt-trial-verdict/; Spencer S. Hsu, "Proud Boys Leader Tarrio, 4 Top Lieutenants Charged with Seditious Conspiracy In Widening Jan. 6 Case," *Washington Post*, June 16, 2022, https://www.washingtonpost.com/dc-md-va/2022/06/06/tarrio-proud-boys-seditious-conpiracy/; Spencer S. Hsu et al, "Mich. Gubernatorial Candidate Arrested on Jan. 6 Capitol Riot Charge," *Washington Post*, June 9, 2022, https://www.washingtonpost.com/national-security/2022/06/09/ryan-kelley-arrested-michigan-jan-6/.

[13] Isaac Chotiner, "Making Sense of the Racist Mass Shooting in Buffalo [interview with political scientist Kathleen Belew)," *New Yorker*, May 15, 2022, https://www.newyorker.com/news/q-and-a/making-sense-of-

Notes

the-racist-mass-shooting-in-buffalo?s_src=9J68Z&mkt_tok=MjUwLUNRSC05MzYAAAGEu22QPFhOnL4nHAKj5-MsuLolxTHpcUtxqxGbS83YKUWESOcbHTxmilqaq2tr6LwvHXeGEXwaF9yC42cu2yyWmKRTuwwhY6tgrHWnmSfXhasd; David Bauder, "Explainer: White 'Replacement Theory' Fuels Racist Attacks," Associated Press, May 16, 2022, https://apnews.com/article/great-white-replacement-theory-explainer-c86f309f02cd14062f301ce6b9228e33; Isaac Stanley-Becker and Drew Harwell; "Buffalo Suspect Allegedly Inspired by Racist Theory Fueling Global Carnage," *Washington Post*, May 15, 2022, https://www.washingtonpost.com/nation/2022/05/15/buffalo-shooter-great-replacement-extremism/; John Kunza, "White Replacement Theory's Antisemitic Origins," Unpacked, May 18, 2022, https://jewishunpacked.com/white-replacement-theorys-antisemitic-origins/; Yair Rosenberg, " 'Jews Will Not Replace Us': Why White Supremacists Go after Jews," *Washington Post*, August 14, 2017, https://www.washingtonpost.com/news/acts-of-faith/wp/2017/08/14/jews-will-not-replace-us-why-white-supremacists-go-after-jews/.

[14] The general facts stated in this subsection are drawn from Terrence Ball and Richard Dagger, "Communism," *Encyclopedia Britannica Online*, accessed May 15, 2022, https://www.britannica.com/topic/communism, as well as my recollection of the writings of Karl Marx, Friedrich Engels, and Vladimir Lenin that I last read during the 1960s.

[15] Hill, *There Is Nothing for You Here*, chaps. 5 and 6 passim, Kindle; Snyder, *Road to Unfreedom*.

[16] Helen Pluckrose and James Lindsay, *Cynical Theories: How Activist Scholarship Made Everything about Race, Gender, and Identity—And Why This Harms Everybody* (Durham, NC: Pitchstone, 2020), chap. 2, loc. 917 of 6361 (italics added), Kindle (citing Andrew Jolivétte, *Research Justice: Methodologies for Social Change* [Bristol, UK: Policy Press, 2015]).

[17] Rochelle Gutiérrez, "Political Conocimiento for Teaching Mathematics: Why Teachers Need It and How to Develop It," in *Building Support for Scholarly Practices in Mathematics Methods*, ed. Signe E. Kastberg et al. (Charlotte, NC: Information Age, 2017), chap. 2, Kindle. As is often the case with postmodern authors, Gutiérrez's chapter contains some observations that are shared by other thinkers who do not adhere to the rigid applied postmodernist ideology.

[18] For detailed discussion, citation of, and quotations from postmodern authors, see Pluckrose and Lindsay, *Cynical Theories*. Such an extensive account is beyond the scope of the present book. See also James A. Lindsay and Mike Nayna, "Postmodern Religion and the Faith of Social Justice," *Areo*, December 18, 2018, https://areomagazine.com/2018/12/18/postmodern-religion-and-the-faith-of-social-justice/; Hicks, *Explaining Postmodernism*; Noretta Koertge, ed., *A House Built on Sand: Exposing Postmodernist Myths about Science* (New York: Oxford University Press, 1998); and Robert Hanna, *The Philosophy of the Future: Uniscience and the Modern World* (2022), § 2.3.1, https://www.academia.edu/62653411/THE_PHILOSOPHY_OF_THE_FUTURE_Uniscience_and_the_Modern_World_2022_version_. Please note that I do not endorse everything in these publications or in other public statements of these authors.

[19] John McWhorter, *Woke Racism: How a New Religion Has Betrayed Black America* (New York: Portfolio / Penguin, 2021); Bonnie Kerrigan Snyder, *Undoctrinate: How Politicized Classrooms Harm Kids and Ruin Our Schools—And What We Can Do about It* (New York: Bombardier Books, 2021); Michael Powell, "New York's Private Schools Tackle White Privilege. It Has Not Been Easy," *New York Times*, August 27, 2021, https://www.nytimes.com/2021/08/27/us/new-york-private-schools-racism.html?searchResultPosition=1. Again, I do not necessarily agree with everything in the foregoing

publications or with everything these authors have stated in other venues.

[20] Society of Professional Journalists, *Code of Ethics*, revised September 6, 2014, https://www.spj.org/ethicscode.asp.

Chapter 6. Political Ethics

[1] Plato, *Seventh Letter* 326a–b, trans. Jonah Radding, in *Plato at Syracuse: Essays on Plato in Western Greece with a New Translation of the "Seventh Letter" by Jonah Radding*, ed. Heather L. Reid and Mark Ralkowski (Sioux City, IA: Parnassos Press, 2019). Radding's translation is also available at https://www.jstor.org/stable/j.ctvcmxptk.7.

[2] James Madison, *Federalist No. 10*, November 22, 1788, Founders Online, National Archives, https://founders.archives.gov/documents/Madison/01-10-02-0178.

[3] Plato, *Gorgias*, 503a–504e.

[4] James H. Nichols Jr., preface to Plato, *Gorgias*, trans. and ed. James H. Nichols Jr. (Ithaca, New York: Cornell University Press, 1998), vii–viii.

[5] Plato, *Republic* 457c–d, trans. Sachs.

[6] Bloom, "Interpretive Essay," 409-10.

[7] Sachs, "Glossary," in Plato, *Republic*, trans. Sachs, 351; see also *Republic* 544c.

[8] The remainder of this paragraph is adapted from pages 9-10 of my 1971 Master's Essay, "The Teaching of Plato's *Seventh Letter*," which can be accessed online at https://www.academia.edu/22999496/The_Teaching_of_Plato s_Seventh_Letter.

[9] Plato, *Seventh Letter*, trans. Radding, 326b–d.

[10] The basic facts stated in this subsection on Stalin are well known. See, for example, Ronald Francis Hingley, "Joseph Stalin," *Encyclopedia Britannica Online*, March 14, 2022, https://www.britannica.com/biography/Joseph-Stalin; Stephen Kotkin, *Stalin: Paradoxes of Power, 1878–1928* (New York: Penguin Books, 2014), Kindle; Stephen Kotkin, *Stalin:*

Notes

Waiting for Hitler, 1929-41 (New York: Penguin Books, 2018), Kindle; Robert Service, *Stalin: A Biography* (Cambridge, MA: Belknap Press of Harvard University Press, 2005); *Memoirs of Nikita Khrushchev*, vol. 1, *Commissar (1918–1945)*, vol. 2, *Reformer (1945–64)*, ed. Sergei Khrushchev, trans. George Shriver and Stephen Shenfield (University Park, PA: Pennsylvania State University Press, 2004 [vol. 1], 2006 [vol. 2]); and Svetlana Alliluyeva, *Twenty Letters to a Friend: A Memoir*, trans. Priscilla Johnson McMillan (New York: Harper Perennial, 2016), Kindle.

[11] Anne Applebaum, *Red Famine: Stalin's War on Ukraine* (New York: Doubleday, 2017).

[12] Kotkin, *Stalin: Waiting for Hitler*, 131.

[13] Constitutional Rights Foundation, "The Stalin Purges and 'Show Trials,' " accessed June 2, 2022, https://www.crf-usa.org/bill-of-rights-in-action/bria-7-4-a-the-stalin-purges-and-show-trials.

[14] Khrushchev, *Reformer*, 67.

[15] Khrushchev, 83.

[16] Khrushchev, 83.

[17] Khrushchev, 85.

[18] Alliluyeva, *Twenty Letters to a Friend*, 231, 242.

[19] Alliluyeva, 244.

[20] Alliluyeva, 143–44.

[21] Alliluyeva, 10.

[22] Among the many books on Hitler and Nazism, see Evans, *The Coming of the Third Reich*; Richard J. Evans, *The Third Reich in Power* (New York: Penguin Books, 2005), Kindle; Richard J. Evans, *The Third Reich at War, 1939–1945* (New York: Penguin Books, 2008), Kindle; and John Toland, *Adolph Hitler: The Definitive Biography* (New York: Anchor Books, 1992), Kindle.

[23] The facts stated in the present subsection are based on the following: Applebaum, *Twilight of Democracy*; *Encyclopedia Britannica Online*, s.v. "Vladimir Putin," accessed June 5, 2022, https://www.britannica.com/biography/Vladimir-Putin;

Notes

Ben-Ghiat, *Strongmen*; Gessen, *The Future Is History*; Masha Gessen, *The Man without a Face: The Unlikely Rise of Vladimir Putin* (New York: Riverhead Books, 2012), Kindle; Masha Gessen, *Words Will Break Cement: The Passion of Pussy Riot* (New York; Riverhead Books, 2014), Kindle; Hill, *There is Nothing for You Here*; Fiona Hill and Clifford G. Gaddy, *Mr. Putin: Operative in the Kremlin*, new and expanded ed. (Washington, D.C.: Brookings Institution Press, 2015), Kindle; Snyder, *Road to Unfreedom*; Snyder, "We Should Say It: Russia Is Fascist"; Katie Stallard, *Dancing on Bones: History and Power in China, Russia, and North Korea* (New York: Oxford University Press, 2022), Kindle; Angela E. Stent, *Putin's World: Russia against the West and with the Rest* (New York: Twelve, 2012), Kindle; and Wikipedia s.v. "Vladimir Putin," accessed June 5, 2022, https://en.wikipedia.org/wiki/Vladimir_Putin.

[24] Snyder, *Road to Unfreedom*, 79.

[25] Snyder, 16.

[26] YouTube video of remarks by President George W. Bush, April 18, 2006, https://www.youtube.com/watch?v=6Z7sg_VwkXw.

[27] Scott McClellan, *What Happened: Inside the Bush White House and Washington's Culture of Deception* (New York: Public Affairs, 2008), 127, Kindle.

[28] Ron Suskind, "Faith, Certainty, and the Presidency of George W. Bush," *New York Times*, October 17, 2004, https://www.nytimes.com/2004/10/17/magazine/faith-certainty-and-the-presidency-of-george-w-bush.html; see this op–ed for additional details about Bush's governing style.

[29] See Meg Kinnard, "In Widely-Seen Gaffe, George W. Bush Decries 'Brutal' Invasion of Iraq—Meant Ukraine," NBCDFW, May 19, 2022, https://www.nbcdfw.com/news/local/george-w-bush-compares-zelenskyy-to-churchill-calls-iraq-invasion-unjustified-in-gaffe/2972585/. This article contains a link to a YouTube clip of Bush's May 18, 2022 remarks at his presidential library.

Notes

[30] Suskind, "Faith, Certainty, and the Presidency of George W. Bush," https://www.nytimes.com/2004/10/17/magazine/faith-certainty-and-the-presidency-of-george-w-bush.html.

[31] CNN.com, "Transcript: Bush-Putin News Conference," http://edition.cnn.com/2001/WORLD/europe/06/18/bush.putin.transcript/.

[32] Peter Baker, "The Seduction of George W. Bush," *Foreign Policy*, November 6, 2013, https://foreignpolicy.com/2013/11/06/the-seduction-of-george-w-bush/. It is true that Putin's public statements and conduct in the early 2000s gave little indication of his later authoritarian intentions and actions. Still, as a responsible political leader, Bush should have approached Putin in a more rational, skeptical, and guarded manner. The next subsection of this book shows how Bush's error about Putin was repeated in a more grotesque fashion by President Donald J. Trump at a time when Putin's authoritarian ways were observable to all who took time to study them. See Snyder, *The Road to Unfreedom*. But then, Trump openly admired dictators, whereas Bush did not.

[33] For an excellent detailed account and evaluation, see James P. Pfiffner, "The Contemporary Presidency: Decision Making in the Bush White House," *Presidential Studies Quarterly* 39, no. 2 (June 2009), 366–81, https://www.jstor.org/stable/41427364.

[34] Sarah Zhang, "Trump's Most Trusted Advisor Is His Own Gut," *The Atlantic*, January 13, 2019, https://www.theatlantic.com/politics/archive/2019/01/trump-follows-his-gut/580084/.

[35] Alana Abramson, "How Donald Trump Perpetrated the 'Birther' Movement for Years," *ABC News*, September 16, 2016, https://abcnews.go.com/Politics/donald-trump-perpetuated-birther-movement-years/story?id=42138176.

[36] Johnson, *The Electoral College*, 2nd ed., 101–2 (an endnote detailing supporting references is omitted here).

Notes

[37] "Full Interview: President Trump With C&B From Mar-A-Lago," *The Clay Travis and Buck Sexton Show*, February 22, 2022 (transcript), https://www.clayandbuck.com/president-trump-with-cb-from-mar-a-lago/.

[38] David D. Kirkpatrick, Maggie Astor, and Catie Edmondson, "Trump Praises Putin, Leaving Republicans in a Bind," *New York Times*, February 24, 2022, https://www.nytimes.com/2022/02/24/world/europe/trump-putin-russia-ukraine.html; Davey Alba and Stuart A. Thompson, " 'I'll Stand on the Side of Russia': Pro-Putin Sentiment Spreads Online," *New York Times*, February 25, 2022, https://www.nytimes.com/2022/02/25/technology/pro-russia-pro-putin-sentiment-spreads-online.html.

[39] Wikipedia s.v. "Veracity of Statements by Donald Trump," last modified December 20, 2022, 00:37, https://en.wikipedia.org/wiki/Veracity_of_statements_by_Donald_Trump#:~:text=During%20his%20term%20as%20President,of%20about%2021%20per%20day.

[40] Christina A. Cassidy, "Far Too Little Vote Fraud to Tip Election to Trump, AP Finds," Associated Press, December 14, 2021, https://apnews.com/article/voter-fraud-election-2020-joe-biden-donald-trump-7fcb6f134e528fee8237c7601db3328f; Lisa Mascaro and Eric Tucker, "1/6 Panel: Told Repeatedly He Lost, Trump Refused to Go," Associated Press, June 10, 2022, https://apnews.com/article/donald-trump-capitol-riot-hearing-67ec5f32b1dd050a24c3312570fa6c67?user_email=7e64d43f939de26e986b1b53cbc65a113597cdde95d317077c5ddaa40d2b0a72&utm_source=Sailthru&utm_medium=email&utm_campaign=June11_MorningWire&utm_term=Morning%20Wire%20Subscribers; Lisa Mascaro, Mary Clare Jalonick and Farnoush Amiri, "Capitol Riot Panel Blames Trump for 1/6 'Attempted Coup'," Associated Press, June 10, 2022, https://apnews.com/article/jan-6-capitol-riot-hearings-live-updates-eefb79f2cffb705f04bf43ea164db20f?user_email=7e64d43f93

Notes

9de26e986b1b53cbc65a113597cdde95d317077c5ddaa40d2b0a72&utm_source=Sailthru&utm_medium=email&utm_campaign=June10_MorningWire&utm_term=Morning%20Wire%20Subscribers; Catie Edmondson, " 'So the Traitors Know the Stakes': The Meaning of the Jan. 6 Gallows," *New York Times*, June 17, 2022, https://www.nytimes.com/2022/06/16/us/politics/jan-6-gallows.html. For additional details and corroborating evidence, see the website of the U.S. House of Representatives Select Committee to Investigate the January 6th Attack on the U.S. Capitol, https://january6th.house.gov/. See also Chapter 5 of Johnson, *The Electoral College*, 2nd ed.

[41] Bob Woodward and Carl Bernstein, "Woodward and Bernstein thought Nixon defined corruption. Then came Trump," *Washington Post*, June 5, 2022, https://www.washingtonpost.com/outlook/2022/06/05/woodward-bernstein-nixon-trump/.

[42] Posner, *Unholy*; Freedom From Religion Foundation and the Baptist Joint Committee for Religious Liberty, *Christian Nationalism and the January 6, 2021 Insurrection*, n.d., https://ffrf.org/uploads/legal/Christian_Nationalism_and_the_Jan6_Insurrection-2-9-22.pdf; Rowley, "Prophetic Populism and the Violent Rejection of Joe Biden's Election"; Zack Stanton, "It's Time to Talk about Violent Christian Extremism," *Politico*, February 4, 2021, https://www.politico.com/news/magazine/2021/02/04/qanon-christian-extremism-nationalism-violence-466034; Elizabeth Dias and Ruth Graham, "How White Evangelical Christians Fused with Trump Extremism," *New York Times*, January 19, 2021, https://www.nytimes.com/2021/01/11/us/how-white-evangelical-christians-fused-with-trump-extremism.html; Michelle Boorstein, "For Some Christians, the Capitol Riot Doesn't Change the Prophecy: Trump Will Be President," *Washington Post*, January 14, 2021, https://www.washingtonpost.com/religion/2021/01/14/prophets-apostles-christian-prophesy-trump-won-biden-capitol/.

Notes

[43] See especially Chapter 23 of Ted Sorensen, *Counselor: A Life at the Edge of History* (New York: HarperCollins, 2008), Kindle.

Epilogue

[1] See, for example, the sections "Ethical Relativism" and "Modern Moral Sentiment/Emotion" in Chapter 1, above; see also Chapter 1 ("Arguments against Free Will") passim in Johnson, *Free Will and Human Life*.

[2] See Johnson, *The First American Founder: Roger Williams and Freedom of Conscience*, and the appendix to the present book.

Appendix: Conflicts among the Claims to Revelation

[1] For a discussion of the historical backgrounds and principal tenets of the major religions, see Robert S. Ellwood and Barbara A. McGraw, *Many Peoples, Many Faiths: Women and Men in the World Religions*, 11th ed. (London: Routledge, 2022).

[2] The source of most of the facts set forth in this subsection is James Henry Breasted, *A History of Egypt from the Earliest Times to the Persian Conquest*, 2nd ed. (New York: Charles Scribner's Sons, 1912).

[3] The term "pharaoh" comes to us from the Torah, in which the word was a transliteration of the Egyptian word "Per-o," meaning "Great House." The Egyptians considered it irreverent to refer to their ruler by name. Thus, the practice developed of referring to the ruler and the ruler's government by the term "Great House," perhaps in a manner similar to which Americans refer to the president and the executive branch of the federal government as the White House. See Breasted, 74. It is another curious historical fact that the ancient Egyptian treasury was called the White House. Breasted, 237.

[4] "[I]n religion they were already dimly conscious of a judgment in the hereafter, and they were thus the first men whose ethical intuitions made happiness in the future life dependent upon character." Breasted, 144. The myth of Osiris

Notes

listed forty-two sins that would affect a person's status in the afterlife, including murder, stealing, lying, deceit, false witness, slander, reviling, eavesdropping, sexual impurity, adultery, blasphemy, and the theft of mortuary offerings. Breasted, 173.

[5] The account herein of Ikhnaton and his new religion is based largely upon chapter 18 ("The Religious Revolution of Ikhnaton") of Breasted's *History of Egypt*. As is discussed in that work, some of the thought behind Ikhnaton's new religion of Aton was not entirely unprecedented. Amenhotep III, the immediately preceding pharaoh and Ikhnaton's father, had instituted the acknowledgment of Aton on a small and inconspicuous scale and may have instructed Ikhnaton regarding the new religion. In addition, Ikhnaton may have been influenced by the priests of Ptah (the artificer god of Memphis), who had begun interpreting their religion in philosophical terms.

[6] Breasted, 365. Notwithstanding the fact that Breasted's *History of Egypt* was written more than century ago, it remains a great and fascinating study of the history of ancient Egypt in general and of Ikhnaton in particular. Breasted himself spent much time in Egypt, leading archeological expeditions and reading and translating the ancient hieroglyphics.

[7] Breasted, who independently translated these and a vast quantity of other Egyptian writings from the originals, sets forth his English translation of this hymn, along with parallel passages in Psalm 104, in *History of Egypt*, 371–76.

[8] Breasted, 392 (italics in the original).

[9] Mary Boyce, *Zoroastrianism: Its Antiquity and Constant Vigour* (Costa Mesa, CA: Mazda Publishers, 1992), Chapter 2; Mary Boyce, ed. and trans., *Textual Sources for the Study of Zoroastrianism* (Chicago: University of Chicago Press, 1984), 22. Boyce points out that the society in which Zoroaster lived eventually migrated southward into what is now Iran, and thus Zoroastrianism is associated in recorded

historical periods with Persia (the former name for the land now occupied by Iran).

[10] The following interpretation of the *Gathas* is my own. In arriving at this interpretation, I consulted the following English translations: the respective translations of Irach J.S. Taraporewala and Christian Bartholomae in Irach J.S. Taraporewala, ed., *The Divine Songs of Zarathushtra: A Philological Study of the Gathas of Zarathushtra, Containing the Text with Literal Translation into English, a Free English Rendering and Full Critical and Grammatical Notes, Metrical Index and Glossary* (1951; repr., New York: AMS Press, Inc., 1977); and the translation of Mary Boyce in her *Textual Sources for the Study of Zoroastrianism*, 34–45. Unfortunately, Boyce's translation is not complete. In addition, Taraporewala's translation and interpretation are marred by his assumption, unsupported in the text of the *Gathas*, that Zoroaster intended to communicate the same messages as Hinduism or Christianity on certain subjects. The *Gathas* of Zoroaster constitute Chapters 28–34, 43–51, and 53 of a Zoroastrian scripture called *Yasna*, which is part of the Zoroastrian holy book of *Avesta*. Accordingly, the references in the following discussion are to chapters and verses (separated by a colon) of *Yasna*, as referenced in the above cited translations. It should be emphasized that my interpretation of the *Gathas* is selective, focusing on the great ethical themes of that work without attempting to set forth the details of its theology.

[11] *Yasna* 34:13, 43:5–16, 45:3–5, 50:1–11, 51:7.

[12] *Yasna* 31:8, 50:6.

[13] *Yasna* 31:11.

[14] *Yasna* 31:12, 33:1, 48:4.

[15] *Yasna* 32:6.

[16] *Yasna* 30:3. Evidently, the Avestan text is literally translated "the better and the bad." Zoroaster may have had some reason for putting "the good" in a comparative grammatical form, though it is not clear what that reason is. It is consistent with the entirety of the *Gathas* to interpret this

passage as the juxtaposition of good and evil, and such contrast, as understood in contemporary English, is probably what Zoroaster meant.

[17] *Yasna* 30:4.

[18] *Yasna* 30:2–3, 31:22, 32:7.

[19] *Yasna* 30:3.

[20] *Yasna* 30:4, 31:14.

[21] *Yasna* 28:8, 28:10, 30:7–8, 30:10–11, 34:1, 34:3–4, 34:13–14, 43:5, 43:12, 43:16, 45:3, 45:7, 46:11–12, 47:1, 50:2–3, 51:6, 51:8–9, 51:13.

[22] *Yasna* 28:4, 33:13, 34:1, 45:3, 43:5, 43:16, 45:3, 47:1, 49:11, 51:1–3, 51:21.

[23] *Yasna* 29:1–11, 30:6, 31:15, 31:18, 32:10–11, 32:16, 34:5, 43:14, 48:7, 48:12.

[24] *Yasna* 28:1–11, 29:8, 29:10–11, 30:9, 31:2–5, 31:21–22, 33:4–9, 33:14, 34:10, 43:5–16, 45:1–11, 46:9–10, 46:13–19, 47:1, 48:3, 49:5–10, 50:2–11, 51:1–3, 58:8, 53:1.

[25] *Yasna* 31:14–17, 32:16, 34:5–12, 34:15, 43:11, 44:6–20, 46:1–8, 46:11, 48:2, 48:8–11, 49:1–4, 49:11–12, 50:1, 51:12.

[26] *Yasna* 53:4–5.

[27] *Yasna* 28:2, 33:10, 43:3, 51:17, 53:4–5.

[28] *Yasna* 43:2.

[29] Although the first three Gospels (Matthew, Mark, and Luke) as well as the Epistle of James in the Christian Bible do not promote any notion of justification by faith, indicating instead that salvation is obtained by repentance and by practice of a certain moral code, Paul the Apostle introduced the doctrine of justification by faith in his Epistle to the Romans. Lutheranism and most Protestant denominations of Christianity advanced the doctrine of justification by faith as one of the most important tenets of their religious doctrines. The issue is fraught with a historical ambiguity regarding the word "works": a ritualistic meaning (e.g., ecclesiastical observances) and an ethical meaning. Luther taught that only faith, not works (in both senses of the word), could bring salvation, but Luther also taught that a person who truly had

faith would strive to follow the Christian moral code. This issue is further complicated by the fact that Augustine (in his later works), Luther, and Calvin all denied human free will, insisting instead that every human's fate was predestined by God before birth. See Johnson, *Free Will and Human Life*, 7–17.

[30] Plato, *Alcibiades I* 122a.

[31] Charles Caldwell Ryrie, *Ryrie Study Bible*, expanded ed. (Chicago: Moody Press, 1995), 1499, 1512.

[32] Ryrie, 1499.

[33] Much scholarship has addressed this question during the last few centuries. See, for example, E. P. Sanders, *The Historical Figure of Jesus* (London: Penguin Books, 1993), 132–68; A. N. Wilson, *Jesus: A Life* (New York: Fawcett Columbine, 1992); A. N. Wilson, *Paul: The Mind of the Apostle* (New York: W.W. Norton, 1997); and the many books authored by Bart Ehrman.

[34] Although Muhammad himself evidently did not claim to perform or to have been the recipient of any miracles other than the circumstances involving the revelation of the Qur'an, his followers later attributed as many as 3,000 miracles and prophecies to him. Edward Gibbon, *The History of the Decline and Fall of the Roman Empire*, vol. 6, chap. 50, 234–35 (London: Folio Society, 1988).

[35] Breasted, *History of Egypt*, 392.

[36] See Exodus 23:23–24, 35, 34:13, 24; Leviticus 18:24, 20:23–24; Numbers 21:1–3, 21–35, 25:16–18, 31:1–18, 33:50–56; Deuteronomy 1:8, 2:24–25, 30–36, 3:1–10, 7:1–26, 11:23–25, 18:14, 31:3–8, 20:16–17; Joshua, 3:10, 6:21, 8:21–29, 9:24, 10:1, 19–20, 26–42, 11:7–23; and Judges 1:1–20.

[37] With regard to Hindu nationalist discrimination against Muslims, see, for example, Sheikh Saaliq, "A Long-Dead Muslim Emperor Vexes India's Hindu Nationalists," Associated Press, June 3, 2022, https://apnews.com/article/politics-narendra-modi-new-delhi-india-religion-

Notes

98335c46c3ecbe599699ee391248c664?user_email=7e64d43f939de26e986b1b53cbc65a113597cdde95d317077c5ddaa40d2b0a72&utm_source=Sailthru&utm_medium=email&utm_campaign=June03_MorningWire&utm_term=Morning%20Wire%20Subscribers; Sheikh Saaliq and Krutika Pathi, "Dispute over Mosque Becomes Religious Flashpoint in India," Associated Press, May 26, 2022, https://apnews.com/article/politics-india-religion-3ce634c6ab34c4d5c12ecc572e9ad3b6?user_email=7e64d43f939de26e986b1b53cbc65a113597cdde95d317077c5ddaa40d2b0a72&utm_source=Sailthru&utm_medium=email&utm_campaign=May26_MorningWire&utm_term=Morning%20Wire%20Subscribers.

SELECTED BIBLIOGRAPHY

This selected bibliography includes only cited works that thematically discuss the principal issues addressed in this book. Other writings, including news articles, are not cited in more than one chapter or are identified in each endnote citation with a URL designation.

Adams, John. Letter to Mercy Otis Warren. April 16, 1776. In *Founders Online*, National Archives, https://founders.archives.gov/documents/Adams/06-04-02-0044.

Adorno, T. W., Else Frenkel-Brunswik, Daniel J. Levinson, and R. Nevitt Sanford. *The Authoritarian Personality*. 1950; Reprint, Brooklyn, New York: Verso, 2019. Kindle/

Allen, Colin, and Jacob Neal. "Teleological Notions in Biology." In *The Stanford Encyclopedia of Philosophy*, spring 2020 ed., edited by Edward L. Zalta. https://plato.stanford.edu/entries/teleology-biology/.

Alliluyeva, Svetlana. *Twenty Letters to a Friend: A Memoir*. Translated by Priscilla Johnson McMillan. New York: Harper Perennial, 2016. Kindle.

Applebaum, Anne. *Red Famine: Stalin's War on Ukraine*. New York: Doubleday, 2017.

Applebaum, Anne. *Twilight of Democracy: The Seductive Lure of Authoritarianism*. New York: Doubleday, 2020. Kindle.

Arain, Mariam, Maliha Haque, Lina Johal, Puja Mathur, Wynand Nel, Afsha Rais, Ranbir Sandhu, and Sushil Sharma. "Maturation of the Adolescent Brain." *Neuropsychiatric Disease and Treatment* 9 (2013): 449–61. Doi:10.2147/NDT.S39776. https://www.ncbi.nlm.nih.gov/pmc/articles/PMC3621648/.

Selected Bibliography

Arendt, Hannah. *The Origins of Totalitarianism*. New ed. New York: Harvest Book, 1994. Kindle.

Aristotle. *Eudemian Ethics*. Translated and edited by Brad Inwood and Raphael Woolf. Cambridge: Cambridge University Press, 2013.

Aristotle. *Metaphysics*. In *Aristotle's "Metaphysics"*, translated and edited by Joe Sachs. Santa Fe, NM: Green Lion Press, 2002.

Aristotle. *Nicomachean Ethics*. In *Aristotle's "Nicomachean Ethics"*. Translated and edited by Robert C. Bartlett and Susan D. Collins. Chicago: University of Chicago Press, 2011.

Aristotle. *On Sophistical Refutations*. Translated by E. S. Forster. Loeb Classical Library. Cambridge, MA: Harvard University Press, 1955.

Aristotle. *Physics*. In *Aristotle's "Physics": A Guided Study*, translated with introduction, commentary, and explanatory glossary by Joe Sachs. New Brunswick, NJ: Rutgers University Press, 1995.

Arp, Robert, Steven Barbone, and Michael Bruce, eds. *Bad Arguments: 100 of the Most Important Fallacies in Western Philosophy*. Hoboken, NJ: Wiley-Walton, 2018. Kindle.

Attenborough, David. "A Life on Our Planet." 2002. https://www.imdb.com/title/tt11989890/.

Attridge, Harold W., and Wayne A. Meeks, eds. *HarperCollins Study Bible*. Rev. ed. New York: HarperCollins, 2006. Kindle.

Australian Academy of Science. "What's Killing the Bees?" Accessed May 9, 2022. https://www.science.org.au/curious/earth-environment/whats-killing-bees.

Bacon, Francis. *The Advancement of Learning and New Atlantis*. Edited by Thomas Case. London: Oxford University Press, 1906.

Baghramian, Maria, and Annalisa Coliva. *Relativism*. Oxford, UK: Routledge, 2020. Kindle.

Selected Bibliography

Baghramian, Maria, and J. Adam Carter. "Relativism. In *Stanford Encyclopedia of Philosophy*, spring 2021 ed., edited by Edward L. Zalta. https://plato.stanford.edu/archieves/spr2021/entries/relativism/.

Baker, Peter. "The Seduction of George W. Bush." *Foreign Policy*, November 6, 2013. https://foreignpolicy.com/2013/11/06/the-seduction-of-george-w-bush/.

Ball, T., and Richard Dagger. "Communism." *Encyclopedia Britannica*, November 13, 2019. https://www.britannica.com/topic/communism.

Belew, Kathleen. *Bring the War Home: The White Power Movement and Paramilitary America*. Cambridge, MA: Harvard University Press, 2018. Kindle.

Ben-Ghiat, Ruth. *Strongmen: Mussolini to the Present*. New York: W. W. Norton, 2020. Kindle.

Block, Gregory L. "Appeal to Ridicule." In Arp, Barbone, and Bruce, *Bad Arguments*, chap. 2.

Bonazzi, Mauro. "Protagoras." In *Stanford Encyclopedia of Philosophy*, fall 2020 ed., edited by Edward L. Zalta. https://plato.stanford.edu/archives/fall2020/entries/protagoras/.

Booth, Wayne C. *Now Don't Try to Reason with Me: Essays and Ironies for a Credulous Age*. Chicago: University of Chicago Press, 1970.

Boyce, Mary. *Textual Sources for the Study of Zoroastrianism*. Chicago: University of Chicago Press, 1984.

Boyce, Mary. *Zoroastrianism: Its Antiquity and Constant Vigour*. Costa Mesa, CA: Mazda Publishers, 1992.

Breasted, James Henry. *A History of Egypt from the Earliest Times to the Persian Conquest*. 2nd ed. New York: Charles Scribner's Sons, 1912.

Burnett, Anne Pippin. *Revenge in Attic and Later Tragedy*. Berkeley: University of California Press, 1998.

Butler, Heather A. "Why Do Smart People Do Foolish Things? Intelligence Is Not the Same as Critical Thinking—and the

Selected Bibliography

Difference Matters." *Scientific American,* October 3, 2017. https://www.scientificamerican.com/article/why-do-smart-people-do-foolish-things/.

Calvin, John. "Articles concerning Predestination." In *Calvin: Theological Treatises,* 178–80. Philadelphia: Westminster, 1954.

Calvin, John. *Institutes of the Christian Religion.* Translated by Henry Beveridge. 1845. Reprint, Grand Rapids, MI: Wm. B. Eerdmans, 2001.

Calvin, John. *Theological Treatises.* Translated and edited by J. K. S. Reid. Philadelphia: Westminster, 1954.

Carson, Rachel. *Silent Spring.* New York: Houghton Mifflin Harcourt, 2002.

Cicero. *Cicero's Tusculan Disputations.* Translated by C. D. Yonge. New York: Harper & Brothers, 1899.

Confucius. *The Analects.* Translated and edited by Simon Leys. New York: W. W. Norton, 1997.

Confucius. *The Analects of Confucius: A Philosophical Translation.* Translated and edited by Roger T. Ames and Henry Rosemont Jr. New York: Ballantine Books, 1998.

Confucius. *The Great Learning.* Translated and edited by James Legge. In Legge, *The Life and Teachings of Confucius,* 2nd ed., 264–67. Vol. 1 of *The Chinese Classics,* translated and edited by James Legge.

Confucius and Tsze-tse, *The Doctrine of the Mean,* in Legge, *The Life and Teachings of Confucius,* 2nd ed., 282–320.

Constitutional Rights Foundation. "The Stalin Purges and 'Show Trials.' " Accessed June 2, 2022. https://www.crf-usa.org/bill-of-rights-in-action/bria-7-4-a-the-stalin-purges-and-show-trials.

Cooper, William S. *The Evolution of Reason: Logic as a Branch of Biology.* Cambridge: Cambridge University Press, 2001.

Cropsey, Joseph. *Polity and Economy: With Further Thoughts on the Principles of Adam Smith.* South Bend, IN: St Augustine's Press, 2001.

Culver, Jennifer. "False Dilemma." In Arp, Barbone, and Bruce, *Bad Arguments,* chap. 81.

Selected Bibliography

de Tocqueville, Alexis. *Democracy in America*. Translated and edited by Harvey C. Mansfield and Delba Winthrop. Chicago: University of Chicago Press, 2000.

de Waal, Frans. *The Age of Empathy: Nature's Lessons for a Kinder Society*. New York: Three Rivers, 2009.

de Waal, Frans. *The Bonobo and the Atheist: In Search of Humanism among the Primates*. New York: W. W. Norton, 2014.

de Waal, Frans. *Primates and Philosophers: How Morality Evolved*. Princeton: Princeton University Press, 2006.

Deacon, Terrence W. *Incomplete Nature: How Mind Emerged from Matter*. New York: W. W. Norton, 2013.

DeMarco, Patricia M. *Pathways to Our Sustainable Future: A Perspective from Pittsburgh*. Pittsburgh: University of Pittsburgh Press, 2017.

Doidge, Norman. *The Brain That Changes Itself: Stories of Personal Triumph from the Frontiers of Brain Science*. New York: Penguin, 2007.

Driver, Julia. "The History of Utilitarianism." In *The Stanford Encyclopedia of Philosophy*, winter 2014 ed., edited by Edward L. Zalta, https://plato.stanford.edu/entries/utilitarianism-history/.

Ellwood, Robert S., and Barbara A. McGraw. *Many Peoples, Many Faiths: Women and Men in the World Religions*. 11th ed. London: Routledge, 2022.

Encyclopedia Britannica Online, s.v. "Achilles Paradox," accessed December 7, 2021, https://www.britannica.com/topic/Achilles-paradox.

Encyclopedia Britannica Online, s.v. "Vladimir Putin," accessed June 5, 2022, https://www.britannica.com/biography/Vladimir-Putin

Evans, Richard J. *The Coming of the Third Reich*. New York: Penguin, 2005. Kindle.

Evans, Richard J. *The Third Reich at War, 1939–1945*. New York: Penguin Books, 2008. Kindle.

Evans, Richard J. *The Third Reich in Power*. New York: Penguin Books, 2005. Kindle.

Selected Bibliography

Fearnside, W. Ward, and William B. Holther. *Fallacy: The Counterfeit of Argument*. Englewood Cliffs, N.J.: Prentice-Hall, Inc., Spectrum Paperbacks, 1959.

Fischer, David Hackett. *Historians' Fallacies: Toward a Logic of Historical Thought*. New York: HarperPerennial, 1970.

Foot, Philippa. *Natural Goodness*. Oxford: Clarendon, 2001.

Freedom From Religion Foundation and the Baptist Joint Committee for Religious Liberty. *Christian Nationalism and the January 6, 2021 Insurrection*. N.d. https://ffrf.org/uploads/legal/Christian_Nationalism_and_the_Jan6_Insurrection-2-9-22.pdf.

Gambarotto, Andrea, and Auguste Nahras. "Teleology and the Organism: Kant's Controversial Legacy for Contemporary Biology." *Studies in History and Philosophy of Science* 93 (2022): 47–56. https://www.academia.edu/75441507/Teleology_and_the_Organism_Kants_Controversial_Legacy_for_Contemporary_Biology.

Gessen, Masha. *The Future Is History: How Totalitarianism Reclaimed Russia*. New York: Riverhead Books, 2017. Kindle.

Gessen, Masha. *The Man without a Face: The Unlikely Rise of Vladimir Putin*. New York: Riverhead Books, 2012. Kindle.

Gessen, Masha. *Surviving Autocracy*. New York: Riverhead Books, 2000. Kindle.

Gessen, Masha. *Words Will Break Cement: The Passion of Pussy Riot*. New York; Riverhead Books, 2014. Kindle.

Gibbon, Edward. *The History of the Decline and Fall of the Roman Empire*. Vol. 6. London: Folio Society, 1988.

Ginsburg, Tom, and Aziz Z. Huq. *How to Save a Constitutional Democracy*. Chicago: University of Chicago Press, 2018. Kindle.

Goldberg, Elkhonon. *The New Executive Brain: Frontal Lobes in a Complex World*. New York: Oxford University Press, 2009.

Goodall, Jane. *In the Shadow of Man*. 1971. Reprint, New York: Mariner Books, 2000.

Selected Bibliography

Gopnik, Adam. "How to Build a Twenty-First-Century Tyrant: Autocracies Are Resurgent, and Today's Would-Be Strongmen Are Using a New Set of Tools." *New Yorker*, May 16, 2022. https://www.newyorker.com/magazine/2022/05/23/how-to-build-a-twenty-first-century-tyrant-the-revenge-of-power-spin-dictators.

Greene, Nathanael, ed. *Fascism: An Anthology*. New York: Thomas Y. Crowell, 1968.

Grimes, David Robert. *Good Thinking: Why Flawed Logic Puts Us All at Risk and How Critical Thinking Can Save the World*. New York: The Experiment, 2019. Kindle.

Groarke, Leo. "Informal Logic." In *The Stanford Encyclopedia of Philosophy*, fall 2021 ed., edited by Edward L. Zalta. https://plato.stanford.edu/entries/logic-informal/.

Gruter, Margaret, and Roger D. Masters. "Balancing Altruism and Selfishness: Evolutionary Theory and the Foundation of Morality." *Jahrbuch Für Recht Und Ethik / Annual Review of Law and Ethics* 4 (1996): 561–73. http://www.jstor.org/stable/43593571.

Gutiérrez, Rochelle. "Political Conocimiento for Teaching Mathematics: Why Teachers Need It and How to Develop It." Chap. 2 in *Building Support for Scholarly Practices in Mathematics Methods*, edited by Signe E. Kastberg, Andrew M. Tyminski, Alyson E. Lischka, and Wendy B. Sanchez. Charlotte, NC: Information Age, 2017. Kindle.

Haidt, Jonathan. "The Emotional Dog and Its Rational Tail." *Psychological Review* 108, no. 4 (2001): 814–34. https://psycnet.apa.org/doiLanding?doi=10.1037%2F0033-295X.108.4.814.

Haidt, Jonathan. "The New Synthesis in Moral Psychology." *Science* 316, no. 5827 (2007): 998–1002. http://www.jstor.org/stable/20036276.

Haidt, Jonathan. *The Righteous Mind: Why Good People Are Divided by Politics and Religion*. New York: Pantheon, 2012. Kindle.

Selected Bibliography

Hanna, Robert. *Deep Freedom and Real Persons—A Study in Metaphysics*. New York: Nova Science, 2018. Vol. 2 of Hanna, *The Rational Human Condition*.

Hanna, Robert. *The Philosophy of the Future: Uniscience and the Modern World*. 2022. https://www.academia.edu/62653411/THE_PHILOSOPHY_OF_THE_FUTURE_Uniscience_and_the_Modern_World_2022_version_.

Hansen, Hans. "Fallacies." In *The Stanford Encyclopedia of Philosophy*, summer 2020 ed., edited by Edward L. Zalta. https://plato.stanford.edu/cgi-bin/encyclopedia/archinfo.cgi?entry=fallacies.

Hansen, Hans V., and Robert C. Pinto. *Fallacies: Classical and Contemporary Readings*. University Park, PA: Pennsylvania State University Press, 1995.

Harman, Gilbert. "Moral Relativism Is Moral Realism." *Philosophical Studies: An International Journal for Philosophy in the Analytic Tradition* 172, no. 4 (2015): 855–63. http://www.jstor.org/stable/24704141.

Hicks, Stephen R. C. *Explaining Postmodernism: Skepticism and Socialism from Rousseau to Foucault*. Expanded ed. Roscoe, IL: Ockham's Razor, 2014. Kindle.

Hill, Fiona. *There Is Nothing for You Here: Finding Opportunity in the Twenty-First Century*. New York: Mariner Books, 2021. Kindle.

Hill, Fiona, and Clifford G. Gaddy. *Mr. Putin: Operative in the Kremlin*. New and expanded ed. Washington, D.C.: Brookings Institution Press, 2015. Kindle.

Hingley, R. Francis. "Joseph Stalin." *Encyclopedia Britannica*, March 14, 2022. https://www.britannica.com/biography/Joseph-Stalin.

Hitchcock, David. "Critical Thinking." In *The Stanford Encyclopedia of Philosophy*, fall 2020 ed., edited by Edward L. Zalta. https://plato.stanford.edu/entries/critical-thinking/.

Hobbes, Thomas. *Body, Man, and Citizen: Selections from Thomas Hobbes*, Edited by Richard S. Peters. New York: Collier Books, 1962.

Selected Bibliography

Holmes, Oliver Wendell. *The Common Law*. Edited by Mark DeWolfe Howe. Boston, MA Little, Brown, 1936. Originally published in 1881.

Hume, David. *An Enquiry Concerning Human Understanding*. In *Hume: An Enquiry Concerning Human Understanding and Other Writings*, edited by Stephen Buckle. Cambridge: Cambridge University Press, 2007.

Hume, David. *An Enquiry Concerning the Principles of Morals*. Edited by J. B. Schneewind. Indianapolis: Hackett, 1983.

Hume, David. *The Letters of David Hume*. Edited by J. Y. T. Greig. Oxford: Clarendon, 1932.

Hume, David. *A Treatise of Human Nature*. Edited by L. A. Selby-Bigge. Oxford: Clarendon, 1896.

Hursthouse, Rosalind. *On Virtue Ethics*. Oxford: Oxford University Press, 1999.

Hursthouse, Rosalind. "Virtue Ethics." In *The Stanford Encyclopedia of Philosophy*, winter 2018 ed., edited by Edward L. Zalta, https://plato.stanford.edu/entries/ethics-virtue/.

Hurwitz, Lisa (director). "Automat" (film documentary). 2022. https://www.amazon.com/Automat-Mel-Brooks/dp/B0B1MDV2RB/ref=sr_1_1?crid=3MSRWHFGTNGLC&keywords=automat&qid=1655639140&s=instant-video&sprefix=Automat%2Cinstant-video%2C54&sr=1-1.

Hutcheson, Francis. *Philosophiae Moralis Institutio Compendiaria with A Short Introduction to Moral Philosophy*. 2nd ed. Edited by Luigi Turco. Indianapolis: Liberty Fund, 2007.

Hutcheson, Francis. *A System of Moral Philosophy*. Vol. 1. Glasgow, 1755.

Johnson, Alan E. *The Electoral College: Failures of Original Intent and Proposed Constitutional and Statutory Changes for Direct Popular Vote*. 2nd ed. Pittsburgh, PA: Philosophia Publications, 2021.

Johnson, Alan E. *The First American Founder: Roger Williams and Freedom of Conscience*. Pittsburgh, PA: Philosophia Publications, 2015.

Selected Bibliography

Johnson, Alan E. *Free Will and Human Life*. Pittsburgh, PA: Philosophia Publications, 2021.

Johnson, Alan E. "The Teaching of Plato's *Seventh Letter*." Master's essay, University of Chicago, 1971. https://www.academia.edu/22999496/The_Teaching_of_Platos_Seventh_Letter.

Johnson, Ralph H. and J. Anthony Blair. *Logical Self-Defense*. New York: IDEA Press, 2006.

Johnson, Stephen. "Why Is 18 the Age of Adulthood If the Brain Can Take 30 Years to Mature?" Big Think: Neuropsych. January 31, 2022. https://bigthink.com/neuropsych/adult-brain/.

Kahneman, Daniel. *Thinking, Fast and Slow*. New York: Farrar, Straus and Giroux, 2011.

Kant, Immanuel. *Anthropology from a Pragmatic Point of View*. Translated by Robert B. Louden. In *Anthropology, History, and Education*, 227–429.

Kant, Immanuel. *Anthropology, History, and Education*. Edited by Günter Zöller, Robert B. Louden, Mary Gregor, Paul Guyer, Holly Wilson, Allen W. Wood, and Arnulf Zweig. New York: Cambridge University Press, 2007. Kindle.

Kant, Immanuel. *Critique of Practical Reason*. Translated by Mary J. Gregor. In *Practical Philosophy*, 133–271.

Kant, Immanuel. *Groundwork of the Metaphysics of Morals*. Translated by Mary J. Gregor. In *Practical Philosophy*, 37–108.

Kant, Immanuel. "Idea for a Universal History with a Cosmopolitan Aim." Translated by Allen W. Wood. In *Anthropology, History, and Education*, 107–21.

Kant, Immanuel. *The Metaphysics of Morals*. Translated by Mary J. Gregor. In *Practical Philosophy*, 353–603.

Kant, Immanuel. "On a Supposed Right to Lie from Philanthropy." Translated by Mary J. Gregor. In *Practical Philosophy*, 605–15.

Kant, Immanuel. *Practical Philosophy*. Translated and edited by Mary J. Gregor. Cambridge: Cambridge University Press, 1996.

Selected Bibliography

Katz, Leonard D., ed. *Evolutionary Origins of Morality: Cross-Disciplinary Perspectives*. Thorverton, UK: Imprint Academic, 2000.

Kauffman, Stuart A. *A World Beyond Physics: The Emergence and Evolution of Life*. New York: Oxford University Press, 1999. Kindle.

Koertge, Noretta, ed. *A House Built on Sand: Exposing Postmodernist Myths about Science*. New York: Oxford University Press, 1998.

Kolbert, Elizabeth. *The Sixth Extinction: An Unnatural History*. New York: Henry Holt, 2014.

Kotkin, Stephen. *Stalin: Paradoxes of Power, 1878–1928*. New York: Penguin Books, 2014. Kindle.

Kotkin, Stephen. *Stalin: Waiting for Hitler, 1929-41*. New York: Penguin Books, 2018. Kindle.

Khrushchev, Nikita. *Memoirs of Nikita Khrushchev*. Vol. 1, *Commissar (1918–1945)*; Vol. 2, *Reformer (1945–64)*. Edited by Sergei Khrushchev. Translated by. George Shriver and Stephen Shenfield. University Park, PA: Pennsylvania State University Press, 2004 (vol. 1), 2006 (vol. 2).

LaBossiere, Michael. *76 Fallacies*. N.p.: [Amazon Digital Services?], 2012. Kindle.

Legge, James, trans. and ed. *The Life and Teachings of Confucius*, 2nd ed. London: N. Trüber, 1869. Vol. 1 of *The Chinese Classics*, translated and edited by James Legge.

Leijenhors, Cees. "Hobbes's Theory of Causality and Its Aristotelian Background." *The Monist* 79, no. 3 (July 1996): 426. https://www.jstor.org/stable/27903492.

Lennox, James G. "Darwin *Was* a Teleologist." *Biology and Philosophy* 8 (1993): 409–21. https://inters.org/files/lennox1993.pdf.

Levitin, Daniel J. *A Field Guide to Lies: Critical Thinking with Statistics and the Scientific Method*. New York: Dutton, 2016. Kindle.

Levitsky, Steven, and Daniel Ziblatt. *How Democracies Die*. New York: Crown, 2018. Kindle.

Selected Bibliography

Lincoln, Abraham. "The Perpetuation of Our Political Institutions." Address Before the Young Men's Lyceum of Springfield, Illinois. January 27, 1838. http://www.abrahamlincolnonline.org/lincoln/speeches/lyceum.htm.

Lindauer, Miriam. "The Biology of Morality: Why People Are More Often Good Than Bad." March 2, 2019. https://www.academia.edu/16610786/The_Biology_of_Morality_Why_People_Are_More_Often_Good_Than_Bad.

Lindsay, James A. and Mike Nayna. "Postmodern Religion and the Faith of Social Justice." *Areo*. December 18, 2018. https://areomagazine.com/2018/12/18/postmodern-religion-and-the-faith-of-social-justice/.

Luther, Martin. *The Bondage of the Will*. Translated by J. I. Packer and O. R. Johnston. Grand Rapids, MI: Fleming H. Revell, 1957. Originally published in 1525.

Luther, Martin. "A Commentary on St. Paul's Epistle to the Galatians." Translated by Philip S. Watson. In *Martin Luther: Selections from His Writings*, edited by John Dillenberger. New York: Anchor Books, 1962.

MacIntyre, Alasdair. *After Virtue*. 3rd ed. Notre Dame, IN: University of Notre Dame Press, 2007. Kindle.

Madison, James. *Federalist No. 10*. November 22, 1788. Founders Online, National Archives. https://founders.archives.gov/documents/Madison/01-10-02-0178.

Madison, James. Speech in the Virginia Ratifying Convention. June 20, 1788. In *Documentary History of the Ratification of the Constitution, Digital Edition*, edited by John P. Kaminski and Gaspare J. Saladino. Charlottesville: University of Virginia Press, 2009, 10:1412–19. http://rotunda.upress.virginia.edu/founders/RNCN-02-10-02-0002-0009.

Manninen, Bertha Alvarez. "Weak Analogy." In Arp, Barbone, and Bruce, *Bad Arguments*, chap. 2.

McClellan, Scott. *What Happened: Inside the Bush White House and Washington's Culture of Deception*. New York: Public Affairs, 2008. Kindle.

Selected Bibliography

McCraw. Benjamin W. "Appeal to the People." In Arp, Barbone, and Bruce, *Bad Arguments*, chap. 16.

McWhorter, John. *Woke Racism: How a New Religion Has Betrayed Black America*. New York: Portfolio / Penguin, 2021.

Mill, John Stuart. *A System of Logic, Ratiocinative and Inductive, Being a Connected View of the Principles of Evidence and the Methods of Scientific Investigation*. 8th ed. New York: Harper & Brothers, 1882.

Mill, John Stuart. *Utilitarianism: With Related Remarks from Mill's Other Writings*. Edited by Ben Eggleston. Indianapolis: Hackett, 2017.

Mitford, Nancy. *Voltaire in Love*. Pleasantville, New York: Akadine, 1998.

Muniz, Michael J. "Hasty Generalization." In Arp, Barbone, and Bruce, *Bad Arguments*, chap. 84.

Naím, Moisés. *The Revenge of Power: How Autocrats Are Reinventing Politics for the 21st Century*. New York: St. Martin's, 2022. Kindle.

Nichols Jr., James H. Preface to Plato, *Gorgias*, trans. Nichols, vii–xi.

Norman, Andy. *Mental Immunity: Infectious Ideas, Mind-Parasites, and the Search for a Better Way to Think*. New York: Harper Wave, 2021. Kindle.

Norris, Pippa, and Robert Inglehart. *Cultural Backlash: Trump, Brexit, and Authoritarian Populism*. New York: Cambridge University Press, 2019. Kindle.

Olson, Walter. "Reasonable Doubts: Invitation to a Stoning." *Reason*. November 1998. https://reason.com/1998/11/01/invitation-to-a-stoning/.

Pangle, Lorraine Smith. *Reason and Character: The Moral Foundations of Aristotelian Political Philosophy*. Chicago: University of Chicago Press, 2020. Kindle.

Passingham, Richard E. and Steven P. Wise. *The Neurobiology of the Prefrontal Cortex: Anatomy, Evolution, and the Origin of Instinct*. Oxford: Oxford University Press, 2014.

Selected Bibliography

Pesticide Action Network (PAN). "The DDT Story." Accessed May 9, 2022. https://www.panna.org/resources/ddt-story#:~:text=Banned%20for%20agricultural%20uses%20worldwide%20by%20the%202001,the%20transition%20to%20safer%20and%20more%20effective%20alternatives.

Pfiffner, James P. "The Contemporary Presidency: Decision Making in the Bush White House." *Presidential Studies Quarterly* 39, no. 2 (June 2009), 366–81. https://www.jstor.org/stable/41427364.

Pinker, Steven. *Rationality: What It Is, Why It Seems Scarce, Why It Matters*. New York: Viking, 2021. Kindle.

Plato. *Alcibiades I*. Translated by Carnes Lord. In *The Roots of Political Philosophy: Ten Forgotten Socratic Dialogues*, edited by Thomas L. Pangle, 175–221. Ithaca: Cornell University Press, 1987.

Plato. *Apology of Socrates*. Translated by Harold North Fowler. Loeb Classical Library. Cambridge, MA: Harvard University Press, 1914.

Plato. *Gorgias*. Translated and edited by James H. Nichols Jr. Ithaca, NY: Cornell University Press, 1998.

Plato. *Phaedrus*. Translated and edited by James H. Nichols Jr. Ithaca, NY: Cornell University Press, 1998.

Plato. *Republic*. In *The Republic of Plato*. 2nd ed., translated and edited by Allan Bloom. New York: Basic Books, 1991.

Plato. *Republic*. Translated and edited by Joe Sachs. Newbury, MA: Focus, 2007.

Plato. *Seventh Letter*. Translated by Jonah Radding. In *Plato at Syracuse: Essays on Plato in Western Greece with a New Translation of the "Seventh Letter" by Jonah Radding*, edited by Heather L. Reid and Mark Ralkowski. Sioux City, IA: Parnassos Press, 2019. Radding's translation is also located at https://www.jstor.org/stable/j.ctvcmxptk.7.

Plato. *Theaetetus*. In *Plato's Theaetetus*, translated by Seth Benardete. Chicago: University of Chicago Press, 1986.

Pluckrose, Helen, and James Lindsay. *Cynical Theories: How Activist Scholarship Made Everything about Race, Gender, and Identity—And Why This Harms Everybody*. Durham, NC: Pitchstone, 2020. Kindle.

Selected Bibliography

Posner, Sarah. *Unholy: How Christian Nationalists Powered the Trump Presidency, and the Devastating Legacy They Left Behind.* New York: Random House, 2021. Kindle.

Priest, Graham. *Beyond the Limits of Thought.* Oxford: Clarendon Press, 2002.

Priest, Graham, Francesco Berto, and Zach Weber. "Dialetheism." In *Stanford Encyclopedia of Philosophy*, fall 2018 ed., edited by Edward N. Zalta. https://plato.stanford.edu/archives/fall2018/entries/dialetheism/.

Priest, Graham, Koji Tanaka, and Zach Weber. "Paraconsistent Logic." In *Stanford Encyclopedia of Philosophy*, summer 2018 ed., edited by Edward N. Zalta, https://plato.stanford.edu/archives/sum2018/entries/logic-paraconsistent/.

Psychology Tools. "Fight or Flight Response" Accessed June 17, 2022. https://www.psychologytools.com/resource/fight-or-flight-response/.

Rand, Ayn. "How Does One Lead a Rational Life in an Irrational Society?" Chap. 8 in *The Virtue of Selfishness: A New Concept of Egoism.* New York: Signet, 1964.

Ricks, Thomas E. *First Principles: What America's Founders Learned from the Greeks and Romans and How That Shaped Our Country.* New York: Harper, 2020. Kindle.

Ridley, Matt. *The Origins of Virtue: Human Instincts and the Evolution of Cooperation.* New York: Penguin Books, 1996.

Rowley, Matthew. "Prophetic Populism and the Violent Rejection of Biden's Election: Mapping the Theology of the Capitol Insurrection." *International Journal of Religion* 12, no. 2 (December 2021): 145–164. https://www.academia.edu/67060884/Prophetic_Populism_and_the_Violent_Rejection_of_Joe_Bidens_Election_Mapping_the_Theology_of_the_Capitol_Insurrection

Russell, Daniel C. *Practical Intelligence and the Virtues.* Oxford: Clarendon, 2009. Kindle.

Ryrie, Charles Caldwell. *Ryrie Study Bible.* Expanded ed. Chicago: Moody Press, 1995.

Selected Bibliography

Sachs, Joe. Introduction to Plato, *Republic*, translated and edited by Joe Sachs.

Sanders, E. P. *The Historical Figure of Jesus*. London: Penguin Books, 1993.

Sapolsky, Robert M. *Behave: The Biology of Humans at Our Best and Worst*. New York: Penguin Books, 2017.

Sauer, Hanno. *Moral Judgments as Educated Intuitions*. Cambridge, MA: MIT Press, 2017. Kindle.

Sauer, Hanno. *Moral Thinking, Fast and Slow*. Oxford, UK: Routledge, 2019.

Schagrin, Morton L., and G. E. Hughes. "Formal Logic." *Encyclopedia Britannica*, November 2, 2018. https://www.britannica.com/topic/formal-logic.

Schwartz, Jeffrey M., and Sharon Begley. *The Mind and the Brain: Neuroplasticity and the Power of Mental Force*. New York: HarperCollins, 2002.

Service, Robert. *Stalin: A Biography*, Cambridge, MA: Belknap Press of Harvard University Press, 2005.

Sheldon, Garrett Ward. *The Political Philosophy of Thomas Jefferson*. Baltimore: Johns Hopkins University Press, 1991.

Sinnott-Armstrong, Walter. "Consequentialism." In *The Stanford Encyclopedia of Philosophy*, fall 2021 ed., edited by Edward L. Zalta. https://plato.stanford.edu/entries/consequentialism/.

Sinnott-Armstrong, Walter, ed. *The Evolution of Morality: Adaptations and Innateness*. Vol. 1. *Moral Psychology*. Cambridge, MA: MIT Press, 2008.

Sinnott-Armstrong, Walter. *Think Again: How to Reason and Argue*. New York Oxford University Press, 2018. Kindle.

Smith, Adam. *An Inquiry into the Nature and Causes of the Wealth of Nations*. Edited by Edwin Cannan, with an introduction by Max Lerner. New York: Modern Library, 1937.

Smith, Adam. *The Theory of Moral Sentiments*. Edited by E. G. West. Indianapolis: Liberty Classics, 1976.

Snyder, Bonnie Kerrigan. *Undoctrinate: How Politicized Classrooms Harm Kids and Ruin Our Schools—And What

Selected Bibliography

We Can Do about It. New York: Bombardier Books, 2021. Kindle.

Snyder, Timothy. *On Tyranny: Twenty Lessons from the Twentieth Century*. New York: Tim Duggan Books, 2017. Kindle.

Snyder, Timothy. *The Road to Unfreedom: Russia, Europe, America*, New York: Tim Duggan Books, 2018. Kindle.

Snyder, Timothy. "We Should Say It. Russia Is Fascist." *New York Times*. May 19, 2022. https://www.nytimes.com/2022/05/19/opinion/russia-fascism-ukraine-putin.html.

Society of Professional Journalists. *Code of Ethics*. Revised September 6, 2014. https://www.spj.org/ethicscode.asp.

Sorensen, Ted. *Counselor: A Life at the Edge of History*. New York: HarperCollins, 2008. Kindle.

Stallard, Katie. *Dancing on Bones: History and Power in China, Russia, and North Korea*. New York: Oxford University Press, 2022. Kindle.

Stanovich, Keith E. *The Bias That Divides Us: The Science and Politics of Myside Thinking*. Cambridge, MA: MIT Press, 2021. Kindle.

Stanovich, Keith E. *What Intelligence Tests Miss: The Psychology of Rational Thought*. New Haven: Yale University Press, 2009.

Stent, Angela E. *Putin's World: Russia against the West and with the Rest*. New York: Twelve, 2012.

Stoddard, Ross. *Rise Up: How to Build a Socially Conscious Business*. Boise, ID: Elevate, 2017.

Strauss, Leo. *Natural Right and History*. Chicago: University of Chicago Press, 1953.

Strauss, Leo. "On Plato's *Apology of Socrates* and *Crito*." In *Leo Strauss: Studies in Platonic Political Philosophy*, edited by Thomas L. Pangle. Chicago: University of Chicago Press, 1983.

Strauss, Leo. "Relativism." Chap. 7 in *The Rebirth of Classical Political Rationalism: An Introduction to the Thought of Leo Strauss; Essays and Lectures by Leo Strauss*, selected and introduced by Thomas L. Pangle. Chicago: University of Chicago Press, 1989.

Strauss, Leo. *Socrates and Aristophanes*. New York: Basic Books, 1966.

Suskind, Ron. "Faith, Certainty, and the Presidency of George W. Bush." *New York Times*. October 17, 2004. https://www.nytimes.com/2004/10/17/magazine/faith-certainty-and-the-presidency-of-george-w-bush.html.

Sunstein, Cass R., ed. *Can It Happen Here?: Authoritarianism in America*. New York: HarperCollins, 2018. Kindle.

Taraporewala, Irach J. S., ed. *The Divine Songs of Zarathushtra: A Philological Study of the Gathas of Zarathushtra, Containing the Text with Literal Translation into English, a Free English Rendering and Full Critical and Grammatical Notes, Metrical Index and Glossary*. 1951. Reprint, New York: AMS Press, Inc., 1977.

Toland, John. *Adolph Hitler: The Definitive Biography*. New York: Anchor Books, 1992. Kindle.

Toulmin, Stephen. *An Introduction to Reasoning*. 2nd ed. New York: Macmillan, 1984.

Trochim, William M. K. "Establishing a Cause-Effect Relationship" Accessed June 17, 2022. https://conjointly.com/kb/establishing-cause-and-effect/.

United Nations Intergovernmental Panel on Climate Change (IPCC). Website. https://www.ipcc.ch/.

vos Savant, Marilyn. *The Power of Logical Thinking: Easy Lessons in the Art of Reasoning . . . and Hard Facts About Its Absence in Our Lives*. New York: St. Martin's Griffin, 1996.

Wallace-Wells, David. *The Uninhabitable Earth: Life after Warming*. New York: Tom Duggan Books, 2020.

Walton, Douglas. *Informal Logic: A Pragmatic Approach*. New York: Oxford University Press, 2008. Kindle.

Watson, Jamie Carlin, and Robert Arp. *Critical Thinking: An Introduction to Reasoning Well*. 2nd ed. London: Bloomsbury Academic, 2015. Kindle.

Wilson, A. N. *Jesus: A Life*. New York: Fawcett Columbine, 1992.

Selected Bibliography

Wilson, A. N. *Paul: The Mind of the Apostle*. New York: W.W. Norton, 1997.

Wilson, Edward O. *Half-Earth: Our Planet's Fight for Life*. New York: Liveright, 2016.

Woodward, Bob, and Carl Bernstein. "Woodward and Bernstein thought Nixon defined corruption. Then came Trump." *Washington Post*. June 5, 2022. https://www.washingtonpost.com/outlook/2022/06/05/woodward-bernstein-nixon-trump/.

World Wildlife Fund. "Nearly 70 Percent of Wildlife Lost since 1970." September 10, 2020. https://www.trtworld.com/life/wwf-nearly-70-percent-of-wildlife-lost-since-1970-39628.

World Wildlife Fund. "Why Some Species Are Unwelcome." Accessed May 9, 2022. https://wwf.panda.org/discover/our_focus/wildlife_practice/problems/invasive_species/.

Zhang, Sarah. "Trump's Most Trusted Advisor Is His Own Gut." *The Atlantic*. January 13, 2019. https://www.theatlantic.com/politics/archive/2019/01/trump-follows-his-gut/580084/.

INDEX

abortion, 110
Adams, John, 116–18, 127
Akhenaten. *See* Ikhnaton
Akhenaton. *See* Ikhnaton
Akhnaton. *See* Ikhnaton
Alliluyeva, Svetlana, 142–43
Amenhotep IV. *See* Ikhnaton
Amon-Re or Amon (Egyptian god), 9, 162–63, 164, 178
anger, 73–74, 107n13
Aquinas, Thomas, 10
Aton (Egyptian god), 9, 163–65
Aristotle, vii, x, 5–9, 10–11, 16, 21, 26, 31–33, 38, 40, 65–69, 75–79, 84, 87
Aristotelianism. *See* Aristotle
Augustine of Hippo (Saint Augustine), 172
authoritarianism, vii, viii, 19, 50, 51, 81, 118, 120–24, 128, 134–48, 151–56, 158, 159
Bahá'í, 10
Bacon, Francis, 11, 32
Beria, Lavrentiy, 143
Biden, Joe, 46–47, 155
Booth, Wayne, 31
Buddhism, 9, 25
Burnett, Anne Pippin, 107n13
Bush, George W., viii, 148–51, 156

Index

Calvin, John, 11, 12, 181

Calvinism: See Calvin, John

categorical imperative. *See* Kant, Immanuel

Christian nationalism, 121, 156

Christian Reconstructionism, 11

Christianity, 10, 11–12, 13, 24, 33, 50, 52, 121, 128, 156, 163, 169, 171, 172, 173, 174–76, 177, 179, 180–82. *See also* Jesus

Churchill, Winston, 47

classical reason. *See* reason

communism, 119, 131, 122–24, 140–43, 147

conformism, 70–71

Confucianism. *See* Confucius

Confucius, ii, iv, vii, x, 1, 9, 25, 63, 75–76, 78, 85–86, 87, 92, 93, 111–12, 113

conspiracies—actual, probable, possible, and fictional, 60–62

Constitutional Rights Foundation, 141

courage, 78–84

critical thinking, 54–62. *See also* reason

Crowley, Aleister. *See* Thelema

Darwin, Charles, 27

Delphic oracle. *See* Homeric gods

demagoguery, 19, 118, 120, 121, 133, 137–38, 152, 155, 156. *Compare* rhetoric, political

Duterte, Rodrigo, 153

emotivism, 2

Erdoğan, Recep Tayyip, 153

ethics: basis of, 1–35, 159–60; citizen, 115–26; environmental, 106–9; ethical mean, vii, 75–78, 84, 87; individual, 63–87; media, 127–30; nonhuman animals, 108, 138n21; pandemic mitigation, 110–11, 126, 139n29; political, 132–58; social, 88–131

evolutionary biology, ix, 1, 27–29, 39–40, 81–82

Index

fact-value dichotomy, 2, 19, 26, 29
fallacies, 40–54. *See also* reason
family, 97–98
fascism, 119–20, 144–48
Foot, Philippa, 25–27
force and fraud, 109–111
friendship, 95
Gnosticism, 10, 171
Goldberg, Elkhonon, 27–28
Golden Rule, 92–93
Great Replacement Theory, 121–22
Haidt, Jonathan, 13, 18–19, 29
Hamilton, Alexander, 127
Harman, Gilbert, 3–4
Hinduism, 9, 25, 172–73
historicism, 2–3, 5
Hitler, Adolph, vii, 4, 35, 51, 70, 81, 91, 120, 122, 144, 152, 179
Hobbes, Thomas, 11, 32
Homeric gods, 10, 173
Hume, David, 13, 15–17, 18–19, 25, 26, 29, 30, 34
Hutcheson, Francis, 13–16, 19, 25
ideology, viii, 119–26, 138, 144, 145, 147, 157
Ikhnaton, 9, 161, 163–66, 170, 178
intemperance, 73
is-ought distinction, 16, 26, 29
Islam, 10, 13, 170, 173, 174, 176, 179–80, 182
Israel. *See* Judaism
January 6, 2021 insurrection, 19, 48–49, 51–52, 60, 118, 121–22, 154–55
Jefferson, Thomas, x, 118, 127–28

Index

Jesus, 4, 67, 73, 88–89, 91, 92, 113, 168, 172, 174–76, 177. *See also* Christianity

Jews. *See* Judaism

Jong-un, Kim, 153

Judaism, 9, 13, 32, 111–12, 122, 144, 173–75, 176, 179–80

judging others, 88–92

Kant, Immanuel, 1, 20–21, 94

Kennedy, John F., viii, 61–62, 157, 158

Khrushchev, Nikita, 141–42

Kotkin, Stephen, 140

Latter-day Saints, 10, 177–78

Lee, Mother Anne. *See* Shakers

Levitin, Daniel, 53–54, 58–59

Lincoln, Abraham, 60, 115, 118

Lindauer, Miriam, ix, 106, 190n63

Lindsay, James, 124–26

logic. *See* reason

Luther, Martin, 11, 181

Madison, James, 116–17, 127, 132–33

Mani. *See* Manicheism

Manicheism, 10, 171, 172

Massachusetts Bay theocracy, 12, 181–82

materialism, 71–72

McClellan, Scott, 148

mental laziness, 69–70

Mill, John Stuart, 22–25, 26, 43–44

Mithraism, 170–71

moderation, 84

Mormonism. *See* Latter-day Saints

Muhammad. *See* Islam

Index

Muslims. *See* Islam

Mussolini, Benito, 120, 122, 144

Nazism and neo-Nazism, 21, 46, 120–22, 144, 155, 179

Norman, Andy, 129

Norse mythology, 10

pandemics, 110–11, 120, 126, 139n29

Pence, Mike, 52, 155

Pinker, Steven, 193n11, 196n22

Plato, viii, x, 2, 5–9, 16, 18–19, 26, 31–32, 35–38, 55, 63, 92, 132, 133, 135-40, 170

Pluckrose, Helen, 124–26

postmodernism, 36, 124–26, 128, 159

power, love of, 74

prefrontal cortex, 27–28, 65, 86

prejudice and discrimination, 93–94

principle of (non)contradiction, 6–8, 37, 56–57

Protagoras, 2

Protestantism, 11, 50, 169, 181

Putin, Vladimir, viii, 51, 81, 123, 144–48, 151–52, 153–54

QAnon, 50, 52, 60, 62, 132, 156

Rand, Ayn, 89–91

Re (Egyptian god), 9, 162, 163, 164

reason: 5–9, 31–74, 86, 115–19, 130, 135, 156–60

relativism, 1–5, 19, 29, 126, 137, 159

revelation. *See* religion

religion, 1, 9–13, 30, 45, 49, 50, 94, 127–28, 137, 146–47, 161–82

rhetoric, political, 133–34. *Compare* demagoguery

Ricks, Thomas E., 117

Roberts, Oral, 10

Index

Robertson, Pat, 10
romantic relationships, 95–97
Rousseau, Jean-Jacques, 24
Sauer, Hanno, 19
Scholasticism, 7, 11, 32
Seneca, 107n13
Shakers, 10
Shakespeare, William, 74, 107n14
Sikhism, 10, 182
Smith, Adam, 13, 15, 18, 19
Smith, Joseph. *See* Latter-Day Saints
Snyder, Timothy, 115–16, 119–20, 146, 147
Socrates: character in Plato's dialogues, 35–37, 55–56, 133, 135–38; historical person, ii, iv, x, 1, 55–56, 71, 133
Social Darwinism, 27, 36, 184n7
Stalin, Joseph, viii, 51, 140–43, 144
Stanovich, Keith, 38, 184n7, 194n16
Strauss, Leo, 5
Suskind, Ron, 149–50
Swedenborgism, 10
Taoism, 173
Taliban, 12–13, 149–50, 182
Thrasymachus, 35–37
teleology, vi, 1, 9, 11, 26, 29–33, 87, 93, 160
theocracy, 12–13, 51, 149–50, 156, 174, 179, 181–82
Thelema (Aleister Crowley), 10
totalitarianism, vii, 118, 120, 123, 124, 140–48, 158
Trump, Donald J., viii, 10, 46–47, 48, 50–52, 62, 121, 122, 136, 151–56
utilitarianism, 1, 17, 22–25

Index

veracity, 94–95
virtue, public, vii, 116–18, 133. *See also* ethics
virtue ethics, 1, 25–27
Washington, George, 118, 127, 153
Weber, Max, 2, 19
Wilson, Jack (Wovoka), 10
work, 98–105
Wovoka (Jack Wilson), 10
Zarathustra. *See* Zoroaster
Zoroaster (and Zoroastrianism), 10, 161, 166–70, 171, 172, 173, 178–79

ABOUT THE AUTHOR

Alan E. Johnson, an independent philosopher and historian, is the author of *Reason and Human Ethics*; *Free Will and Human Life*; *The First American Founder: Roger Williams and Freedom of Conscience*; *The Electoral College: Failures of Original Intent and Proposed Constitutional and Statutory Changes for Direct Popular Vote*, Second Edition; and other publications in the fields of philosophy, history, law, and political science.

He holds an A.B. (political science) and an A.M. (humanities) from the University of Chicago and a J.D. from Cleveland State University, Cleveland-Marshall College of Law. He retired in 2012 from a long career as an attorney in which he focused primarily, though not exclusively, on constitutional and public law litigation.